Taiwan Cinema

Taiwan Cinema

A Contested Nation on Screen

Guo-Juin Hong

First published in hardcover in 2011 by PALGRAVE MACMILLAN® in the United States—a division of St. Martin's Press LLC, 175 Fifth Avenue, New York, NY 10010.

Where this book is distributed in the UK, Europe and the rest of the world, this is by Palgrave Macmillan, a division of Macmillan Publishers Limited, registered in England, company number 785998, of Houndmills, Basingstoke, Hampshire RG21 6XS.

Palgrave Macmillan is the global academic imprint of the above companies and has companies and representatives throughout the world.

Palgrave® and Macmillan® are registered trademarks in the United States, the United Kingdom, Europe and other countries.

ISBN: 978–1–137–29009–0

The Library of Congress has cataloged the hardcover edition as follows:

Hong, Gou-Juin, 1967–
    Taiwan cinema : a contested nation on screen / Guo-Juin Hong.
      p. cm.
    Includes bibliographical references and index.
    ISBN 0–230–11162–9
      1. Motion pictures—Taiwan. I. Title.

PN1993.5.T28H66 2010
791.43095124'9—dc22   2010030643

A catalogue record of the book is available from the British Library.

Design by Newgen Imaging Systems (P) Ltd., Chennai, India.

First PALGRAVE MACMILLAN paperback edition: February 2013

D 10 9 8 7 6 5 4 3

For my parents; for Edward

Contents

Illustrations

Acknowledgments

I originally conceived the title of this book to be *Dire Straits*, invoking Taiwan's place in the world as defined in relationship to the Mainland, on the one hand, and Japan, on the other. The writing and eventual publication of this book have gone through several phases and many incarnations, but my conviction remains the same. To understand Taiwan means emphatically to consider also China and Japan, as well as the larger global context. The national is the framework we cannot evade and with which we must contend. The current title says directly that my interpretive history of Taiwan's film industry is also a history of this contested nation on the cinematic screen.

That is seemingly a very simple statement, yet I have come to appreciate its complexities with help and challenges from others. I have many people to thank who have been with me through different times and places in my life. Recounting those names is my way of affirming my gratitude. To begin, parts of the book are reworked from my dissertation and I wish to thank my cochairs, Linda Williams and Chris Berry, and two other committee members, Trinh T. Minh-ha and Andrew F. Jones, whose guidance is still keenly felt.

I was very privileged to join Duke University upon graduating from the University of California, Berkeley. The transition from a large public institution to a small private one, as well as from the San Francisco Bay area to the Research Triangle, was surprisingly smooth, even enjoyable, thanks to my colleagues both in- and outside the Department of Asian and Middle Eastern Studies. Many senior colleagues immediately took me under their wings so that I could test my own. I thank miriam cooke, Hae-Young Kim, Ralph Litzinger, Tomiko Yoda, Anne Allison, Jane Gaines, Walter Mignolo, Bruce Lawrence, Negar Mottahedeh, Stan Abe, Gennifer Weisenfeld, Kristine Stiles, Rob Sikorski, Robyn Wiegman, Michael Hardt, Ken Surin, Fredric Jameson, and, of course, Leo Ching. Other colleagues who joined us later have also played an important role in my intellectual life at Duke: Rey Chow, Sean Metzger, Shai Ginsburg,

Nayoung Aimee Kown, and Carlos Rojas. I am proud to call them my friends.

Under the directorship first of Srinivas Aravamudan and then Ian Baucom, and with the excellent administrative magic of Christina Chia and John Orluk, I had the good fortune of presenting my manuscript at Duke's Franklin Humanities Institute Faculty Manuscript Workshop in the fall of 2009. Tani Barlow, Yomi Braester, Ken Wissoker, and Rey Chow offered extensive productive criticism, complemented by that of other participants from Duke, the University of North Carolina–Chapel Hill, and North Carolina State University: David Ambaras, Leo Ching, Shai Ginsburg, Michael Hardt, Nayoung Aimee Kwon, Ralph Litzinger, Sean Metzger, Negar Mottahedeh, Maria Pramaggiore, and Robin Visser. I thank them for their support and encouragement and I regret not being able to fully incorporate all their excellent suggestions. To do that would require half a dozen different books but, for now, I humbly present this one.

Duke Libraries have been most supportive in my research, particularly when Taiwan collections, such as Taiwanese-dialect films, have not always been easy to come by. My heart-felt gratitude goes to Luo Zhou, subject librarian for China, and Danette Pachtner, film, video, and digital media librarian, for their tireless assistance. Jui-An Chao provides me with most excellent research assistance, to whom I owe many thanks.

Many colleagues and friends outside of Duke have continued to be an important part of my intellectual and personal life: Linda Williams, Scott Combs, David Eng, Lydia Liu, Shu-Mei Shi, Jean Ma, Weihong Bao, Siyen Fei, Zhang Zhen, Michael Berry, Song Hwee Lim, Wenchi Lin, Daw-Ming Lee, Homay King, Olivia Khoo, and Chunchi Wang. Special thanks go to Martin Jay, Andrew F. Jones, Sylvia Chong, and Jason McGrath, who have read my manuscript from beginning to end without ever doubting that it would eventually all be worth it, even at those times when I was uncertain myself.

Parts of this book have previously appeared elsewhere. A portion of the introduction first appeared in the introduction to a special issue on Taiwan cinema's "missing years" that I guest edited for the *Journal of Chinese Cinemas*, vol. 4, no. 1 (2010). Part of chapter 3 is included in the forthcoming *The BFI Chinese Cinema Book*. Lastly, a shorter version of chapter 5 was included in *Futures of Chinese Cinema: Technologies and Temporalities in Chinese Screen Cultures* (2009), coedited by Olivia Khoo and Sean Metzger, and published by Intellect.

Various drafts of chapter 1 were presented on several occasions: "Reflections on the Decolonial Option and the Humanities: An International Dialogue," Duke University, February 2008; the Inter-Asia Cultural Studies Society Summer Theory Camp, Yonsei University, Seoul,

Korea, June 2008; and "Taiwan under Japanese Rule: Cultural Translation and Colonial Modernity," Center for Taiwan Studies, University of California, Santa Barbara, June 2010. The Interlude has also benefited greatly from the following conferences: "Relocating Ozu: The Question of an Asian Cinematic Aesthetic," Centers for Chinese Studies, University of California, Berkeley, February 2010; and "History, Literature, and Auteurs: Revisiting Taiwan New Cinema," Academia Sinica, Taipei, Taiwan, October 2010. I wish to thank the organizers of those events as well as the participants who offered invaluable feedback.

Finally, I offer unending gratitude to my family, especially my parents to whom this book is dedicated. Much love goes to Andrew F. Jones, Lanchih Po, Evan Joseph, Yu-Fen Ko, Chu-Joe Hsia, Xiao-Wei Hong, Daniel Bao, Martin Jay, Huei-Ling Christina Tsuei, Shuo Lin, Mickey Chen, and Jeng-Guo and David Chen.

To Edward I give all my love. Without him, nothing is possible.

Names and Romanization

I list personal names in Chinese style, surname first, followed by given name; for example, Lee Hsing rather than Hsing Lee. I reverse it only when the person has a name commonly known in English publications which may put the given name first, such as Yingjin Zhang, Edward Yang, and Sung-Sheng Yvonne Chang. I follow the standard pinyin in the United States except for those names commonly known in English under other romanization systems, such as Hou Hsiao-Hsien, Chiang Kai-Shek, Taipei, etc. For names originating in Taiwan, I hyphenate the given name if composed of two characters and put both in upper case; for example, Lu Su-Shang, Lee Daw-Ming, and Ye Long-Yan. The guiding principles are to comply with common usage and to be consistent throughout. Names of important historical persons and filmmakers, as well as film titles, are listed in their original Chinese in the appendices.

Introduction

Taiwan Cinema and the Historiography of Absence

National Cinema in Question

I took my first film history course in the United States in 1993, less than a month after I had left the island of Taiwan for the first time. And it was then when I read and was struck by the account of Taiwan cinema in the widely used textbook, *Film History: An Introduction*. With evident delight not unlike that at encountering a serendipitous anthropological find, Kristin Thompson and David Bordwell exclaimed, "In 1982, Taiwan was an unlikely source of innovative filmmaking. Its products were notorious for being either stultifyingly propagandistic or rudimentary, low-budget entertainment. Yet by 1986 [Taiwan cinema] had become one of the most exciting areas of international film culture."[1] Looking back almost two decades later, students of Taiwan might very well be struck by such a dismissal of its pre-1982 cinema as either "propagandistic"—politics overruling media—or "rudimentary," lowbrow entertainment overriding art.

For Thompson and Bordwell, it was "unlikely" that Taiwan had created any "innovative" filmmaking before the New Cinema, and it was "exciting" to find Taiwan at the center of the global art cinema by 1986. What happened between 1982 and 1986 may be a familiar story, but some questions remain. How about those years before 1982? What was Taiwan cinema really like before it burst onto the international scene? What kinds of films were made and why? Was there no merit at all to a cinema under an authoritarian state, and with an impoverished industrial infrastructure and encroaching international pressure? In short, how should we interpret the absence of Taiwan cinema before 1982?

So what might Taiwan cinema have been like before it was admitted to the world cinema scene? The keywords Thompson and Bordwell use offer some clues. First, "innovation" assumes that New Cinema is new and, tautologically, different from what it was before; with some optimism, it also suggests that New Cinema anticipates what is still to come, again tautologically, as differentiated from what it is at present. In other words, "innovation" is not just a moment in time; it designates a duration of time that includes *represented* time—the time before what this innovation is believed to renew—and *projected* time—the time the said innovation points toward a future to which the newness of this alleged advancement may lead. The history of Taiwan cinema is therefore written through a double mediation. For one, Taiwan cinema has no history before film historians write about it; for the other, that written history is predicated on a stunning lack of *pre*-history. Taiwan's cinema is thus *written* into the Western historiography of global cinema, but never on its own terms. Indeed, one cannot miss the glaringly *ahistorical* account of Taiwan before 1982, which remains locked in absence throughout the several decades and numerous revisions of *Film History: An Introduction.*

There is yet a different challenge that renders Taiwan cinema invisible before 1982, specifically in terms of the study of intra-Chinese-language cinemas by another version of world cinema. In that account, Taiwan is admitted into global film history by way of China's fifth generation filmmaking. In *A World History of Film*, Robert Sklar introduces Taiwan by singling out Hou Hsiao-Hsien, one of the central figures of Taiwan's New Cinema of the 1980s and beyond, casting Hou in the light of his involvement in the production of *Raise the Red Lantern* by China's Zhang Yimou—a fact, Sklar claims, that "might have startled any spectator knowledgeable about Asian film."[2] What is doubtlessly startling is that Taiwan should deserve mentioning not because of some filmmakers' own contribution to world cinema but, rather, it is validated by its connection to the cinema of the Mainland. Even though Hou's directorial career predated Zhang's, the former's place in film history, with Taiwan as a definite subcategory under "China," is nothing more than an accessory to the latter.

Different then from Thompson and Bordwell's mapping of the world, Sklar's views zoom in closer on the particular region in question. With all their complicated histories, Chinese-language cinemas coincide and collide with the equally complex histories of world cinema, a continuing interlacing of the contentious and uneven transformations through the tumultuous twentieth century until today. At the heart of both historiographies is a stratified structure wherein history is organized in spatial terms, following the logic of center and periphery and, most importantly, a dialectics of visibility and *absence*. This book intervenes with a temporal measure whereby history is deepened, also in spatial terms, by advancing Taiwan as a place to be historicized on its own terms.

*   *   *

The core question I pose in this book is a simple but persistent one: What is Taiwan's national cinema? I ask whether the notion of the "national" is adequate to frame and produce a narrative of Taiwan's film history. If the national has been a functional category that helps non-American cinemas to resist Hollywood's domination, is it still operable in the age of globalization when the transnational reigns supreme? In short, what is national cinema?

In "The Concept of National Cinema," Andrew Higson attempts a comprehensive look at the term. Basing his extrapolation on the British cinema, Higson lists four discursive frameworks by which national cinema may be defined: economy; exhibition or consumption; film texts; and film criticism.[3] The categorical distinctness of those terms betrays a certain Eurocentrism whereby regional specificities are ignored, as Higson himself would later admit, in favor of a "theory of national cinema in the abstract that is assumed to be applicable in all contexts."[4] In an effort to "reconceptualize" national cinema, however, Stephen Crofts expands Higson's formulation into non-Western films, proposing a more complex consideration of the diverse global contexts and various modes of production, such as European-model art cinemas, Third Cinema, totalitarian cinemas, regional/ethnic cinemas, and cinemas that "ignore" Hollywood.[5] National cinema thus becomes different sets of dialectics, to quote from Higson's own later theorization, between "nationalism and transnationalism" and between "cultural diversity and national specificity." Such tensions would lead to the exit of the national from the once-definitive framings of national cinema. For "the contingent communities that cinema imagines are much more likely to be either local or transnational than national."[6] The concept of national cinema must be grasped, finally, as unstable, as changeable, and as historical. As we shall see throughout the book, "history" itself is consistently under siege and "nation" always contested.

*   *   *

This book complicates the framework of the national by investigating its relationship to cinema in the muddied history of Taiwan.

Multiple internal and external pressures form the dynamic and unstable forcefield that is Taiwan, including the Japanese colonial legacy, the Nationalist government's cultural policies, various nativist movements' entanglement with "China", and the more recent challenge of globalization. By addressing these pressures, I show that the history of Taiwan cinema—its formal representation and contexts of exhibition and reception, its generic diversification and stylistic exploration—is a history of its ever-changing imagination of the "nation" that shapes and is contested by the cinema.

Transnational from the beginning, as the following chapter on the colonial period begins to demonstrate, Taiwan cinema is best understood by treating the "nation" as a nexus of internal and external contentions and by seeing the national and the transnational as a dialectic. I insist that Taiwan be positioned not only in relation to the Mainland, but also to the East Asian region as a whole, and even in a global context. By doing so, we avoid mistaking the national as a mere essentialized or outdated concept and thereby overlooking its persistent ideological function which is still prevalent today. Otherwise, we risk overemphasizing the transnational as overcoming accepted boundaries but neglecting the specific histories and conditions of those entities it is mistakenly assumed to transcend.

Two interrelated problematics help to further analyze this tension. First, any quick dismissal of the national as an outdated category in the name of a transnationalized, or even globalized, cinema does not explain how and why the national for non-Hollywood cinemas is still the predominant framework within which critical discourse is constructed and political rhetoric is mobilized. Second, if the national still operates, however contested, what is the history of the notion of "nation" and, as a contested term, how has it been figured into various discursive and cinematic manifestations? Dudley Andrew has advocated an "oceanic view" of national cinema, especially in the form of various new waves that demand assessment in national terms. His metaphor, "islands in the sea of cinema," encourages close attention to those new cinemas as crucial parts of, and filmic responses to, their divergent global contexts.[7] National cinema is never a self-enclosed territory that excludes the transnational; the transnational is the precondition of the national. To study the composition of transnational Chinese-language cinemas, I argue, we must first examine how "nation" has been shaped historically, discursively, and cinematically.

At issue is Taiwan's historical specificity. What Chen Kuan-Hsing has called a "global nativism" which characterizes Taiwan cinema, although a useful starting point, ends up flattening out a complex history.[8] For if both "global" and "nativist" are the key operative terms that bracket an understanding of Taiwan cinema today, they must also be complicated by an acknowledgement of the historically specific density of coloniality that shapes the formation of the nativism and affects its forms of contention with the global. Furthermore, the place of Taiwan has been provocatively termed "insignificant" by Shi Shu-Mei precisely to call attention to its very significance.[9] An impressive number of Taiwan filmmakers' accomplishments in the last two decades have contributed to an ironic erasure of a historically specific Taiwan in the global circulation of cinema. Especially striking in the case of individual filmmakers labeled as "national" icons—film auteurs standing in for the nation—the transnational feeds on the nationalist discourse and turns "national cinema" into discrete identifiable objects—directors, films, awards—for global consumption.

This book intervenes by insisting on historical rigor and theoretical flexibility. I situate "nation" in the historical, political, cultural, and, last but not least, discursive contexts that construct it in the first place. The national must thus be viewed as a contested site in order to fully appreciate its dynamic tension with the transnational. In this light, this book is also a historiographical project on national cinema in general because, through the examination of Taiwan cinema, it provides a template for writing film history by attending to both its contextual contingency and categorical instability. Both conditions have much to teach us about cinema's constructive and contentious relationship with the nation, and they lay the ground for a renewed understanding of the transnational.

But crucial difficulties arise. Does the struggle in cinema to deal with the national question mirror changes in general attitudes toward the nation? Does it anticipate those changes, acting as a kind of bellwether for what is to come? Does it contradict them, showing that there is more than one way to conceptualize Taiwanese identity? Are there turning points in the changes that do occur, and if so, what are they? That is, with Taiwan's film history deeply imbricated with its multiple colonial histories and international politics, how can the critical framework of the national, suspended and sustained at the same time by the political, yield a productive revision of Taiwan's "national" film history under transnational influences?

In what follows, I begin to broach these questions by going back to Taiwan cinema's history itself—films, written texts, archives—and to refocus the historiographic lens by looking closely at how those texts, filmic and otherwise, may lead us through the terrain of the "nation" as both discursive and cinematic problematics. In my conceptualization of national cinema, nation does not come before cinema to frame it; nation is imagined and imaged in cinema and, in turn, shapes cinema's continuing and changing construction of nation.

I approach Taiwan's film history by seeing "nation" and "cinema" as mutually constitutive. This relationship is particularly crucial in the case of the Chinese nation, which is not one. The split between Communist China and Nationalist Taiwan, not to mention Colonial Hong Kong, does not even begin to describe the dauntingly complicated diversity and contentious histories among numerous ethnic and regional communities vis-à-vis different constitutions of the nation-state in the last century and beyond. Out of this messiness, Chris Berry suggests that cinema be considered as a collective agency, categorized not by any unified or stable criteria but always in the plural and manifested in the performative. Such a "collective model of agency," in place of a "national" one, enables a productive engagement with films. Indeed, Berry encourages a "potential for the mobilization of a...collectivity that...exceeds the unified collectivities invoked by the nation-state and modern nationalism at the same time that it registers the violence perpetrated by them."[10]

*   *   *

To be sure, the embedded histories of colonial and postcolonial Taiwan have informed post-1945 cinematic genres and styles, and those dispersed histories have made up the matrix of the formation of what "nation" has meant at different times for Taiwan. Precisely because "nation" is impossible and inoperable in the Taiwan context, it becomes necessary. This antinomy registers itself in filmic representation in a number of historically specific ways, which form the core of my analysis. I emphasize that filmic form makes legible the spectral and contingent quality of nation and nationhood in the context of Taiwan's multiple and overlapping colonizations as various sets of forces that are different and apart from, and yet closely implicated by, the Mainland influences, the Japanese colonial legacies, and the changing international pressures. Taiwan and its cinema as a historically and geopolitically determinate case, therefore, help us to question and resituate the notion of national cinema in existing Chinese-language film studies. In order to do so, my book employs not only a historiographic approach to the national in dialectic with the transnational, but also the specific history of Taiwan cinema's formal transformation as it relates to that dialectic. To understand post-1945 Taiwan cinema, one must begin by returning to the colonial archives. In chapter 1, "Colonial Archives, Postcolonial Archaeology: Pre-1945 Taiwan and the Hybrid Texts of Cinema before Nation," I first present a case study of Taiwan's colonial film history and how the change in the writing of that history shows a distinctive postcolonial historiography under two salient conditions: *film history without film,* and *national cinema without nation.* The latter half turns to the role film exhibitors play and shows how exhibition practices as cultural translation demonstrate the *transnational* roots of Taiwan's colonial cinema. In so doing, this chapter emphasizes two major rubrics—*genre* and *style*—that will continue to organize my ensuing elaboration. Both sets of formal considerations enable a productive investigation of post-1945 Taiwan cinema with important implications for broader inquiries about nation and cinema. By illuminating the conditions of colonial modernity as processes of cultural translation, this chapter traces the transnational history of pre-1945 Taiwan cinema and identifies *generic* diversity as its long-lasting legacy.

Seemingly still outside strict regulations by any clear cultural policies, the first two decades after Taiwan's restoration were indeed remarkable for their generic diversity. Chapter 2, "Cinema among Genres: An Unorthodox History of Taiwan's Dialect Cinema, 1955–1970," underlines the *unclean severance* from Japan's colonial legacy and the *vernacular hybridity* prevalent in genre films (Western, Japanese as well as domestic, recycled Shanghai films as well as newly made dialect films) which thrived despite the Nationalist monolithic ideology soon to be imposed with full force. This chapter follows the chronology of its development and is divided into three periods; it shows the increasing complexity of dialect film as mobilized and implicated in nation-building on both the ideological and the vernacular levels. First, I describe the early years after Taiwan's restoration and lay the groundwork for an analysis of the "nation" after colonization. Second, I focus on one of the earliest Taiwanese-dialect films, *Descendants of the Yellow Emperor* (1956), to anchor my discussion of this cinema's first wave between 1956–1960, highlighting two major modes of representation: the operatic and the realist. Finally, I examine two prominent genres—comedy and melodrama—and sketch their development, decline, and eventual demise under the pressure of Mandarin-language films. The contest between dialect and Mandarin films paves the way for the rise of the latter cinema's Healthy Realism.

If "nation" in Taiwan's dialect cinema was not yet a clearly posed question, we would see from 1964 the beginning of increasing efforts from the ruling regime to impose a nation-building agenda in cultural policies, on the one hand, and burgeoning nativist movements, on the other. Chapter 3, "Tracing a Journeyman's Electric Shadow: Healthy Realism, Cultural Policies, and Lee Hsing, 1964–1980," focuses on this cinematic movement, which was launched by the leading state-owned studio in the mid-1960s, and on one particular filmmaker, Lee Hsing, whose career spans more than half a century and parallels the complex trajectories of Taiwan cinema most prominently in the 1960s and 1970s. I aim, first, to contextualize the inception of Healthy Realism in relation to the changing cultural policies in Taiwan since the mid-1940s; second, to describe Healthy Realism's salient features through Lee's *Beautiful Duckling* (1964) while comparing it with his other major works; third, to demonstrate how Lee's narrative themes of family and nation carry his aesthetics and style over to other genres and exert strong influences on other contemporary filmmakers; fourth, to show that the Healthy Realist movement was a distinct body of films, across genres notwithstanding, that resisted the dominance of commercial cinemas while being deeply implicated in them; and, finally, to engage with the radical shift of international politics in the 1970s and show how the stylistics of Healthy Realism would be swiftly transposed to policy films of that decade. That the movement's aesthetic paradigm eventually reached an impasse between aesthetics and politics—becoming an "aesthetics of politics"—leads us to the next conception of film aesthetics *repoliticized* with the emergence of Taiwan's New Cinema of the 1980s.

The three years between 1980 and 1982 was an important period largely neglected by existing scholarship and this interlude explores its significance. "Hou Hsiao-Hsien before Hou Hsiao-Hsien: Film Aesthetics in Transition, 1980–1982" analyzes Hou's first three films from 1980 to 1982, which embody the transition between Healthy Realism's polymorphous uses of realist aesthetics and New Taiwan Cinema's repoliticization of realism. From *Lovable You* (aka *Cute Girl*, 1980), to *Play While You Play* (1981), to *Green, Green Grass of Home* (1982), I seek to open up new ways of apprehending the historical development of the period by bringing to light Hou's connection with Healthy Realism. That is, instead of subscribing to the fantasy scenario in which Taiwan's New Cinema simply bursts forth and takes the global art cinema scene by surprise, I take the notion of transition dialectically. Transition does not mean a middle point in a linear course, a mere passageway for history to move from one stage to the next. Rather, this transition is one of dynamic tension that shows historical transformation as struggle and negotiation and, in the case of Taiwan cinema, as a historically specific form of resistance to previous paradigmatic structure; it anticipates the emergence of a new aesthetic sensitivity in contention with the sociopolitical reality it represents. What I call *"durée at a distance"* in Hou's early films not only prefigures that emerging film realism, but it also signals a renewed historiography of nation pursued in the next few decades.

Chapter 4 begins an intensive study of Taiwan cinema's engagement with history and style. "A Time to Live, a Time to Die: New Taiwan Cinema and Its Vicissitudes, 1982–1989," traces the commencement, development, and quick demise of this movement by following the works of Hou Hsiao-Hsien and Edward Yang. By concentrating on two of the best-known Taiwan directors, this chapter emphasizes two predominant sets of dialectics: urban/rural and personal/collective. It also marks a critical shift to auteurist and stylistic discursive practices from the early 1980s onward. "Nation" has now to be articulated as subject position and identification, foreshadowing the heated debate between "native Taiwanese" and "emigrant Mainlanders" detailed in chapter 5. "Realism" in this context departs from the generic into a *politics of aesthetics*. A distinctive style was formed, the salient features of which included most notably the long take and a countermelodramatic narrative structure, expanding the characteristic of *"durée at a distance"* to the specific temporal and spatial terms of the New Cinema. I focus on Hou's *Dust in the Wind* and Yang's *Terrorizers*, both from 1986, and demonstrate this new cinema's filmic strategies for a representation of modernity in contention with nationalism. Considering other films and the collective critical discourses surrounding this cinematic movement, I show the desire for a "Taiwanese" identity in the making and how that desire enables cinema's continuous *search for a national history*, on the one hand, and its eventual *loss of historical specificity*, on the other: two dominating conditions of Taiwan cinema after the New Cinema I expound upon in the final two chapters.

Chapter 5, "Island of No Return: Cinematic Narration as Retrospection in Wang Tong's Taiwan Trilogy and Beyond," argues for a mode of cinematic representation of colonial history in a postcolonial context, a cinematic space wherein national identity is articulated in temporal terms. The complexity of Taiwan's multiple colonial histories often finds its cinematic representation in the form of *retrospection*. By exploring this specific filmic temporality, this chapter illustrates the backward temporal movement in historical representation. Through a review of the changing notions and practices of film historiographies of New Taiwan Cinema, I establish the tension between public history and private memory as a predominant trope in the 1980s and early 1990s. The tension between public and private is further complicated when competing identifications—most notably between commonly labeled "native Taiwanese" and "emigrant Mainlanders"—are interlaced with contested public histories and personal memories. With Wang Tong's Taiwan dramas as my primary examples, this chapter elaborates three major modes of retrospection—diegetic, extra-diegetic, and meta-diegetic—each of which designates a unique relationship between narration and spectatorship. The questionable figure of a national subject is presented through these different levels of retrospection of a yet attainable national history.

Much of the inquiry in films after New Cinema is performed in temporal terms, as chapter 5 shows, especially in their retrospective gaze at Taiwan's colonial history and experience of modernization. That leaves vacant the present space of Taiwan in cinematic representation. Chapter 6, "Anywhere but Here: The Postcolonial City in Tsai Ming-Liang's Taipei Trilogy," homes in on the seemingly deterritorialized contemporary Taiwan cinema. It shows that Tsai Ming-Liang's urban dramas of the past decade portray a Taipei in which, under the recent pressure of globalization, multiple modernities coexist with multiple colonial histories. My discussion of Tsai's work places film form in relation to its filmic subject, one that is both homeless (wanderer in a postcolonial city) and ahistorical (everywhere alike yet anywhere but here in a global city). The lack of spatial immediacy and the alienation of urban spaces from any historical moorings cinematize in Tsai's distinctive style an impossibility of the Now as the central problem of the postcolonial city. Tsai's films, in short, depict the impoverishment of history adrift, further and further away from the wished-for foundation of either a nativist or nationalist anchor posited just a decade earlier. Two peculiar conditions best characterize this loss of historicity: *homelessness at home* and *connectedness by separation*. And it is in this place of the impossible Now that we begin to catch glimpses of an emerging local space, as transnational as that in the colonial period, as contentious as in the struggle against the new universal order of the global, after and beyond nation.

I

Genres

Colonial Archives, Postcolonial Archaeology: Pre-1945 Taiwan and the Hybrid Texts of Cinema before Nation

1945, Taiwan at the Great Divide

Atomic bombs fell in Hiroshima and Nagasaki on August 8 and 9, 1945. A week later, on August 15, Emperor Hirohito announced Japan's unconditional surrender. After fifty years under Japanese colonization, Taiwan was soon to be returned to China. More than four decades later, in 1989, the emperor's radio address provided the opening for famed Taiwan director Hou Hsiao-Hsien's *A City of Sadness.* Monotonous and impassionate, the emperor's voice is as opaque as the screen is dark. When a candle is finally lit at a family shrine, the flash of light is a profound reminder of Taiwan's history in cinematic representation. Diegetically, the scene takes place during a power outage; the Japanese emperor's radio address must then be issued from elsewhere and made to coexist with the unknowing subjects on screen.

The articulation of these two simultaneous events by the cinematic apparatus, despite their incongruity, is but one way the cinema represents history. Between the radio issuance of the official end of Taiwan's colonization and the everyday life of its populace beneath its wavelength, the cinematic suture of these two specific loci characterizes an important aspect of postcolonial historiography in Taiwan cinema. Between light and darkness, and under filmic reconstruction, seems to be the most fitting setting in which Taiwan's muddied histories reside. Between silence and speech as well, *City* entrusts its history-telling to a deaf-mute protagonist, allowing the diegesis to be flooded with divergent and intertwined storylines, with multiple linguistic environments, and with voiceover and captions. By bringing to light both Taiwan's darkened history as deeply implicated in its colonial legacies, and by giving voices to the heretofore voiceless so as to compete against the authoritarian official speech with increasingly emphatic vernacular contrapuntal sounds, *A City of Sadness* illustrates the cinematic imagining and representation of Taiwan's history. The cinema is Taiwan's historiography.

Half a century of Japanese colonization was the framework with which generations of people in Taiwan lived between China and Japan, in addition to the unending pressure from the West. But what of Taiwan itself? This question is particularly pertinent because the history of Taiwan has been in a transitional state for more than four hundred years. If the year 1945 indeed marked yet another transition, one has to ask from what to what. Questions of the "nation" itself would need to be posed if the return to China is indeed the return home, its assumed national origin. Is it a matter of sovereignty or governance? Considering the seventeenth century when Taiwan was passed from the hands of the Dutch and the Spanish to the Ming loyalists, and then to the Qing Dynasty, what would make this particular transition from the Japanese Empire to the Chinese Nationalists a definitive one, especially when the latter would soon lose its rule over the Mainland to the Communists? The road home for Taiwan keeps extending toward the horizon while no single act of looking back shows where it all came from.

It is possible, however, to imagine an origin in the future, a history without nation. When the character in the opening sequence of *A City of Sadness* finally manages to bring the lights back on, all the while as the Japanese emperor's voice permeates the entire sonic field, it is a moment when history comes to a standstill, a rupture in time in order for history to find its place. It is also a moment when the decolonial takes place—different from the colonial it seeks to eradicate, more insistent than the colonial that refuses to relinquish its hold, and almost tentative in its opening up of a fissure without filling it—where the horror of colonization never ceases and which an easy exit from colonial time cannot fix.

To understand post-1945 Taiwan, one must begin by returning to the colonial archives, even when this endeavor is inevitably obscured by absences and gaps, muddled with much hearsay and authenticated by few extant materials. To put it another way, in order to understand Taiwan cinema in the postcolonial years, it is crucial to investigate how the knowledge of colonial Taiwan is produced, and how the production of that knowledge changes over time. Any history of film must be grasped within the specific context in which it is produced, exhibited, and received. For as a technology at once cultural and industrial, film represents as well as precipitates how the modern is implicated in the East–West dichotomy in the colonial/postcolonial drama of nation-building, a set of conditions that will continue to impact postcolonial Taiwan after 1945.

* * *

If the colonial conditions entail a loss or erasure, or at least a suppression or denial, of the history of the colonized, to revitalize the research and the writing of colonial history must be an important part of any decolonial project. In the following pages, I begin by presenting a case study of Taiwan's colonial film history. I show how the changes in the writings of that history reveal a distinctive postcolonial historiography hard at work to decolonize film history from its past, and how that historiography is deeply entrenched in the very history it seeks to exorcise, that which still haunts it. After explaining the unique dilemma in writing Taiwan's colonial film history—paradoxical conditions I call *film history without film* and *national cinema without nation*—the second half of the chapter looks at film exhibition practices in colonial Taiwan. The role that film exhibitors play presents a vantage point from which to see decolonial forces already in existence during the colonial occupation.

Those two examples present two drastically different temporal schemas of coloniality. The first instance shows a decolonial race for a national origin of film that seeks to overcome the colonizer's dominion of time, only to come to a supposed national origin already marked by another imperial power—cinema as the Western technology *par excellence*—and always nonnational and already colonized. The other case goes back into colonial time to find the decolonial already in motion, not by a simplistic longing for a national origin but, rather, by a distinct movement toward the transnational which works to defy its colonial confines. Whereas the former finds the energy that fuels the pursuit of nation in writing and rewriting national history, the latter illuminates the field of history-making and nation-building as always already beyond nation.

* * *

Racing for the National Origin in Colonial Time

To start let us ask this: When was film first introduced to Taiwan? The history of how such a seemingly straightforward question has been answered demonstrates great intrigue and sheds much light on Taiwan's film historiography. For over three decades after Lu Su-Shang published *The History of Taiwan's Film and Drama* in 1961, long considered the earliest and most definitive account of Taiwan film and drama, the beginning of Taiwan's film history was believed to be November 1901, five years behind that of China and Japan.[1] Many publications after Lu simply copied that date without verifying it. Du Yun-Zhi's *The Film History of China* is a significant case in point. First published in 1972 and winner of the grand prize of the Chiang Kai-Shek Literary Awards later in 1975, Du's book was reprinted in 1988 under the auspices of the Council for Cultural Affairs, a government department under the Administrative Yuan. The later edition claimed to have expanded its coverage to 1983, as well as to have been revised based on new archival materials. The title was even changed to *The Film History of the Republic of China*, clearly a move to distinguish the Republic on Taiwan island from the communist People's Republic on the Mainland.

The sections on Taiwan's colonial period in these two versions of Du's history are only different in tone, while the historical data cited remains the same. The earlier edition emphasizes that Taiwan is part of China and that the Japanese rulers used film merely as an "enslavement" (*nuhua*) tool, and that domestic production at the time was an "insult to Chinese people" because Taiwanese/Chinese were uniformly depicted as submissive and willing subjects of the Japanese regime.[2] However, the later version softens its rhetoric about Japan's occupation by highlighting Shanghai film imports as the key influence on the commencement and subsequent development of Taiwan's film industry.[3] Doubtless, as a historian officially sanctioned by the Nationalist government, Du Yun-Zhi needed to sustain an ideological slant that regards Taiwan during the Japanese occupation as inferior, insignificant, and even aberrant. However, the subtle difference in tone between the two editions reveals a shift in film historiography, reflecting a much broader change in the political climate as well. More than four decades after the Nationalist retreat from the Mainland, and in the wake of the lifting of martial law in 1987, Taiwan, as depicted in its film history, is finally treated as an entity with its own history.

A further manifestation of such politically informed historiographic shifts, however, takes some surprising turns in a new wave of research done by historians in the early 1990s, only a few years after Du's second edition. Some scholars began to retrace Taiwan's film history and endow it with even greater significance in its own right by means of reentering the colonial archives. By doing so, the more recent film research attempts to write a history of Taiwan that, on the one hand, is not subordinate to China's film history, and, on the other, allows closer examination of the history of Japan's colonization, all done with a strong decolonial conviction. In other words, colonial Taiwan is no longer a mere stain on national history; colonial history is Taiwan history.[4] What remains to be accounted for is the tension between the two seemingly incompatible categories of (Chinese) "nation" and "Taiwan" which continues to shape and be shaped by the cinema.

One way to do this is to return to the question I just posed: When was film first introduced to Taiwan? "November 1901" as the beginning of Taiwan cinema, based on Lu Su-Shang's account, was not challenged until as late as 1992, five years after martial law was lifted and a burgeoning Taiwanese consciousness was on the rise. Film historian Lee Daw-Ming visited the National Film Center at the National Museum of Modern Arts in Tokyo, Japan, and there he chanced upon a 1941 publication by Ichikawa Sai, entitled *The Creation and Development of the Motion Pictures in Asia*. It turned out that Lu's account was based on a chapter from this monograph, and, after Lee's further research, it was proven erroneous.[5] Eventually, Lee's research was able to date the first film screening in Taiwan back one year to June 1900, when Oshima Inoshi and his projectionist Matuura Shozo exhibited the Lumière Brothers' Cinématographes in Taipei and other cities—significantly in this version, only three and four years after they arrived in Japan and China respectively.[6] If the colony was deemed to have lagged behind, this new discovery successfully closed the time gap by a year.

Clearly from a pro-Nationalist perspective, Li Tian-Duo bemoans the "lateness" of film's introduction to Taiwan via Japan, instead of the "consanguine" (*xieyuan xiangyi*) China, a historical occurrence which was the direct result of "the order of colonial dependency in the world system."[7] History is never short of irony, however. As further research continued to unearth heretofore buried facts mostly from newspaper advertisements and some fragmented reports, more and more documents surfaced to suggest that film exhibitions in Taiwan had taken place earlier. In August and September of 1899, an unnamed businessperson brought an Edison projection system from the United States and showed a documentary short on the Spanish-American War.[8] Encouraged by these new historical findings, Ye Long-Yan dug deeper into the colonial archives and was greeted by an even greater surprise. In August 1896, less than a year after the "invention" of cinema in 1985, a time coinciding with Japan's acquisition of Taiwan, a Japanese merchant brought with him to Taipei some ten Edison short films. And that was the very first exhibition of Kinetoscope in Asia, three months *before* the same technology arrived in Kobe, Japan.[9]

The colony has, all of a sudden, leapt ahead of its colonizer in time: film-time and technology-time. Ye's delight in Taiwan's introduction of cinema before Japan is apparent, while his disappointment that the more advanced film technology, specifically Lumière's Cinématographes which were considered closer to the cinema proper, did not arrive sooner than it did in Shanghai, is barely concealed. In the field of historical research into Taiwan cinema, the search for its origin has become a retrospective race against time, one that attempts to reset the clock of film history against the received colonial timeline. The former colonial subject's quest into the archives is, finally, a postcolonial archaeology that has raced ahead of its colonizer in time, modern-time.

*   *   *

Film History without Film, National Cinema without Nation

It remains an open question whether the founding moment of Taiwan's film history may be revised again. What is certain, however, is that film activities in Taiwan after the technology was introduced were a mixture of Japanese colonial government propaganda; Japanese, Taiwanese, and later Mainland Chinese entrepreneurs' commercial exhibitions and infrequent filmmaking; and numerous imports from

Japan, Hollywood, Europe, and China. A key figure is Takamatsu Toyojiro, who first arrived in Taiwan in 1903 and subsequently brought various newsreels and shorts from Japan and Europe. Following great successes in the touring exhibition business, Takamatsu went on to build a total of eight theaters in different cities all over the island. He even established an acting school in 1909 and began inviting film celebrities from Japan to appear on stage in 1910. According to Ye Long-Yan, Takamatsu's commercial achievement in the film business had largely to do with his personal connection with a high-ranking official in the colonial government.[10] The colonial regime supported and influenced the kinds of films exhibited because those films were believed to help educate the Taiwanese to become better colonial subjects.[11] The political utility of film was, not surprisingly, the backbone of Takamatsu's financial gains.

Takamatsu's savvy maneuvering between colonial politics and film as a commercial enterprise also marked the first film production in Taiwan. Commissioned by the colonial government, in February 1907 Takamatsu began filming the first documentary produced in Taiwan. Two months of shooting took the crew to more than one hundred towns and cities all over the island and the production was closely followed and reported by a leading newspaper, *Taiwan Nichinichi Shimpo*. The film premiered in Taipei on May 8 of that year and was later screened in Osaka, Tokyo, and other major cities in Japan. This documentary, entitled *Introducing Taiwan Today*, served two purposes. It was the colonial regime's concerted effort to showcase progress made in the colony *both* to the colonized and to the people in the mother country, a dual effort to legitimize its colonial enterprise to the former and to garner further support from the latter in order to advance its imperialist ambitions.[12]

While newsreels and documentaries remained central to early cinema in Taiwan, and while exhibition of foreign imports continued to flourish, domestically made narrative film did not begin until 1922 with the production of *The Eyes of the Buddha* by Tanaka King. Significantly, the production crew included several Taiwanese locals, particularly Liu Xi-Yang, who later cofounded the Taiwan Cinema Research Association in 1925. Even though the Association was short-lived, it inspired the first all-Taiwanese produced film, *Whose Fault Is It?*, written and directed by and starring Liu himself.[13] According to Edmund K. Y. Wong, a total of 16 feature-length films were produced between 1922 and 1943.[14]

Japanese-Taiwanese coproduction was the norm, with two exceptions. First, a Taiwanese businessman, Zhang Han-Shu, founded a film company with a branch office in Shanghai. The company produced *Love Waves* in 1926 but was soon disbanded due to the film's failure at the box office. The other exception was *Blood Stains*, shot in 1929 and released the following year. Produced entirely by a Taiwanese crew, this film was lauded as the first domestic blockbuster.

The coproduction mode was inevitable, largely because of crippling financial and technological deficiencies, as well as strict censorship imposed by the colonial government. Similar conditions would limit Taiwan's film industry after the island was handed over to the Nationalist government; the new regime not only took over film equipment left by the Japanese, but also took control of the technology and the talent. Tight censorship under colonial rule, furthermore, dictated that domestic production comply with Japanese policy and propagate colonial indoctrination. As in other colonial contexts, the colonized were granted only selective and regulated access to highly limited resources, entertainment included. Taiwanese were denied admittance to theaters that were for Japanese only, high prices in first-run theaters precluded a large portion of the local population from attending, and language remained a barrier. One account summarizes the situation well:

> The late 1920s context, in both film exhibition and production, was twofold in character: the Japanese had permanent movie theaters and a strong film industry at home to back up their film production in Taiwan, while Taiwanese film exhibition was still mainly itinerant, with the exception of one permanent movie theater in Taipei, [and] the film production industry was still dependent on Japan's specialized skills. During Japanese rule, Taiwan never managed to set up an independent film industry.[15]

Under such dire circumstances, domestic film industry was close to nonexistent. However, three important aspects of Taiwan's cinema in the colonial period warrant further attention: the role of the *benzi* (commentators of silent films, the equivalent of Japanese cinema's *benshi*); traveling exhibitions; and imported films (from China, especially Shanghai, as well as from elsewhere around the globe). Together they weave the fabric of colonial Taiwan cinema which drapes over postcolonial Taiwan's film development after the island's return to its ostensible "motherland" China after 1945.

* * *

The *Benzi*, Cultural Translator and National Warrior in One

Film historians have long attributed great significance to the Japanese *benshi* in their functions as exhibitors, translators, and creative interpreters.[16] Mediating between foreign imports and local audiences, the *benshi* acted as a kind of protector of culture by both narrating the story and mimicking the voices of the characters.[17] When the *benshi* practices were adopted and re-termed the *benzi* (*bianshi*) in Taiwan, they performed an additional task of explaining the plot to the audience who might be unfamiliar with the Japanese context or tradition. One can easily imagine the Japanese *benshi* taking on the same function when performing for non-Japanese programs. However, it is important to consider the added layers of mediation and translation for the Taiwanese *benzi* in the colonial context. The role of the *benzi* allows us to see a specific everyday practice of the colonized in the complex cultural and political life during the occupation period.[18]

The *benshi* from Japan were first introduced in one of the earliest permanent movie houses in Taipei, Fang-Nai Pavilion Theater, which was established in 1911 and served Japanese audiences only. In the beginning, untrained theater employees were called upon to comment on the films, and, as a result, the quality of those ad hoc commentators was nowhere near the well-trained and highly regarded *benshi* masters in Japan. By 1923, however, Fang-Nai Pavilion had to hire A-list *benshi* from Japan due to increasing competition from rival movie houses. Meanwhile, a Japanese entrepreneur had opened a theater in 1921 in a district largely populated by Taiwanese locals and found himself immediately in need of a commentator fluent in the Taiwanese dialect. A young Taiwanese musician Wang Yun-Feng was hired because he had worked at Fang-Nai Pavilion for several years and learned the skills while playing in the band. Wang not only became one of the top Taiwanese *benzi* masters throughout the occupation period, but he also was credited with training a younger generation of *benzi* during that time.[19] Other famous *benzi* included Zhan Tian-Ma, whose Tian-Ma Teahouse would later become a historical site when the event that triggered the 2/28 Incident and later government suppression took place on its front steps[20] and Lu Su-Shang, the author of the first Taiwan film history in 1961 discussed earlier.

The Taiwanese *benzi* were later lauded by historians for being potentially subversive by negotiating between the well-established tradition of the Japanese *benshi* and the ruling regime's tight censorship. But how so? Existing accounts are scant and vague at best. For example, the only concrete evidence several historians cite is the use of words like "dogs," a common way for the Taiwanese to refer implicitly to the Japanese. As daring as that sort of act of defiance might have been because a Japanese policeman and a fire marshal were routinely present at screenings for local audiences, it would seem farfetched to call its performers "the pioneers of [Taiwan's] nationalist movement."[21] One needs to look deeper into the context of the exhibition practices to see that.

Citing similar incidents when the colonizers were ridiculed by way of linguistic play, Ye Long-Yan, for one, believes that the subversive power lies elsewhere, namely in the manipulation, even re-creation, of film texts. The most noted was the Mei-Tai Troupe (which literally means Beautiful Taiwan Troupe). Ye distinguishes the *cultural benzi* from the *political benzi*. The former were a select group of intellectuals, well trained in speech and rhetoric, and thus capable of utilizing their knowledge of language and culture to connect the film texts with current affairs. Those skills ensured their popular status as entertainment celebrities, beloved by the local audiences but feared and closely watched by the colonial authorities. However, some of the *benzi* ventured further into politicizing the authorship of film texts even when film commentaries were supposed to be scripted word-for-word by the ruling regime. In so doing they carved out a space, if only for an instant of mutual acknowledgement with the audience, that allowed a Taiwanese consciousness to emerge.[22] Therefore, whenever the word "dog" was uttered, it became a poignant moment rich with mutual recognition of the colonial structure shared by the *benzi* and their audiences. Those moments of linguistic play were potential forms of subaltern subversion, undermining the *authorship* of the films, and, by extension, the authoritarian hold the colonial regime had on the meaning of film texts.

The *benzi* continued to exert considerable influence after the coming of sound in cinema. There are several reasons, the first of which is still language. Japan's colonial government did not enforce an all-out Japanese language policy until the Sino-Japanese War broke out in 1937. Few Taiwanese audiences could understand Japanese films, not to mention European or Hollywood imports, especially in the rural areas with high illiteracy rates; even Mandarin-language films from Mainland China would require oral commentary.[23] Second, the *benzi*'s role in film exhibition went far beyond mere translation or interpretation. Their individual styles, and, often, the nativist slant they demonstrated in moments of vernacular linguistic play, were so integrated into the viewing experience for the local audiences that their presence was strongly desired. Finally, as there were few permanent film theaters on the island and those were in major cities only, the presence of the *benzi* was imperative for touring exhibitions.

* * *

The Hybrid Texts of Taiwan's Colonial Cinema

Touring exhibitions started out as a necessity. From the late 1910s to the early 1920s, there were less than a handful of permanent movie theaters in Taipei, and one each in Tainan and Kaohsiung, the two major cities in southern Taiwan. In other words, a quarter century after cinema was introduced into Taiwan, it would have remained a modern entertainment not accessible to people outside of a few urban centers had it not been for touring exhibition merchants who brought to rural areas many films from divergent sources. The heterogeneity of film texts thus exhibited characterized Taiwan's colonial cinema under Japanese rule.

In 1904, Taiwanese Liao Huang acquired a number of documentaries and comic shorts and began touring the island with his arbitrarily assembled repertoire.[24] Although permanent movie theaters were slow to emerge, especially outside Taipei City, the touring business flourished, practically unregulated, throughout the early 1920s. Individual entrepreneurs would acquire simple projectors and films from whatever available sources, even smuggling in illegal prints from Japan.[25] In 1923, the colonial government began to enforce regulations on the island.[26] Touring exhibitions, however, continued to travel all over the island, bringing a great variety of films to cities, towns, and villages alike. Because individual touring exhibitionists relied on their own means of securing film sources, and because they had to be responsible for the marketing and the screenings themselves, most of them performed all the tasks for the show, often including acting as the *benzi*.

Here we have to be cautious when parsing the various aspects prevalent in the history of colonial Taiwan cinema. First of all, the diversity of film genres and texts exhibited in pre-1937 Taiwan was due to a combination of political and economic factors. As counterparts to propaganda from the colonial regime, commercial cinemas, as embodied by those touring exhibitions, presented not an alternative or even illicit film culture; instead, they were very much part of normal film practices, coexisting with the officially sanctioned activities precisely because they served certain popular needs that the colonial regime could not provide. Such practices meant, therefore, a constant, if haphazard, supply of film entertainment in areas other than major cities (with the Mei-Tai Troupe as one significant exception which will be described later). Ye Long-Yan lists 22 touring businessmen and small companies on record between 1921 and 1937. Furthermore, besides imports from Japan, Europe, and Hollywood, it is striking to see the large number of films from Shanghai exhibited in Taiwan.[27] It has been, from the beginning, a three-way traffic; not only were films being imported from China and Japan, but a significant number of Taiwanese also traveled to those places. While some of them focused on learning film technology to bring home, or on establishing connections with film studios to set up distribution channels in China and Japan—acting as film compradors of sorts—others enjoyed impressive film careers as actors, mostly in China.[28]

Among the most notable Taiwanese working in the Shanghai film industry was Liu Na'ou, a famous New Sensationalist writer whose film-related career began in 1932. It ended abruptly in 1941, however, when he was assassinated at a restaurant in Shanghai for being suspected as a collaborator.[29] Another major figure was He Fei-Guang. Starting as a trainee in Shanghai's Lianhua Studio in 1929, he rose to stardom in 1933, acting opposite major movie stars such as Ruan Lingyu. He later became a director, working with high-profile actors like Hu Die. During the Sino-Japanese War, He Fei-Guang worked with the Nationalist government and made anti-Japanese propaganda. After the 2/28 Incident in 1947, He was commissioned to make *Hua-Lien Harbor* in Taiwan to promote harmony between the Taiwanese and the newly arrived Nationalist regime. After the Communists took over the Mainland, He was not able to partake in any more film activity but stayed on in China until he died in 1997.

In colonial Taiwan, on the other hand, imports from China were highly popular. There were three major ways of acquiring films: purchasing screening rights to current films from studios in Shanghai or via their branch offices in Taiwan; recycling older film prints initially exported to Southeast Asia; and re-releasing older films from Xiamen, also known as Amoy, a coastal city in Fujian Province on the Mainland directly across the Strait from Taiwan.[30] The Xiamen connection will continue to have great significance in post-1945 film history, particularly in relation to Taiwan's dialect cinema in the 1950s and 1960s. It is important to note that more than 300 titles from Shanghai in the 1920s and 1930s were imported to Taiwan. Even a quick glance at this impressive repertoire reveals that, between 1913 and 1944, most major films in Shanghai of all genres and political leanings had in fact toured Taiwan. The list extends from the 18 installments of *The Burning of the Red Lotus Temple* (the most popular martial arts film of the late1920s), *The Song of the Fisherman* (the first Chinese film to win an international award at the Moscow Film Festival in 1935 and later dubbed as a classic of the Shanghai leftist film movement), to socially conscious works such as *The Goddess* and *Toys*, and to blockbusters, for instance, Hu Die's star-vehicle, *Sisters*, and popular music diva Zhou Xuan's biggest box office success, *Street Angels*.[31] It is clear then, that although their access to films was regulated by the colonial government and limited by affordability, audiences in Taiwan were by no means an isolated populace that lacked exposure to world cinema, be it from Europe, Hollywood, Japan, or China.

Transnational from the beginning, despite not having a national film history with its own production, Taiwan cinema was forged on a unique foundation, messy and unstable, exemplifying the contentious relationship between nation and cinema in a colonial context. A hybrid mixture of film texts with every provenance but Taiwan's own traveled the island in the first half-century of global cinema. That film history was nonetheless made Taiwan's own. To demonstrate the transnational characteristic of Taiwan's national cinema without nation, I return to the *benzi* by focusing on the practices of touring exhibitions by arguably the most important Taiwanese group, the Mei-Tai Troupe.

*   *   *

Vernacularizing the Other, Externalizing the Self

It would be bestowing too much credit, or imputing too much responsibility, to single out one group to explain the budding national consciousness in pre-1945 colonial Taiwan. It is possible, however, to gain valuable insight by tracing the brief history of the Taiwan Cultural Association and its touring film exhibition sector, the Mei-Tai Troupe.

The Association was founded by prominent Taiwanese intellectuals such as Chiang Wei-Shui, Lin Hsien-Tang, Tsai Pei-Huo, and Yang Zhao-Jia; all were and would continue to be influential political figures during the occupation period and beyond.[32] The Association's first meeting was held on October 17, 1921, at an all-girls high school located in a Taiwanese-populated section of Taipei City. With "nurturing the development of Taiwan culture" as its core mission,[33] the Association offered public lecture tours, organized summer schools, and staged theater performances of spoken dramas.

Some historians consider the Association's theatrical performances groundbreaking. For example, Harry J. Lamley credits the Association for the creation of a "new mode of [Taiwan] drama." He claims, "performance in the colony now reflected recent developments in the Chinese and Japanese theatrical productions as well as the influence of political and social change and the Western impact in East Asia."[34] The Association's groundbreaking endeavor could be understood as bringing colonial Taiwan *in sync* with the world, not only regarding the specific media in question but also the larger global picture within which arts, entertainment, and representation were embedded. In other words, to "develop Taiwan culture" would mean to break out of the colonial cage, to bring the world to it, and to meet the world head on.

As we have seen, however, colonial Taiwan was never in an iron house, isolated completely from the outside world. As Japan's model colony, Taiwan had long been the testing ground for the construction of, one might say, a *semi*-state, a loyal subject to the Japanese Empire according to its grand modernizing projects. In the realm of cinema, on the other hand, we have also seen that, despite the impossibility of having its own film industry under the colonial regime, Taiwan had long been exposed to major films produced in Europe, Hollywood, Japan, and China, from newsreels to all popular genres. Finally, given the previous two conditions, we have learned that Taiwan's experiences with modernity as well as with global cinema had not only been regulated and framed by the colonial regime and its changing imperatives throughout the occupation period, but had also been mediated by a great number of cultural agents until 1937 when the war in China halted most, if not all, nonsanctioned activities. The Taiwan Cultural Association provides an exemplary case study.

* * *

The Association was extremely successful during its short-lived active years, with a reported number of attendees to the touring lectures and other activities exceeding 110,000.[35] The leading members of the Association were dissatisfied, however, because of their inability to reach out to the largely illiterate Taiwanese population outside urban areas. At the 1924 annual meeting, a consensus was reached that a film exhibition sector would be crucial to extend the pedagogical reach of the Association. As the key players planned the organization of a film sector, an occasion in 1925 made it all possible. On Tsai Pei-Huo's mother's seventy-first birthday, a large sum of gift money was collected. Tsai used a small portion of the money to buy some token gifts for his mother but took the rest to Tokyo where he purchased a projector and several educational films.

Thus began the Mei-Tai Troupe. The first screenings did not begin, however, until April 1926 when the films Tsai had brought back from Japan were finally approved by the colonial government for exhibition.[36] The Mei-Tai Troupe enjoyed a warm reception in Taipei, Tainan, and other parts of Taiwan, and, according to a newspaper at the time, its popularity was attributed to three major factors: first, affordable admission fees; second, local audiences' emotional affinity to the Troupe; and third, Taiwanese locals' strong "desire for knowledge" (*qiuzhi yu*). In fact, the Troupe was so successful that a second and then a third unit were organized soon afterward, bringing more films to more people in more areas of Taiwan.[37]

If we pause for a moment and examine more closely what those three reasons for success suggest, they shed more light than first meets the eye on the struggling nascent national consciousness in colonial Taiwan. "Affordable admission fees" seems straightforward enough since high-priced movie theaters in big cities were largely inaccessible for most locals because, pure and simple, they did not have the means for such luxury. When the Mei-Tai Troupe toured the second-tier cities, and especially rural areas, charging only a small fraction of the fees in Taipei, those screenings were in popular demand. Furthermore, the cultural-cum-political *benzi*, particularly those affiliated with the Mei-Tai Troupe, were keen on bringing social and political reality into their interpretive performances of film texts. Whatever subjects were narrated and explained, they satisfied the audiences' need for entertainment, on the one hand, and shared linguistic communal bond, on the other; "emotional affinity" easily prevailed.

But what was the appeal of affordable film exhibitions with interpretations of the film texts aligned with social and political reality catering to the Taiwanese locals' "desire to know"? To know *what*? Having been immersed in secondary materials about this period, without direct access to the history in question, a difficulty also experienced by historians before me, I too must attempt speculative interpretations. Following Ye Long-Yan, Yingjin Zhang stops short of a somewhat elusive suggestion that an emerging sense of a "Taiwanese identity" would best explain, tautologically in my mind, the popularity of the Association's film activities.[38] It may be feasible, however, to venture another interpretation by considering the specific films exhibited by the Mei-Tai Troupe.

When Tsai made purchases in Tokyo, educational films topped his choices. Among the first films he bought back to Taiwan were documentaries about agricultural advancement and farming co-ops in Denmark, as well as animal life in Antarctica.[39] The selection of films revealed some underlying assumptions about the tasks of "cultural development" advocated by the Association. First of all, the emphasis on science and technology suggests a significant link between modernization and the forging of national identity. In other words, nation-building is here imagined as *modernizing* a nation; as will be discussed particularly in chapter 3, similar efforts would be made repeatedly in later periods. More importantly, in terms of the cinematic imagination at work here, instead of documentaries or narrative films made by or for the Japanese colonial regime or commercial genre films already circulating on the island, which would certainly have been easier to get permission to screen, why those films about distant lands?

What I see is a distinctive movement toward a decolonial frame that aims at two goals at once: a *distancing* from the immediate political context, and an *annexing* of Taiwan to the larger world—away from and beyond Japan and China.[40] It is precisely this *transnational* drive that defines the decolonial desire and the making of a Taiwanese identity in the colonial period. How exactly to situate Taiwan in the changing global geopolitical landscape, however, remains a question that this book will attempt to address from different perspectives in different critical moments of Taiwan's post-1945 film history.

To return to the Mei-Tai Troupe, records did show that similar selections of film sources and genres were, nevertheless, a familiar part of other touring exhibitions at the time, especially when imports from China, and even Charlie Chaplin's films from Hollywood, would soon be added to the Troupe's program. In other words, it was not simply the types of films shown by the Mei-Tai Troupe that distinguished them from other practitioners; it was, much more importantly, how those films were exhibited with a nationalistic educational slant. Recall here the incidents I cited earlier when the cultural-cum-political *benzi* of the Troupe went far beyond explaining the film plots and even gave speeches after the screenings. In this vein, we can understand why Chen Feibao calls all the Mei-Tai Troupe screenings "purely political events."[41] What the Mei-Tai Troupe did with the touring exhibitions was in keeping with other activities of the Association. From public lectures to summer schools, from spoken drama performances to film exhibition, education was political, especially in the times of colonial occupation and war, and, as we shall continue to see throughout the book, of constructing the nation *apart* from existing, official "national" histories that would long divide post-1945 Taiwan.

*   *   *

The Taiwan Cultural Association's success was short-lived. By 1927, left-leaning members, such as Tsai Pei-Huo and Lin Xian-Tang, left the group and organized the more politically radical Taiwan Self-Governance Alliance, while Chiang Wei-Shui founded the Taiwanese People's Party. Because the Mei-Tai Troupe was affiliated with, but independent of, those different factions, Tsai was able to transition the Troupe into the People's Party and continue its touring activities. However, due to intensifying conflicts among those political subgroups and worsening harassment by the Japanese police, all three units of the Mei-Tai Troupe completely stopped their screening activities by the summer of 1930. Three years after the Association disbanded, what was arguably the most important exhibition group in colonial Taiwan also ceased to exist. Even though Tsai held on to the projection equipment and the films purchased over the years, they were never put to use again before a U.S. bombing near the end of the war destroyed them all.[42]

When the Sino-Japanese War broke out in 1937, all film imports from China were banned. Japan's colonial government switched from policies in previous years that encouraged "assimilation" (*doka*) to a far more aggressive campaign of "imperialization" (*kominka*). By the time the Pacific War erupted in 1941, not only were Japanese names imposed upon Taiwanese subjects, but Japanese was also strictly enforced as the only language permitted, in media and everyday life alike.[43] Commercial film activities came to an abrupt halt. Those eight wartime years witnessed intensifying political oppression, widespread infrastructural destruction, and escalating economic hardships, especially under the U.S. bombings of Taiwan after the Pearl

Harbor attack. The war machine churned out propaganda films, fiction, and documentaries, promoting Japan's agenda of militarism and imperial ambition, while it was desperately caught in a war it had started but could not finish. Interestingly, however, a small number of films sanctioned by the Japanese government were again permitted to enter Taiwan after Shanghai, the film capital on the Mainland, fell under Japanese occupation in 1941.[44] Sharing a fate suffered by many other countries caught in the crossfire of the Second World War, Taiwan's film-time came to a standstill as the wheels of war rolled thunderously by.

* * *

If we weave the short history of the Taiwan Cultural Association, and the Mei-Tai Troupe in particular, back into the larger fabric of Taiwan's colonial film history I have sketched so far, two significant patterns begin to come into focus. First of all, during the occupation, the technology of film, which had been a source of modern entertainment, was often used as an educational tool by both the colonial regime and a select group of Taiwanese intellectuals, each advancing its own agenda—monitoring and regulation for the former, and education and consciousness-raising for the latter. The two-sided *politics of pedagogy* would continue in post-1945 Taiwan, this time with the Nationalist regime working to instill a nationalist ideology of "China," as various waves of nativist movements attempted to forge a distinctly local Taiwanese identity. The contention between a "Chinese" and a "Taiwanese" nation would fuel the ensuing cinematic movements long before the famed New Taiwan Cinema of the 1980s.

The exhibition practices in colonial Taiwan engendered what I would call a *vernacular hybridity*. The term designates how the multiplicities of diverse genres and sources were not merely a mishmash of random film texts, but, rather, they made up a unique cinemascape molded by Taiwanese *benzi*'s linguistic and cultural translations, and further proliferated in Taiwan's dialect cinemas detailed in chapter 2. Because of a lack of, strictly speaking, domestic production, colonial Taiwan cinema has to be understood as a composite textual field intricately nativized by way of the everyday practices of the *benzi*. The *benzi* did not disappear after the Nationalist government's takeover; instead, they would reappear and thrive, only slowly to wane in the 1960s under various pressures, most significantly the rise of Mandarin-language Healthy Realism after 1964. The last documented regular *benzi* performance was said to have taken place in the spring of 1969 in Pingtung, the southernmost county of Taiwan.[45] Since then, the *benzi* have been resurrected only as a nostalgic tool for marketing.[46] The legacy of nativizing or vernacularizing film genres and film texts, particularly in Taiwanese-dialect films and later in their state-led Mandarin counterparts, would continue to characterize a vital part of 1950s and 1960s Taiwan. Once we understand the multiple forces that shaped Taiwan's films up through the 1970s, we will be ready to engage with Taiwan's New Cinema in the 1980s and beyond. Pre-1945 colonial cinema was a significant step taken in that direction.

2

Cinema among *Genres*: An Unorthodox History of Taiwan's Dialect Cinema, 1955–1970

Many puzzles have intrigued, if also befuddled, historians of Taiwan's colonial film history. One area of confusion is caused by the difficult conditions of "film history without film" and "national cinema without nation" in the colonial period described in chapter 1. In the aftermath of the Nationalist government's arrival in 1945, however, a different set of difficulties in researching Taiwan's film history arises. Reestablishing the film industry, while restructuring political and social order, during the first few years of the Republic of China proved to have lasting impact. That is particularly true in terms of the Nationalist government's cultural policy, the private importation and exhibition of films from various sources, and the 2/28 Incident in 1947, followed by the defeat of the Nationalist regime on the Mainland in 1949. For the most part, in its first decade in Taiwan, the Nationalist government did not put much effort into narrative filmmaking, emphasizing instead documentary and educational films and leaving commercial cinema to the private sector. Taiwan's vibrant dialect cinema emerged from this context between 1955 and 1970.

Messy at best, the history of Taiwanese-dialect cinema presents a great challenge.[1] Without attempting to provide a total picture of the two decades in question, I seek to perform three tasks in this chapter in order to enable future research to amend its gaps and omissions. I follow the chronology of the development of dialect cinema in three periods, showing its increasing complexity as mobilized and implicated in the nation-building project on both the ideological and the vernacular levels. First, I describe the early years after Taiwan's restoration and lay the groundwork for a nuanced analysis of the "nation" after colonization, even when there was only scant domestic film production. Second, one of the earliest Taiwanese dialect films, *Descendants of the Yellow Emperor* (1956) anchors my discussion of dialect cinema's first wave between 1956 and 1960, emphasizing the film's visualization of the nation in two major modes of representation: the operatic and the realist. Finally, I look at two prominent genres of dialect films, comedy and melodrama, which cross over to dialect film's second wave between 1961 and 1970, and I sketch their development, decline, and eventual demise under the pressure of Mandarin-language cinema. The contention between dialect and Mandarin films paves the way for the rise of the latter cinema's Healthy Realism, the focus of chapter 3. It is important to note that, even though only a small fraction survives out of more than one thousand dialect films produced during this time, the existing texts still allow for in-depth formal analyses that support my arguments.

* * *

From Restoration to Restitution

As soon as Japan's colonial occupation was over after the Second World War, another—for some, equally colonizing—regime arrived in 1945, further fracturing the notion of nation: Taiwan changed hands from Imperialist Japan to Nationalist China. Between the end of Japanese colonization and the reclaiming of and subsequent retreat to Taiwan by the Nationalist government after losing the Mainland to the Chinese Communist Party in 1949, there were five turbulent years that foreshadowed Taiwan's future film history.

For some, calling this five-year period "post-war" has significantly different meanings from "post-restoration." While the former carries broad implications that link the island to the larger, general global geopolitics after the Second World War, the latter designates the cultural, political, and social context within which a Taiwan caught between Japan and China is specified historically.[2] Indeed, "restoration" (*guangfu*) not only denotes the fact of Taiwan's return to China's rule but also connotes that it is a return to its national roots after the colonizers' defeat. The very same term would soon be ubiquitous in the Nationalists' official rhetoric in legitimizing its sovereignty in Taiwan and its ultimate goal to reclaim China—to "restore China" to its rightful nationhood, that is, to rule under the Nationalists.

The ideological slogan did not officially change until the late 1980s, although its political signification underwent several subtle shifts which will be discussed in chapter 3 in relation to Taiwan's cultural policies. Of interest here is how the vernacular culture operates, even prospers, under such circumstances.

The atomic bombings of Japan in August 1945 brought an end to the war as well as to Japan's colonial occupation of Taiwan. Their aftershocks were keenly felt in Taiwan in the ensuing months.[3] While film production had already come close to a complete halt during the war years, the end of the war did not revive Taiwan's nearly non-existent film industry, devastated by the destruction in the previous years and further worsened by the hardships that followed. The time between August 15 and October 5, when the first official delegation of the Nationalist government arrived, was a period of political void. The Taiwanese had to live without an official governing body under escalating harsh conditions due to infrastructural damage caused by the U.S. bombings since October 1944. However, the so-called "Seventy Days of Vacuum" was not total chaos, according to some accounts, thanks to local Taiwanese leaders' efforts in organizing volunteer groups to help keep the island stable.[4]

While government buildings were deserted, movies houses were packed. With no more censorship or regulation, at least temporarily, exhibitors were quick to screen whatever films were at hand to eager audiences who had been allowed nothing more than propaganda during the long wartime years. Japanese as well as old Shanghai films were shown. The scarcity of new attractions motivated some entrepreneurs to make efforts to import films directly from Hollywood, whose presence would then take root on the island as in so many other war-afflicted areas of the world. Local production was impossible when talent was hard to regroup and production facilities were not in operational condition. These dire circumstances would begin to change for the better, however, when the second Nationalist delegation arrived on October 15, 1945. Along came Bai Ke, a film veteran, originally from Xiamen (also known as Amoy), who could communicate with the locals, thanks to his ability to speak a dialect very close to Taiwanese. Bai's charge was to receive the film equipment and facilities from the Japanese and to kick-start a state-owned studio in preparation for future government-led production.

Bai's first assignment was, not surprisingly, to document the ceremony on October 25 when Chen Yi, the highest-ranking Nationalist representative and the first governor of Taiwan after the restoration, officially accepted Japan's surrender. The making of the film proved to be a difficult task. The equipment left by the Japanese was scattered and production facilities were in shambles. Several accounts tell the story of how Bai had to rely on technical support from personnel from the colonial period, both Taiwanese and Japanese, and, after shooting the surrender in the morning, how his crew had to resort to using restrooms in the ceremony hall for film printing and a small office for editing and subtitling. Compiled with footage of Taiwanese people lining the streets to welcome the Nationalist delegation and other celebrations, this 35 mm black-and-white newsreel, dubbed Newsreel Number One, was produced despite those extremely impoverished conditions.

Newsreels remained the focus of state production and Bai Ke continued to be its leading figure. Bai located some unused police training facilities in Taipei's Botanical Gardens, and, with some support from the government, the Taiwan Motion Pictures Studios was officially established on June 30, 1946. It was a highly publicized event attended by Governor Chen Yi himself. Several newsreels were produced over the years on subjects including the repatriation of the Japanese, the groundbreaking ceremony of a new railroad line just south of Taipei, and Taiwan's First Annual Games in 1946. Notably, Chiang Kai-Sek and Madame Chiang attended this last event, and the couple in whose hands Taiwan's future lay in the decades to come made their Taiwan film debut in this newsreel. Clearly, what the state-run studio produced was no different from colonial productions, insofar as film was used as a powerful apparatus to serve the propagandistic functions of the ruling regime.

In the private sector, however, the end of colonial rule seemed to promise that the once lucrative practices of importing films from China, Europe, and Hollywood could be profitable again. As early as October 1945, a private-owned distribution company was organized, and films, old and new, from Japan (although these would be banned by the end of 1945), China, Hollywood, and even the USSR were quickly exhibited. Several other companies followed suit. Despite the tight censorship imposed by the Nationalist government which barred films with suspected yellow (pornographic) and red (communist) elements, film exhibition did not slow down in the early years after the restoration.

Besides state-produced newsreels for educational and political purposes, there was no domestic production of narrative film in those few years. Nevertheless, the vibrant exhibition practices nurtured a taste for a wide spectrum of genres, inherited from the colonial period, which would continue into the next few decades and manifest itself in the highly diverse genres of Taiwanese-dialect cinema. This phenomenon is particularly extraordinary given the lack of government support or stable industrial infrastructure. Some studios in Hong Kong and Shanghai did send production teams for location shootings starting in 1946. Famous stars even made occasional public appearances in Taiwan to promote their films. Local production remained nonexistent, with but two significant exceptions.

First, with investment by a Mainland studio, Taiwanese native He Fei-Guang returned to Taiwan and directed *Hua-Lien Harbor* in 1948. A musical noted for its lavish dance and song sequences, this film involved several location shootings, while indoor scenes were shot at the Taiwan Motion Picture Studio and postproduction was done in Shanghai where more advanced equipment was available. The film premiered in Los Angeles and Taipei in 1949 to enthusiastic reception. Later on, however, because of director He's questionable association with the Communist Party, the film was banned in Taiwan in 1951. The legacy of this film was the folksy and highly catchy theme song which was widely popular in dance halls and teahouses for many years.[5]

Hua-Lien Harbor's popularity in Taiwan was reputed to surpass that of the other exceptional productions in Taiwan in the early years after the restoration. In 1947, the Cathay Film Company in Shanghai was one of the earliest to send production teams to Taiwan. Cathay also began distributing films that same year. Two years later, in the early spring of 1949, as the conflict between the Nationalist and Communist factions intensified, Cathay sent a large and considerably well-equipped crew to Taiwan, preparing for a feature-length film, *The Legend of Ali Mountain*. By late April, however, the Communist troops seized the Nationalist capital, Nanjing, and Shanghai was under siege soon after. Even though the management at Cathay was forced to summon the production team to return to the Mainland, the crew understood that the reason that they had been sent to Taiwan in the first place was to keep some equipment safe from potential destruction in the civil war.[6]

After the Communists took over the Mainland, the Cathay crew regrouped as Wan-Xiang Film Company and completed filming *The Legend*, which premiered in Taipei in February 1950. The very first domestically produced narrative film in Taiwan after the restoration was, therefore, produced by a Mainland crew, while the first state-produced narrative film did not appear until Taiwan Agricultural Education Studios released *Awakening from a Nightmare* in November 1950.[7] Even though only some 28 minutes of footage of the former film exists today, it had a far-reaching legacy because of its theme song, "High Mountains Green" (*gaoshanqing*). With lyrics by director Chang Cheh (who later became well known for martial arts films such as *One-Armed Swordsman* in 1967) and aborigine-inspired music, this song, constructed out of the Mainland artists' imagination, was in the following decades used by the Nationalist government as the sonic representation of Taiwan. Thus displaced and appropriated, Lu Feii, for one, laments that the song becomes the codified musical signifier for Taiwan identity and reveals the Nationalists' "colonizing [*zhihua*] attitude of the homeland [*guxiang*] over a foreign land [*yixiang*]."[8]

Lu's assertion follows Homi Bhabha's notion of the "pedagogical," which designates the manner in which the colonizers hold the authority to interpret and instruct the colonized about their own culture.[9] However, as Lu himself is quick to point out, those "colonizers" were themselves only very recently displaced. For the Nationalist government, the struggle was twofold: claiming sovereignty over the Mainland, while asserting legitimacy and establishing authority on Taiwan. This dual challenge had immediate impact on the state-run film sector's production in the first two decades after restoration: an overwhelming emphasis on newsreels, propaganda, and educational films. And it was within this context that private commercial filmmaking, especially Taiwanese-dialect cinema, found space to thrive. Even though they quickly waned once the Nationalist government began its campaign of Mandarin-language films in the mid-1960s, dialect films display a stunning variety of genres. With the low-cost and strongly localized modes of production, promotion, and exhibition, Taiwan's dialect cinema presents a wide spectrum of Taiwan's vernacular culture and shows how the first two decades in Taiwan's film history were rich in genre diversity. Significantly, while this cinema lacks any clearly defined national leaning under the Nationalist regime, one might still detect some nascent, if also suppressed, Taiwanese consciousness—especially in light of the 2/28 Incident in 1947.

The 2/28 Incident is best known outside of Taiwan because of Hou Hsiao-Hsien's 1989 *A City of Sadness*, which situates this event at the most crucial pivotal point of Taiwan's history, the transition from the Japanese to the Nationalist regime. On the evening of February 27, at the front steps of the teahouse owned by famed *benzi* Zhan Tian-Ma, a street vendor of unlicensed cigarettes was injured during a raid by the Wine and Tobacco Monopoly Bureau. Tensions rose and a civilian was shot to death by the Bureau officials. The conflict was further aggravated when enraged Taiwanese locals stormed the Monopoly Bureau the next morning on February 28. As protestors gathered and tempers raged, the military police fired machine guns into the crowd. Governor Chen Yi immediately ordered the entire island put under martial law but unrest continued to spread across the island, a wildfire fueled by dissatisfaction with the Nationalist regime since the handover. On March 8, the military troops from the Mainland that Chiang Kai-shek had ordered arrived in Taiwan and began to suppress the growing civil violence with harsh state violence, causing many casualties and resulting in numerous arrests, including leaders and elite members of local communities regardless of whether or not they were directly involved in the incident.[10] Thus began Taiwan's decades of the "White Terror" under the Nationalist government. This incident sowed the tragic seeds of lasting tension between the Mainlanders and Taiwanese locals. And it was under such dire political circumstances that Taiwan's dialect cinema would have to find space to survive and grow.

* * *

In order to delve into the dizzying dialect film scenes of the 1950s and 1960s, a government production helps set the stage. Directed by Bai Ke for the Taiwan Motion Pictures Studio, *Descendants of the Yellow Emperor* was released in 1956. The oldest dialect film preserved by the Taipei Film Archive and the very first Taiwanese-dialect film produced by a state-owned studio, this film offers great insights into two key characteristics of Taiwan's dialect cinema. By highlighting the hybrid nature of its generic genealogy and its relationship with the Nationalist government's cultural policy, I explore the *vernacular hybridization* of film genres in this cinema, paving the way for an elaboration of its *unclean severance* from Taiwan's multiple colonial histories.

* * *

The Dialectics of Dialect Cinema: The Operatic as National and Vernacular Forms

Descendants of the Yellow Emperor tells the story of a group of elementary school teachers, some native Taiwanese and others from the Mainland, after 1949. The main character, Lin Xi-Yun, is a young woman from Xiamen, Fujian, a province right across the Strait from Taiwan, her background being much like that of director Bai Ke himself. During a home visit to a student's house, she meets the student's grandfather, who turns out to be her father's distant cousin, whose family name is also Lin. Soon afterward, one of Ms. Lin's colleagues is reunited with her own brother, who had been conscripted by the Japanese during the Second War World and with whom she had lost contact. He now returns to Taiwan accompanying a wealthy overseas Chinese businessman from Singapore. As further familial lineages and connections are discovered, four pairs of young lovers spend time in Taipei, later taking a trip to southern Taiwan and eventually returning to the capital. A group wedding ceremony for the four couples closes the film on a celebratory note.

Highly complicated, at times convoluted, *Yellow Emperor* is organized, first and foremost, didactically. A newspaper review of the film, for example, was quick to find issues with, as well as give credit to, its pedagogy. Zhang Sheng (apparently a pen name as it is the Chinese equivalent of a "John Doe" in English) lauded Bai Ke's accomplishment in presenting "a narrative film with materials closer to a documentary" with "on-location historical and geographical knowledge...easily digestible for the local Taiwanese audience."[11] Indeed, the film takes every available opportunity to impart history lessons. Many long sequences are practically extensive lectures on Taiwan's history as an integral part of the grand history of the Chinese nation. Befittingly, the main characters are elementary school teachers and a classical scholar, Grandpa Lin, who has lived through the last years of the Qing Dynasty, the Japanese colonial period, and the recent Nationalist recovery of Taiwan. From classrooms, dinner tables, special events, and ceremonies, to visits to commercial and historical sites, *Yellow Emperor* stages those lectures on history in a stunningly wide variety of ways. This film is a showcase of the kind of generic diversity inherited from the previous period which it in turn helps to propagate. To enumerate all of the generic traits in this film would seem like a laundry list. A few significant examples will suffice, nevertheless, to prepare us for a better appreciation of the outstanding array of genre proliferation and appropriation in this cinema.

One prominent visual characteristic of *Yellow Emperor* is its principal composition of eye-level frontal staging, a setup similar to filmed theater performance. Not only does the film frequently open a sequence with this mise-en-scène, but it also often proceeds to elaborate on the sequence by repeating the same framing. For example, before the schoolteacher visits the Lin family, Grandpa Lin is shown reading classical poetry while sitting in front of the family shrine. The straight-on, symmetrical composition is repeated several times throughout the scene, centralizing the prominence of the family shrine. The film goes still further with this visual arrangement. As Grandpa recounts his life story to Ms. Lin, the film moves swiftly into an extensive flashback with frequent graphically matched shots, culminating in a scene of his own wedding shot in the exact same composition, only this time aided by two gigantic candles bracketing the frame to further accentuate the centrality of the shrine. Symmetry is crucial to the staging in those scenes, from a vantage point afforded only by the best seats in the house.

Since that point of view is offered by the filmic apparatus' advantaged position, what it allows is arguably a visual field closest to the live theater. After the Nationalist government took over Taiwan, the traditional Taiwanese Ge-Zai Opera enjoyed a brief revival, having been suppressed by Japanese colonizers during the Imperialization (*kominka*) period from 1937 to 1945. However, the new regime's attitude toward this vernacular form of entertainment was to impose a nationalist agenda upon it. Locally, opera troupes proliferated with increasingly lowbrow and low-quality production, gradually losing their popularity to other forms of entertainment, especially imported films. By the time domestic film production began, opera film remained its key competitor and initial inspiration. As a matter of fact, the first privately funded dialect film was a Taiwanese opera film, *Xue Ping-Guei and Wang Bao-Chuan*, released several months before *Yellow Emperor*.[12]

Mary Farquhar and Chris Berry call this mode of cinematic representation "shadow opera," through which the viewers are "[hailed] as Chinese people seeing a Chinese spectacle." They claim that "[opera] and opera film signal a national identity during times of crisis."[13] Even though Farquhar and Berry focus on Mainland Chinese cinema, their argument can be extended to the Taiwanese context because opera film was indeed a significant genre in Taiwan's early cinema all the way through the 1960s. But one may ask, What is the "crisis" that a traditional mode of representation is called upon to address in *Yellow Emperor*? If, according to Berry and Farquhar, the operatic mode is a national form of representation, it is important to inquire whether that form, especially when translated into cinematic production, carries the national trait that it purports to bear—What nation? What trait?—or if it signifies something else altogether.

As the first state-produced dialect film more than a decade after the Nationalist government reclaimed Taiwan, *Yellow Emperor* was yet another attempt to bring Nationalist ideology to its Taiwanese-dialect-speaking subjects. Initially, the state policy on spoken language was to discourage the use of dialects other than Mandarin. However, the early imports from Hong Kong were composed of films made in Mandarin, Cantonese, Chaozhou dialect, and Xiamanese (or Amoy), a variation of the southern Hokkienese system and a close cousin of the commonly spoken Taiwanese dialect. While Mandarin and Cantonese films were often made with higher production values, Xiamenese films enjoyed a marketing advantage because of their linguistic affinity with Taiwanese. And they began to arrive in Taiwan as early as 1949. Also popular in other Southeast Asian countries, these Xiamenese films, mostly adaptations of popular operas and folklore, took Taiwan's market by storm.[14]

Yellow Emperor was produced in this context, but, importantly, not as a commercial film. After its completion, the state-owned studio distributed copies to local governments all over the island for free screenings. A Mandarin version was even made and screened once the next year.[15] The use of the operatic mode in *Yellow Emperor* cannot but be a clear indication of the government's willingness to utilize film as a propaganda tool by employing whatever efficient tool was at hand, placing arts and aesthetics in the service of nationalism, the same condition that would haunt Mandarin-language cinema in the 1960s and 1970s.

At the vernacular level, however, the question of "authenticity" for opera film caused great controversy. From the beginning, Xiamenese films were routinely advertised as "Taiwanese." The clamor over that claim reached its peak in 1955, when 23 Xiamenese films were imported, all promoted as Taiwanese with added fanfare: "the king," "the crown," and "the pyramid" of the Taiwanese-dialect film were but a few examples of the flamboyant advertising rhetoric. The appellation that reigned supreme was the "authentic" (*zhengzong*, which also means "orthodox") Taiwanese-dialect film. The issue of authenticity became a heatedly contested issue when more and more privately financed film studios (often with technical support from the state-owned studios) jumped on the moneymaking bandwagon beginning in 1956.[16]

The operatic mode of cinematic representation is, therefore, far more than a mere transposition of one artistic or popular form from one medium to another; it is at the nexus of internal and external forces that have both impacted on and helped with the shaping of Taiwan's vernacular culture. Situated within this context, *Descendants of the Yellow Emperor* takes on even greater significance with added complexity. By adopting a vernacular form for its ideological didactics, the film helps launch a long history of dialectics between cinema and nation which subsequent chapters will continue to explore. The question now with stronger urgency is how the cinema itself, particularly with its indiscriminate inclusion of various genres, imparts the ideological message, for the Taiwanese locals and Mainland emigrants alike, of a great unified Chinese nation of the yellow race.

* * *

Visualizing History: Dialect Cinema's Didactics and Its Realist Drive

To tell the story of the Chinese nation, *Descendants of the Yellow Emperor* employs various visual aids to perform the many reiterations of Taiwan's history as part of the Grand History of the Chinese Nation. Three historical figures stand out: Zheng Cheng-Gong, commonly known in English as *Koxinga*,[17] a Ming Dynasty loyalist who reclaimed Taiwan from the Dutch in the seventeenth century after fleeing from the Qing takeover of China, Wu Feng, a Han settler who, as legend has it, sacrificed his own life to the aboriginal practice of headhunting in order to move them to civilization in the eighteenth century; and, finally, Liu Ming-Chuan, the Qin governor of Taiwan in the late nineteenth century, before Japanese colonization, who was credited with establishing the foundation for the island's modernization. The stories of these three figures are mobilized in *Yellow Emperor* to one end, and one end only: asserting the historical linkage and unbroken lineage between Taiwan and its motherland, China.

Each of these three figures occupies a very complicated place in Taiwan's history, while celebration of and controversy over their legacies abound. Their roles in *Yellow Emperor*, however, are unambiguous. Zheng, Wu, and Liu are here enlisted, if spun effectively, as representative figures in Taiwan's multiple colonial histories, whose lives and legends in their respective historical junctures affirm the ideology of Taiwan as always part of China. And that is precisely what *Yellow Emperor*'s historical lesson professes. Zheng defeated a Western invader to bring Taiwan back under its rightful sovereignty (even though Zheng himself was contending the legitimacy of Qing

governance); Wu sacrificed himself to enlighten the savages to con-
form to the Han civilization (while historical records and existing
scholarship still cannot verify the accuracy of such accounts);[18] and
Liu built the postal, electric, and train systems before Taiwan was
ceded to Japan (although such construction under his governance
was made possible in part by harsh taxation which caused much civil
unrest). To be sure, all parenthetical comments must be put aside in
order for the core message of the film to come to the fore: Taiwan and
China are of one Chinese race, sharing one history, and shall reunite
as one nation when the sole legitimate government, the Nationalist,
reclaims the Mainland. Historical rigor, in short, is trumped by ideological expedience.

To tell the stories of these national heroes and to tell them as part
of the nation's history requires emphatic iteration by reiteration. It
is not enough to say it once; the Grand History bears repeating over
and over again. And *Yellow Emperor* performs such repetition, in
abundance. Starting with a history lesson by Ms. Lin in the class-
room, the film tells the genealogy of the Chinese nation from the
Yellow Emperor on, through dynasty after dynasty, highlighting
Taiwan's inclusion into that history as early as the seventh century.
Hand-drawn illustrations are used as visual aids in Ms. Lin's lecture.
When the time comes for the most recent linkage after the Japanese
occupation, Ms. Lin turns to a movie projector and shows still archival images of Taiwan's restoration, featuring the Nationalist leader,
Chiang Kai-Shek, as the direct descendant of the Yellow Emperor.
The use of drawings, illustrations, animation, and photography
solidifies a sense of historical documentability that later documen-
tation of history further emphasizes, but those still renderings lack
the dynamism of the moving image. The next history lesson utilizes
a more mobile form of expression. When Grandpa Lin recounts his
migration from the Mainland to Taiwan, to show Ms. Lin that both
families are from the beginning part of the same larger Lin clan, an
extensive sequence of reenactment is set in motion, composed of all
on-location shootings, even using a life-size boat for the scene of
crossing the Taiwan Strait.

A particular tendency is evident: history as visual representation.
Even though the stories told are accompanied by verbal commentaries, the weight of their effectiveness lies in their visualization. There
are two distinct and yet interrelated modes of visualization. First is
the frontality of plastic representation in still images and illustrations
that offers an eye-level visual field; its immobility can be and is often

animated by the *operatic* mode of stylization. *Yellow Emperor* not only returns to the same composition many times throughout the film, but it also includes two documentary sequences of actual performances. This leads us to the second mode of visualization, the *realist*. Even in the scenes where theater performances are recorded and then placed centrally on film, *Yellow Emperor* intercuts between the stage and the fictional audience who participate in the actual viewing of a live performance. In other words, the fictional world of the theatrical space is linked to the real physical space of its performance.

Such a realist bent in *Yellow Emperor*, which would continue to manifest itself in subsequent Taiwanese dialect films, is evident in two important, though different, ways. To begin, the film oscillates between ostensibly "staged" spaces—such as those of opera performances—and "real" spaces—including both on-location shooting and sound-stage scenes. In so doing, the apparently fictive field of operatic representation is situated firmly within a realist diegesis more closely akin to that of the cinematic representation. The joining of stage performance with live audiences shows vividly this desired articulation. Furthermore, from one representational space to the other, realism is marked differently by moving from traditional theater to the newly possible national medium, the cinema. By adopting the frontal mise-en-scène as a primary form of composition and by incorporating theatrical performances as a significant way of narrating national history, and yet by containing the operatic firmly within the cinematic mode of indexing the real, *Yellow Emperor* signals a move in visual culture aiming at a higher degree of realism that only the cinematic apparatus could attain.

The moving back and forth between documentary footage and on-location or soundstage enactment is but one dialectics of the real in the film. Between the "staged"—filmed theatrical acts or filmic reenactments—and the "real"—actual historical sites and monuments—*Yellow Emperor* goes still further and capitalizes on the cinema's ability to *physically* move beyond the staged, to the physical real. Before elaborating on this aspect of *Yellow Emperor*, it is important to remember that documentaries, or, more specifically, travelogues, were a dominant cinematic form for both the colonial Japanese and the Nationalist regimes. Film's ability to transpose goes both ways: it brings different times and spaces to the viewer, and it also takes the viewer to them. Colonial travelogues stage a complex temporal-spatial field which showcases the progress of modernization in the colony by highlighting its sameness in otherness, as well as emphasizing at the same time the not-quite-yet and the already-there.[19]

* * *

History as Time Travel

When the characters in *Yellow Emperor* travel in a postcolonial Taiwan, they not only move from north to south, from the Nationalist capital Taipei to the pre-colonial capital Tainan, but they also traverse the present to the past and the future. Rich in history, Tainan and other southern cities house many historical sites and monuments. When the four young couples tour the south by train, they dutifully visit various sites according to two simultaneous trajectories: revisiting the past and looking toward the future. The first, retrospective, tour is quite literal. They visit a temple in Changhua, a place commemorating a so-called Mr. Lin who, according to folktale, appeared out of nowhere some 300 years ago to teach farmers how to build the first irrigation system in Taiwan, only to vanish upon its completion. Next stop is Wu Feng Temple, where the legend of Wu is duly reiterated. When the young tourists finally arrive in Tainan, they spend a lengthy time at the Zheng Cheng-Gong Temple, the oldest and most elaborate sanctuary devoted to Zheng with many artifacts on display. They then visit the Chikan House, built by the Dutch in the seventeenth century, where Zheng accepted their surrender and lived until he himself was defeated by the Qing Dynasty.

If the above description sounds as if the tourists visit those sites and monuments only to repeat the histories associated with them, it is because they do exactly that. A trip down south is a journey back in time. History lessons are not only visualized, but they are presented at the physical locations, mixing vertiginously with stories and legends. Serving as surrogates for the viewers, the four young couples travel to those historical sites and monuments, thereby physically delivering the ideological message of one people and one nation at the core of this didactic film.

But *Yellow Emperor* does more than just affirming the present status quo by reiterating the past; it also gestures toward a future when this imagined Chinese nation will prosper under Nationalist rule. The visualization of this future-oriented trajectory is shown in two temporal ways, both of which are spatialized in keeping with the mode of time travel. First, the extensive journey to the south, taking up almost a quarter of the film's total screen time, is bracketed by the train rides both ways. An emblem for modernization, the train stands at once for progress and for a journey back in time. Images of the train would continue to fascinate later filmmakers. Closer at hand, the location of the train station will occupy a key discussion of melodrama later in this chapter. *Yellow Emperor* evokes both the forward and backward movements emphasized by the jerky editing style for the scenes on the train—the mobile camera equating the movement of modernization—and by the stately composition of the various train stations built in colonial times—architecture embodying the stasis of history. The characters' recounting of Taiwan's railway history, as well as anticipating a bright future enabled by this important infrastructure, reaffirms this bi-directional time travel.

Besides transportation and its significance in both Taiwan's past and future, water conservation and the irrigation system are represented as the backbone of pre-industrial Taiwan's livelihood: agriculture. Indeed, the southern journey portion of *Yellow Emperor* is doubly bracketed. While the train highlights a dialectic between past and future, between history and progress, hydraulic engineering highlights the developmental focus in the 1950s. The trip to the south begins with the first stop at Mr. Lin's temple. That mythical beginning of Taiwan's mass irrigation engineering is paired with the group's final destination at the recently completed site of a massive irrigation system in southern Taiwan.[20] Nothing else in *Yellow Emperor* is more urgently presented and more emphatically ushered to the fore than this moment of display of nation-building with the magnificent images of steel bridges and concrete embankments. As the train takes the four couples back to Taipei, with the same dynamic camera and editing style that began this journey, the film can now charge forward to a promised future of unity and prosperity by staging the long-anticipated group wedding. The final scene shows the four couples now securely contained within the frontal, symmetric composition of the operatic, the national form of visual frame, while the viewers are beckoned by the film's realist representation of nation, in all of its glory of past, present, and future: the total myth of nation.

* * *

Taiwanese-dialect films featuring travel are many. Berry and Farquhar observe that the travelogue format presents an opportunity in that "not only the characters but also the audience, regardless of where they were from [native Taiwanese or Mainlanders], got a chance to see sights composing what was now the existing territory of the Republic of China and their new common home."[21] Perhaps the most famous among these films is Lee Hsing's directorial debut in 1958, *Brother Wang and Brother Liu Tour Taiwan*, a phenomenal commercial success that spawned numerous sequels and knock-offs. Following two lower-class men, a Laurel and Hardy type duo, who strike it rich by winning the lottery, the film travels all over Taiwan and occasions comic scenes as the odd couple encounters one mishap after another. In fact, this film did not only follow in the footsteps of films like *Yellow Emperor*, but it also kept abreast with the government's effort to promote tourism. In 1960, a government branch overseeing tourism was established under the Administrative Yuan; tourism and its representation officially entered the government's purview. The didactic nature of state production would remain at the core of most documentary, educational, and Mandarin-language films until Healthy Realism brought fresh energy to Taiwan cinema in the mid-1960s. Taiwan's cultural and social conditions on the vernacular level would be explored in Taiwanese-dialect films, especially in their fluid representation and generic diversity. Comedy will be the first to help us to navigate this increasingly complex terrain.

* * *

Conflict Resolution and Its Comic Turn

Similar to *Yellow Emperor, Brother Wang and Brother Liu Tour Taiwan* effects a visualization of Taiwan as a part of the Chinese nation. A principal difference between the two is that, the former aims to teach and the latter to entertain. To be sure, *Brother Wang* enjoyed tremendous success largely because of its incorporation of physical comedy into the exotic appeal of the travelogue. The film spawned a significant number of sequels and copycat productions in the ensuing decade, including titles such as *Brother Wang and Brother Liu Have a Happy New Year* (1960), *Brother Wang and Brother Liu Have Hundreds of Children and Thousands of Grandchildren* (1966), and even a hybrid conception with the James Bond franchise, *Brother Wang and Brother Liu 007* (1967), and a composite of opera, martial arts, and fantasy, *Brother Wang and Brother Liu Tour the Underworld* (1967). Spin-offs were even more numerous, either featuring only one of the two heroes or completely different key characters, but the formula of hapless characters visiting various places and the resulting happy endings remained the same.[22] In all cases, these films staged a series of situations in different locations, through which the narrative progressed toward an inevitable denouement of complete resolution. Furthermore, these films are presented in an episodic structure and are extremely fluid in shifting from one generic mode to another, often from segment to segment, and sometimes even within a single segment.

"Comedy" in this context must be understood as a *composite* genre. The generic diversification typical of Taiwan's dialect films is manifest across the larger film scene as well as within a single text, of which the original *Brother Wang and Brother Liu* is exemplary. The film begins with a stunning traveling shot on a motor vehicle, moving straight toward the Presidential Building (formerly the Governor's Building in colonial times). The cheerful music adds to the momentum as the camera makes a right turn and continues at the same swift pace. A quick cut, however, shifts the perspective of the camera to a rear view as the vehicle speeds on. The sense of movement and the embodied representation of travel are enabled by the cinematic apparatus and modern technology. The importance of both is highlighted by the mobile camera coming to a sudden halt in order to introduce the main characters. Wang is a shoe shiner, built like a bear and prone to dozing off, while Liu, though barely half Wang's size, works as a tricycle rickshaw driver. The sight gag is obvious and the film does not hesitate to exploit it by showcasing in quick succession mishaps caused by both Wang's plump flesh and lethargic behavior as well as Liu's straw-like limbs and their inadequacy for his muscular profession. Contrast, not conflict, provides the comedy in this film, and, indeed, the dramatic resolution is achieved through the insistent simultaneous display of such contrast.

Wang wins a big lottery, but the same fortuneteller who has prophesied this windfall has also pronounced Liu's imminent demise in 37 days. To console his dear friend, Wang convinces Liu to embark on a circuminsular tour, leaving the latter's love interest, Ah-Hua, at home. The journey begins as abruptly as it is proposed. With but one quick cut, the film's visual changes into the travelogue mode of representation, swiftly transporting the characters, and the viewers alike, to several tourist sites near Taipei City. As Wang and Liu continue south and around the island, episodic events are similarly structured, alternating between the documentary and the fictive mode. Quick changes from location to location and among different representational modes continue to serve as both temporal and spatial marks, dividing the film into discrete segments for tourism or for comedy, often for both.

But there are two significant exceptions. The first, again, has to do with genre. Even in a comedy like *Brother Wang and Brother Liu*, other distinctive generic modes are prevalent. By "modes," however, I do not mean merely some discernible stylistic techniques or visual elements. In fact, there are complete segments in this film that stand out and apart from its general pattern of physical comedy and documentary travelogue. Two scenes exemplify this. First, after Wang and Liu successfully evade two thugs who have tried in vain to rob them—a hilarious scene in Tainan with the two heroes in full drag, followed by an extensive cat-and mouse chase—they wander in the dark until they chance upon an old and apparently deserted mansion. This sequence begins without a clear transition, appearing as if it were a continuation of the previous chase scene. What is soon clear, however, is that this scene greatly differs from both the comic and the documentary modes; it has moved into the thriller/suspense genre.[23] Similarly, several brief cutaway scenes showing Liu's love interest, Ah-Hua, as she waits tearfully for his return are additional moments of genre shift, this time to the melodramatic.

Even though the film itself shifts fluidly among different genres, with or without plot motivation, the next set of problematics is extraodinarily complex: between fiction and the real; that is, between representation and the "reality" it seeks to represent which is itself a fictive representation of a different order. One of Wang and Liu's earlier tourist arrangements is a hunting trip to the *shandi*—"mountainous region"—inhabited by aboriginal tribes. Accompanied by a conman who schemes to steal their fortune kept in a suitcase, Wang and Liu are adorned with attire suitable for an African safari, with shotguns in tow. The scene is shot on location in southern Taiwan; their physical presence is authenticated by actual roads, buildings, and even a government-erected sign mandating the use of Mandarin once entering the *shandi* region (*jinru shandi qingyong guoyu*). However, their outlandish garments and firearms suggest that something is askew. Indeed, as soon as they wander deep into the mountains, the representational mode of the film changes into something jarringly disparate from what it has started with.

On a sound stage, Wang and Liu find themselves surrounded by "savages" armed with spears and arrows. Dancing to drumbeats around a bonfire, lupine males and serpentine females baffle our heroes with their animalistic gesticulations and chants. Soon a princess-like woman offers her body to Liu despite his righteous but weak protests, while the voracious Wang is treated to a gluttonous feast in the company of a harem of nymphomaniacal women. This orgiastic scene goes far in stereotyping the aborigines on Taiwan as at once barbaric and sexually promiscuous; it is a fantasy on a completely different level that might not be alien in the context of late-1950s Taiwan. Seen today, this sequence might elicit a few nervous giggles, stifling both a sense of outrage and guilty pleasure and whatever else in between.

I do not intend to read any trite political correctness into this "barbaric" or "fantastic" portrayal of the aboriginal people in Taiwan. *Brother Wang and Brother Liu* itself presents another scene that works to retroactively disavow or, at least, correct the barbarity of its own fantasy, this time returning to a more secure combination of comedy and documentary. One of Wang and Liu's last tourist destinations is Sun Moon Lake in the central mountainous region of Taiwan. Famous for its natural beauty and rich in indigenous culture, this location is a must-see site, visited many times in previous travelogues in the colonial period and in many more to come. After a scenic boat ride on the lake, Wang and Liu arrive at a well-manicured village only to discover its indigenous occupants. Frightened by their previous encounter with the aborigines, even though it is clearly a different tribe, Wang and especially Liu recoil with exaggerated fear from a chief-like figure—with a pet monkey on his shoulder and a machete around his waist to boot—and two young women approaching them. The brotherly duo try in vain to hide atop the nearest structure. All done in the on-location, documentary style, the comic moves of the characters' bodies and gestures are perfectly in place and appropriate to the genre. Immediately, the chief introduces himself as the head of the tribal village there *on display* at this actual "cultural village" (*wenhua cun*), and the two women next to him, his daughters, First and Third Princesses,[24] welcome Wang and Liu to their "home." The sequence ends with Wang and Liu watching the tribal women perform a traditional dance before joining them and clumsily mimicking their body movements and comically appropriating their difference thereby rendering them exotic.

What has come before this scene is now cleared for a clean slate. And here filmic characters meet historical subjects; the former's fictional guilt and pleasure is covered over, but not completely erased, by the latter's real-life performance of their selves in the setting of a living museum. The multiple levels of "performance" here are fascinating.

The earlier segment about the aboriginal Taiwanese operates on the level of fantasy and is performed through a cinematic concoction of overly virile males and far too readily available females. Wang and Liu's involvement in that context is a performance of the fictional, reenacting and reinforcing a Han-centric nationalism. In the latter segment, however, the historical subjects—the chief and his daughters, for instance—are wrapped in a second layer of fiction by playing themselves, and they perform what is expected of them—the song and dance, the hospitable natives, the gentle savages—and thus betraying themselves as equally fictitious. Supported by the visual power of the documentary mode of representation, *Brother Wang and Brother Liu* here tries recuperates a sense of realism despite the freewheeling anarchy at the core of its comedy as the heroes complete the eponymous tour around the island.

*   *   *

From opera films to comedy, hybrid-generic productions characterize the first prosperous period of Taiwanese-dialect cinema between 1956 and 1960. Both *Descendants of the Yellow Emperor* and *Brother Wang and Brother Liu Tour Taiwan* exemplify the fluidity of generic hybridity within individual film texts. Furthermore, the cinematic form shows great pliancy in conforming to the nationalistic mandates, particularly with its realist mode of representation. The films also vernacularize cinematic form and film text with the flexible and uneven uses of filmic techniques and strategies of narrativization. The rigid pedagogy of *Yellow Emperor* and its nationalist ideology encourage a diversified use of genre conventions and cinematic forms. Likewise, the anarchistic elaboration of the traveling theme in *Brother Wang and Brother Liu* traverses the diverse landscape of Taiwan despite the uneven treatments of its many divergent subjects. In both cases, what is certain is the notion of synergy and commonality among differences that invokes the wished-for unity of a Chinese nation. As non-propagandistic as *Brother Wang and Brother Liu* seems, it still comes, in some long and roundabout ways, to an eventual resolution, however forced it may be. There is no real conflict—which will have to wait to be explored in the next prominent genre, melodrama—only temporary differences, whose contrast is the cause for historical lessons or, as the case often is, for comic relief.

To be sure, the tension between Taiwanese natives and the recently immigrated Mainlanders may have called for some relief, and comedy provides an ideal venue with less didactic means. For example, *Both Sides Are Happy* (1962) pits a Taiwanese family against another from the Mainland and resolves the frictions between them through the comic means of physical and linguistic play. "Misunderstandings between the older generations [are] undercut by romance between the younger generations;" indeed, this tried and proven plot worked not only in this case but also its immediate source (a Hong Kong production about the "communal tension" between the locals and Mainland refugees after 1949).[25] Interestingly, however, this formula reappears time and again in later dialect films but in two distinct ways. More often than not, generational differences remain at the core of the dramatic conflicts while heterosexual romance continues to be the solution. Class differences, and how they are manifested in terms of spatial differences (such as Taiwan's north and south) between the Mainlanders and Taiwanese slowly recede into the background by the 1960s. A quirky 1967 comedy directed by Xin Qi, *The Ditsy Bride and Her Goofy Groom*, is one such example.

With free love versus arranged marriage as the focus of contention, the film presents obstacles for the bride and her groom not based on family origins, nor even economic or class status. The problem is the disapproval from her widowed mother and his widower father because of their very own failed romance with each other in the past. Social, cultural, and economic differences are completely elided. As a result, the two families are presented symmetrically, each a middle-class family with a single parent and an only child who is college-educated; the cinematic visualization of both families' residences and physical appearances remains clean and proper throughout.[26] The same holds true even at the two weddings at the closure of the film, when the young woman is finally married into the young man's family, mirrored by the groom's father fully dressed as a bride being married to his old-time lover, the mother of his very own daughter-in-law. All the frictions before this odd pair of matrimonial unions are, therefore, props, or building blocks, for the double happiness at the end, whose comic hyperbole—not to mention improbability—is, eventually, only for a laugh.

Laughter, however, is not the only emotive response that other genres of Taiwanese-dialect films seek to elicit. In comedies such as *The Ditsy Bride and Her Goofy Groom* and *Brother Wang and Brother Liu Tour Taiwan*, differences propel the narrative forward and provide occasions for comic action, but their resolution is preordained. Conflicts, in terms of historical contradictions or political contentions, have no place there. Social problems as an inevitable corollary of modernization and change, especially during the rapid growth of the 1960s, though only receiving occasional comic treatment in dialect films, would soon take center stage in another prominent genre of the 1960s dialect cinema, melodrama.

* * *

Melodrama, or the Circumstantial Fate

"Can't you find it in your heart to forgive me, and understand my circumstances, my fate?" Thus pleads the main female character of Liang Zhe-Fu's *The Early Train from Taipei* (1964). Her lover is stoic, even incredulous, because the innocent girl he thought he had known all his life now stands in front of him as a woman he hardly recognizes. Now a dancehall girl (*wunu*), Xiu-Lan has cut her girlish pigtails and donned heavy makeup; in place of plain cotton shirts and pants are a tight blouse and slim-waisted skirt along with ostentatious jewelry. Huo-Tu, on the other hand, is his old self, dressed in his modest Sunday best, wide-eyed in bewilderment. Young lovers have grown irrevocably apart, driven by internal and external forces that the poignant terms "circumstances" and "fate" index.

Seen as a group, Taiwanese-dialect melodrama films in the 1960s share several salient features intimately associated with the widening discrepancies between town and country in a rapidly modernizing society. Together with *Early Train from Taipei*, director Liang's 1963 followup, *The Last Train from Kaohsiung*, exemplify how Taiwanese-dialect melodrama cinematizes modernity as clusters of spatial and temporal problems. While the train and train station figure centrally in this island in transition, the representation of the city provides the locus for class stuggles and gender troubles to play out in this developing country. Realism, as various sets of aesthetic strategies and stylistic devices—artifacts overriding reality—begins to gain prominence over the previous documentary mode that has relied heavily on the physical real, such as historical sites. With increasing intensity, realism serves as a means to organize time and space and resolve cinematically those impasses of modernity, thereby grappling with the contentious relationship between cinema and nation.

The Last Train from Kaohsiung is one of the first Taiwanese-dialect films to focus on the unbalanced development between Taiwan's north and south. The film portrays a Taipei City that is the capital of Taiwan in terms not only of its political and economic status but also its centrality of the social and cultural imagination in cinema. The distinction is subtle but significant. The second largest city, Kaohsiung, has always signified Taiwan's south.[27] Chen Long-Ting, for one, takes the image of Taipei from as early as the 1950s to be the "only" urban center; that "stereotype" (*keban yingxiang*) and its lasting influence map a topography of country/city division while creating a dichotomy of good and evil in the cinematic representation of Taiwan.[28] The conflation of these two binaries is indeed prevalent in many dialect melodrama films, following a supposition of modernization as the corruptor of tradition, urbanity as the center of sin. However, that is only true to some extent as a closer look at the films themselves sheds a different light.

The Last Train tells the story of a young man, Zhong-Yi. While visiting his father's home village, he meets a young girl, Cui-Cui. Their first encounter takes place when she is chased by the village head's overweight son on a suspension bridge, occasioning a dramatic sequence of Cui-Cui hanging on for dear life over the edge of the bridge while Zhong-Yi fights off the predator. They meet again and fall in love. Soon after that, Zhong-Yi's father summons him back to Taipei. In the meantime, Cui-Cui's father has promised her hand to the village head's son due to some outstanding debt. Enraged by his daughter's secret liaison, Cui-Cui's father locks her up on the night of Zhong-Yi's return to Taipei. Cui-Cui sneaks away, only to arrive at the train station too late. Zhong-Yi's sadness, appropriate to the genre, is accompanied by the film's highly popular theme song as the iron wheels of the eponymous last train from Kaohsiung render the ill-fated lovers farther and farther apart. To escape from her forced marriage, Cui-Cui manages to run off to Taipei, just as Zhong-Yi returns to the south to look for her despite his father's order for him to marry the daughter of his company's owner, Mei-Qi. Crestfallen, Zhong-Yi finally agrees to be engaged to Mei-Qi before he goes abroad to study in the United States.

If missed meetings propel the melodramatic plot forward, it is often complemented by chance encounters. Unable to locate Zhong-Yi, a starved and fatigued Cui-Cui faints on the street only to be rescued by Mei-Qi and her father. The rich family takes Cui-Cui in. After learning that Mei-Qi's fiancé is none other than Zhong-Yi, Cui-Cui leaves the family on the eve of his return. In a darkened alley, Cui-Cui and Zhong-Yi run into each other but their reunion is more bitter than sweet. Zhong-Yi manages to convince Cui-Cui to marry him and live a life secret from both his and his fiancé's families. To supplement Zhong-Yi's meager income, Cui-Cui becomes a singer performing on television. By chance, Zhong-Yi's mother finds out where they live and pays Cui-Cui a visit in his absence. The mother begs her to leave Zhong-Yi because, if it is real love, the mother implores, Cui-Cui should put his happiness above her own. Agreeing to do so, Cui-Cui lies to Zhong-Yi that she has fallen in love with someone rich. Enraged, Zhong-Yi slaps her across the face, storms out of the house, and quickly gets hit by a motorcycle.

As Zhong-Yi lies in a hospital bed, Mei-Qi and her father are touched by his repeated calling of his true love's name. Separated from her love as a thunderstorm rages outside, Cui-Cui peeks through the window bars, drenched by rain and tears combined. By the time Mei-Qi decides to give Zhong-Yi back to Cui-Cui, the latter woman is mortally ill from the cold and wet but still decides to perform one last time. As all involved watch Cui-Cui perform live on TV, she collapses. On her deathbed, Cui-Cui places Zhong-Yi's hands over Mei-Qi's as her last breath fades. Ten years later, Zhong-Yi visits Cui-Cui's gravesite; on the soundtrack, a song bemoans how "innocent love is torn to pieces because of the circumstances."

My synopsis of the film, belabored as it may seem, does not actually do full justice to the far more tortuous twists and turns in this melodrama. It does show, nevertheless, several significant aspects that the film poses as the fundamental questions of 1960s Taiwan. The country/city divide not only provides the dramatic loci, but their respective spatial representation also underlines those differences as the key sources of conflict. The city-boy-meets-country-girl narrative of *The Last Train* is a familiar, yet effective, theme because this scenario immediately makes clear what is at stake in spatial, gendered, and economic terms.[29] This spatial division is further implicated in gender and class imbalances compounded by Taiwan's social transformation and economic growth. In short, modernization, the prescriptive path of nation-building, is precisely the "circumstances" that impose themselves, in this and other films, on their subjects' fate.

In *The Last Train*, such a circumstantial fate is nowhere more compelling than near the end when Cui-Cui is again forced to leave Zhong-Yi after the motorcycle accident. Mei-Qi's father has just come with a large sum of money, which she refuses to accept, and she is again asked to sacrifice herself for Zhong-Yi's sakes. A highly charged montage sequence ensues. In a shot/reverse-shot pattern, one after another, images of the key figures who oppose their relationship are superimposed on the walls opposite Cui-Cui. From Zhong-Yi's parents and Mei-Qi's father, to the village hoodlum to whom her father has betrothed her, all these people represent the intertwined familial, social, and economic networks within which Cui-Cui is hopelessly entrapped. The ill fate of her love is preordained, in other words, and the mobility to move from the countryside to the city, to have a love affair with a man of a different class, and, last but not least, to gain a certain economic independence by becoming a TV singer—none of this would free the lovers from the web of their circumstantial fate.

Although *The Last Train* does not articulate these problems in explicit terms regarding modernization, its representation of the human relationship to *technology* offers important clues. To stay with the montage sequence longer, even more striking in those shots is that the shadow on the wall is not Cui-Cui's, as the shot/reverse shot editing implies. The shadow is actually cast by the cameraman in high-key lighting, and the distinct contour of his upper body and the camera itself can be discerned by freezing the frame. Such reflexivity is nowhere else evident in *The Last Train*, so it is difficult to advance a definitive interpretation that the cinematic apparatus itself is intended to be part of the fateful circumstances of the diegesis. The roles of two other distinctive modern technologies, however, move us deeper into this entanglement: transportation (train and motor vehicles) and mass media (popular music, television, and, extradiegetically, the cinema itself). Those two sets of problematics help further illuminate the city/country dynamics at the core of 1960s Taiwanese dialect melodrama.

Both clusters of technology enable a reconfiguration of space, renegotiated through time and in technological terms. For instance, one of the most highly charged dramatic moments in *The Last Train* is when Zhong-Yi is aboard the 10:30 p.m. train to Taipei, anxiously waiting for Cui-Cui to appear and confess something important (her being betrothed by her father to the village head's son) that she has been withholding from him but has promised to disclose at the train station. Set up as a drama of time—Will she make it in time?—this sequence begins as Cui-Cui steals away from her house and gets on an ox cart to rush to the train station. Several close-ups on one rotating cartwheel, an unmistakable sign of rurality and its primitive means of transportation, establish the visual motif. Indeed, this race against time revolves around the many circular objects throughout this breathtaking sequence. The cart tumbles and falls apart, but the determined woman charges on, missing a bus but hitching a ride on a truck. All the while, the furiously turning circles of various wheels are intercut with the circular face of a static clock mercilessly showing the ticking of time and the public address speakers urging ticketed passengers to come aboard. When Cui-Cui finally arrives at the station—too late, of course—the train is already in motion and its roaring wheels of steel wait for no one.

If the spatial divide between Taipei and its south—its rural counterpart, Taiwan's "other" from within—signifies a seemingly unbridgeable gap, these two locations can only be connected by cinematic means. That the visual field focuses on the heavy machinery of the train engine, and that the editing style prolongs the screen time by repeated shots from multiple perspectives, both emphasize the emotional weight of this dialectics of division and connection. The density of the scene warrants careful unpacking, especially when such a multi-layered narrative point is common in other films as well. There are at least three strands of narrational devices at work simultaneously. To be sure, the general function of this scene is to depict a dramatic moment in the film narrative: two lovers are forced to separate from each other due to various pressures, and that separation is further compounded by their spatial, economic, and class differences. The crosscutting between Cui-Cui and Zhong-Yi shows the tension mounting as she moves from one mode of transportation to the next. The fundamental gap that separates them is too great to overcome, however, and their desired union fails to prevail.

Over and on top of the significance of this plot point in *The Last Train* is a popular song on the soundtrack, echoing the situation with lyrics verbosely commenting on its sadness. The song performs another narration in parallel with the image track. This second narrational strand blends with the first and they combine into a totality that is the film narrative proper. Indeed, the uses of highly sentimental songs apropos of the scenes they are coupled with serve as a double iteration. A plot point is narrated twice and both narrations are performed simultaneously, with musical and narrative devices at the same time: melodrama *par excellence*.

* * *

Before going into a more detailed account of the role of music and popular song in Taiwan's dialect cinema, I turn to other films whose representations expand my discussions of melodrama. After the success of *The Last Train*, director Liang Zhe-Fu made another film, *The*

Early Train from Taipei, in the following year; part of a proliferation of generic films common in this period and earlier, such as the *Brother Wang and Brother Liu* series and its many imitators. With the same cast, this later film tackles the issue of the rural/urban divide with even greater urgency.

Narrated by a Western-style painter who wears a trenchcoat and beret and smokes a pipe, *The Early Train* is framed as a flashback, motivated by a friend's inquiry about two portraits: "Why is this girl so beautiful and that one so monstrous?" In a sympathetic, even melancholic tone, the painter recounts the story of a poor country girl named Xiu-Lan, the model for both portraits. The film is another complicated story involving young lovers, this time both from the countryside, whose fate goes from bad to worse when the girl is forced to work in Taipei as a dancehall girl to repay her family debts. By the end of the film, Xiu-Lan, whose face was maimed during a struggle when she killed her two oppressors, serves a life sentence in prison, and her lover, Huo-Tu, having gone blind, becomes a homeless street musician searching in vain for his love all over Taipei.

If *The Last Train* shows a benign urban environment in which the villainy of the circumstances is the inescapable web of socioeconomic relationships, *The Early Train* builds on that entanglement and condemns the city as always already corrupt. Unlike the earlier film which opens with a credit sequence on the train to signal the two locations in contrast, *The Early Train* moves smoothly from the painter's studio to the rustic village where, for an extended period of time, we meet and learn about the youngsters' innocent love in a space of natural beauty. After Xiu-Lan finds out about her family debts, she runs into a childhood friend visiting home from Taipei. The fashionably dressed friend's modern glamour prompts Xiu-Lan to inquire eagerly about possible employment in the city. Her friend hesitates, stuttering about how "complicated" the circumstances are in Taipei. Without warning, a quick dissolve moves the visual field swiftly to Taipei, marked not by some generic landmarks of the city, such as the Presidential Palace which opens *Brother Wang and Brother Liu Tour Taiwan*, but by the flashy neon signs of a dancehall that proclaim in large English letters, "NIGHT PARIS."

Once in the city and, specifically, in the dancehall, the visual style of *The Early Train* changes as abruptly as its location has shifted. The quiet and straightforward style of previous scenes in rural Kaohsiung is now replaced by a quickened tempo of cutting and an emphatic use of close-ups (moving feet, the band's musical instruments, and so on).

In contrast, in *The Last Train* close-ups are reserved almost exclusively for the actors' facial expressions, highlighting the wrought emotions of the scene in question. Here in this later film, the emotive effect is taken over by a fetishistic desire to gaze upon objects of difference, objects of change. The sequence after Xiu-Lan does come to Taipei and is coerced into working as a dancehall girl is a case in point.

Back home, Xiu-Lan's mother is shown in a static medium-long shot, ecstatic at the large amount of money her daughter has been able to make and send home in less than a month. Extremely pleased, the mother asks Huo-Tu to read out loud the letter from Xiu-Lan. His recitation initiates a montage sequence that shows the activities described in the letter. However, the visual styles associated with these two distinct locations are starkly different. Xiu-Lan's apparent transformation from an innocent country girl to a highly desirable dancehall woman is shown with mobile camera movements (often getting closer and closer to her various body parts such as hair, face, and feet, as well as her various dresses and high heels) and sophisticated compositions (involving multiple mirrors and/or male observers in the frame). Both visual styles emphasize her change in appearance and the changing social relationship of that appearance in the urban setting. Through this contrast, the departure from her rural origin and the separation from her hometown lover are shown to be cinematically irrevocable.

A few questions are still unanswered. If modern means of transportation connect the rural and urban areas, how and why is the individual migration to the city so insistently condemned as a journey with no return? If melodramatic narratives like the two representative texts I have discussed so far work toward a resolution and are met only with tragic ends, is the view on modernization in 1960s Taiwan ultimately a pessimistic one? Is Taipei, the capital of Taiwan, a city to which the characters are fatally attracted, an urban hell in which they are forever trapped? To attempt to find some, if only provisional, answers to these questions, we need to go back to the third level of narration suggested earlier by way of the musical sequences ubiquitous in the melodramatic films.

* * *

Dialect Cinema and Its Sonorous Circumstances, Nation within Bounds

The heavily invested scene on the platform in *The Last Train from Kaohsiung* has its counterpart in *The Early Train from Taipei*. The geographical symmetry between the two locations only betrays the imbalanced spatial meanings that both films work categorically to cinematize. On this vast and chaotic field of cinematic representation, if we also look back at comedy, the multi-valence of Taiwanese-dialect film seems unable to mend those fissures, thereby allowing the diegetic to leak into the *extradiegetic*: the third level of narration. To go back even further, what characterizes the dialect cinema in the 1950s—the documentary and the operatic modes—is also what implicates the state policies (government-promoted tourism for the former) and traditional performances (competition against Ge-Zai Opera for the latter). As such, the film text cannot but remain pervious to what lies outside, even when various filmic conventions and operative devices are firmly in place, all with their inevitable cracks: a structure larger than its narrative, genre, or even the entire body of films of a particular time.

The musical sequences help us grasp the complex structure of how cultural production and entertainment products are circulated according to the capitalist logic of dissemination and reproduction. Let us return to the platform in *The Last Train from Kaohsiung*. As the music begins and the singer's baritone belabors the sadness of the imminent separation of two lovers, the lyrics also appear on the screen, providing a verbatim anchor. This practice was not singular to this scene, nor to this film, and not even to Taiwanese-dialect cinema in general. In fact, the marriage between film and popular music dates back at least to 1930s Shanghai. Andrew F. Jones, for example, discusses popular music in that context. Highlighting its daunting ability to cross media boundaries, Jones writes,

> Music, precisely because of its capacity to straddle different media (gramophone records, wireless broadcasting, sound cinema) and places of performance (concert halls, dance halls, and stadium rallies), was also central to the efforts of leftist intellectuals to transform media culture in China and, in so doing, mobilize the citizenry to resist the twin specters of Western imperialism and Japanese territorial encroachment.[30]

Jones's assessment of popular music in 1930s Shanghai bears striking relevance to Taiwan's dialect cinema in the 1960s.

In 1932, *The Peach Girl*, starring Shanghai film diva Ruan Lingyu, was imported to Taiwan. Although it was a silent film, the distributor asked the famed *benzi*, Zhan Tian-Ma, to write lyrics based on the film's narrative with music composed by Wang Yun-Feng. The end result was an immensely successful promotion campaign for the film, dubbed "the first Taiwanese-dialect popular song."[31] A stunning example of how Taiwan's local film circle vernacularized cultural products from outside, this song set a precedent for continuous close ties between film and popular music in Taiwan cinema. By the time Taiwanese-dialect films began to flourish in the mid-1950s and then again in the 1960s, many of the songs were truly hybrid, absorbing traditional opera, Japanese and Mainland Chinese influences, as well as assimilating Western classical music, rock and roll, and jazz.[32] Popular music and film were heavily influenced by each other, and their respective sources of inspiration were diverse as their interaction and interfertilization spawned further hybridization.

Unlike in the 1930s, however, when Shanghai leftist films' avowed mission was to resist encroaching foreign powers, Taiwanese-dialect cinema's marriage to mass entertainment fed on the popularity and potential commercial profit enabled by that coupling. To return again to the scene on the platform at the Kaohsiung station before the last train departs for Taipei, we are now faced with a very different cinematic text. As a matter of fact, the tune so lovingly and painstakingly intoned in that scene was adapted from a popular Japanese song.[33] The musical sequence thus historicized in the film, and in many others, such as those in *The First Train from Taipei*, shows that the general cinemascape of Taiwan's dialect cinema, so rich in its *generic diversity* under either the operatic or the realist mode of representation is, finally, a complex manifestation of its *unclean severance* from various transnational sources of external influences, both colonial and postcolonial, from China, Japan, and beyond. The uniqueness of Taiwanese-dialect cinema's vernacular, recalling here how Andrew Higson theorizes the limits of national cinema, is indeed "more likely to be either local or transnational than national."[34]

* * *

The nearly two decades of Taiwanese-dialect cinema, producing more than a thousand films, are no doubt a significant period in Taiwan's film history as well as in its general cultural history. Something close to being a piece of "national" history, too, the vicissitudes of dialect cinema's rise and demise were so intimately imbricated with the cultural, social, and political transformation of Taiwan that this history awaits further revisions. Besides revisiting the archives and looking for materials that might bring new insights to this period, another possibly productive way forward, I would suggest, is to begin to inquire into Taiwan's later history in relation to what we have learned here and what questions remain.

One such question would be how and why the dialect cinema died out so suddenly around 1970, a year when some 20 films were produced while next to none appeared the very next year. Many historians agree that the major problem with dialect cinema was its quality. Yingjin Zhang, for instance, claims the "the nature of speculation [studios making films catering to specific domestic and oversea markets] restricted the artistic and thematic reorientation in the Taiwanese-dialect film, and speedy production and low production values severely hurt its competitiveness."[35] Besides the overproduction of low-quality films, Ye Long-Yan proposes that two kinds of censorship also contributed to this cinema's rapid decline, on the one hand, by the exhibitors (ensuring that the length of films remained within a commercially viable time for maximum screenings per day), and by the government (in terms of both thematic context control and bureaucratic regulation) on the other.[36]

Perhaps the single most significant factor that caused Taiwanese-dialect cinema's decline and its eventual demise was the rise of Mandarin-language cinema. However, it is important to ask: Were the very different conditions of production between Mandarin and dialect films based solely on their linguistic orientations? Or, were the very designations of "Mandarin" (the official language, the center) vis-à-vis "dialect" (the vernacular, the marginal) already indicative of imbalanced political valences and uneven social resources? As early as 1946, the Nationalist government began its campaign promoting the use of Mandarin Chinese with an emphasis on banning the colonial language, Japanese. Various dialects such as Taiwanese and Hakka were not strictly forbidden, at least in the private sectors. In other words, a broader and deeper change in Taiwan's social and cultural circumstances would have to be in place to bring such devastating impacts on dialect films. Taiwan's Mandarin and dialect cinemas were indeed competitors, but not in mutually exclusive terms. As we shall see, the legacy of generic diversity and aesthetic flexibility of dialect cinema would be key elements that helped Mandarin-language cinema to take flight in the 1960s.

3

Tracing a Journeyman's Electric Shadow: Healthy Realism, Cultural Policies, and Lee Hsing, 1964–1980

Almost 20 years after Taiwan's return to China under Nationalist rule, the first domestic color film was produced in 1964. *Oyster Girls*, codirected by Lee Hsing and Lee Chia (no relation), was an immediate box office success and went on to win the Best Feature Film award the following year at the Asia Film Festival (renamed the Asian Pacific Film Festival in 1983). A landmark for Taiwan cinema's technological achievement and a tremendous commercial and international success, this film marked the beginning of Healthy Realism (*jiankang xieshi zhuyi*). Three decades after the inception of this movement, film critic Chiao Hsiung-Ping lamented that, because of the movement's emphasis on an "impoverished peasantry" instead of "efforts toward modernization," it could at best be considered a "glorious failure."[1] Chiao grouped Healthy Realism with the Yellow Plum Melody costume musicals[2] and melodramas based on popular romance novels by Qiong Yao, all of which, in her words, are "lost in nostalgia and escapism." Her sweeping condemnation is, in retrospect, unjustified, but nonetheless instructive because of its revisionist rhetoric. The grouping of those different films and genres into one historical category overlooks the muddied history of the structures and modes of production within which those different genres had to operate. While Healthy Realist films were mostly produced by the Nationalist Party–owned Central Motion Picture Corporation (CMPC),[3] and the Yellow Plum Melody musicals had strong affiliations with the Hong Kong film industry, Qiong Yao's romantic melodramas were indebted to both.[4]

At a time before any solid industrial infrastructure was established, "culture," vernacular or state-sanctioned, and "policy," explicitly political or inherently ideological, generated highly diverse cinematic imaginings of the nation and its modernization. Reflecting changing political pressures from the Nationalist government, grappling with the colonial legacy, and negotiating intensifying international politics and competition, Taiwan cinema in the 1960s and 1970s must be understood as an active agent that partook in the representation and imaginary construction of the nation in an increasingly transnational context. But how did both industrial and political forces affect culture? The Frankfurt School's critique of the culture industry, with some revision, may help to explain the difficulties faced by Taiwan cinema at that time.

Taiwan cinema in the 1960s and 1970s, albeit largely a commercial endeavor, was not simply designed "from above" for mass consumption,[5] nor was it "from the very beginning" a mere commodity.[6] Instead, it was an intricate operation under shifting cultural and political conditions, including those of language, ethnic identification, distribution and exhibition, and later, volatile international politics and diplomatic crises. This matrix frames Taiwan cinema's highly unstable modes of production and consumption during the years in question. What for Adorno characterizes an industry— "rationalization" and "standardization—manifested itself very differently in Taiwan.[7] On the one hand, the "culture industry" morphed and mutated because of its imbrication with the nationalist cultural policy, both internal and external to film production—*rationalization-cum-nationalization*. On the other hand, the diverse bodies of policy films and popular cinemas were more intermingled than distinctive from one another, mixing the "high" (Healthy Realist cinema) with the "low" (dialect films, melodrama, martial arts)—*standardization-through-proliferation*. These two overlapping force fields make up the spectacular, if spectacularly complicated, cinemascape of a contested "national" cinema.

These two conditions require further explanation, specifically with regard to the Healthy Realist films. To begin, "rationalization-cum-nationalization" designates a process of defining the nation through the movement's insistent pursuit of values, traditions, and characteristics, or, simply put, a "national culture" that both outlines the parameters of and gives rationale to any such definition. Consequently, "nation" becomes a rationalized category by means of cinematization. Even though the rationalization of that category changes over time, the logic of rationalization *as* nationalization remains key. Furthermore, similar to the cornucopia of domestic and imported forms vernacularized in the dialect films discussed previously, genre diversity also characterized Healthy Realism, but it did so by standardizing the deployment and the functioning of aesthetics in the service of the dominant nationalist ideology. The multiplication of generic forms and the further proliferation of those genres to meet shifting demands and pressures eventually compelled aesthetics into a standardized *form* of politics. As we shall see, Healthy Realism was a unique cinematized *stasis of change*, a peculiar condition for a modernizing nation in which the notion of change—progress, movement—is caught in a perpetual state of stagnation wherein film aesthetics is trapped by nationalist ideology.

*   *   *

This chapter focuses on Healthy Realism, a cinematic movement launched by the leading state-owned studio in the mid-1960s, and on one filmmaker in particular, Lee Hsing, whose career spans more than half a century and parallels the long course of Taiwan cinema since the 1950s. Born in Shanghai and well schooled in the dramatic arts, Lee traveled from China to Taiwan, from theater to cinema, from Taiwanese-dialect to Mandarin filmmaking, all the while working in a great variety of genres. Between 1965 and 1980, Lee directed seven Golden Horse Best Feature Film winners and was himself a three-time Best Director recipient. In his prolific career, Lee made films across various genres in different phases of Taiwan's nation-building and is considered one of the most influential filmmakers in Taiwan. In 1990, Lee was chosen to lead a delegation of Taiwan's filmmakers across the Strait to visit Beijing, ending four decades of official segregation of the two film industries.

Lee's representative status does not belie any aesthetic judgment of the quality of his films, however; nor should it be taken as a basis for any intimation of his close ties with the government. Instead, he represented Taiwan cinema in the 1960s and 1970s not simply as a filmmaker in an auteurist sense, but, more importantly, as a major producer of that cinema. Lee had to work closely with both private and state-run studios as well as with pressures from commercial demands and political mandates. Focusing on this representative figure provides us with historical and historiographic lenses through which the movement of Healthy Realism and its intricate imagination of the "nation" may be examined. To be sure, throughout his stunningly prolific career, Lee has helped establish a variety of genres and has aided in their subsequent development. Film historian Lu Feii, for example, credits Lee's work as pioneering in Taiwanese-dialect comedy, family melodrama with Confucian ethics, reinventing romantic melodrama (importantly with filmic adaptations of Qiong Yao's romantic novels), and introducing nativist ideology into filmic exploration of the "China/Taiwan complex."[8] By paying close attention to Lee's films, we can trace the trajectories of Taiwan cinema in the 1960s and 1970s and begin to broach the questions of the nation on this island.

A road map here will be helpful. First, I begin by contextualizing the inception of Healthy Realism in relation to the changing cultural policies in Taiwan since the mid-1940s. Second, I describe Healthy Realism's salient features through Lee's *Beautiful Duckling* (1964) while comparing it with his other major works. Third, I show how Lee's narrative themes of family and nation carry his aesthetics and style over to other films of various genres and to works by other contemporary filmmakers. Fourth, I argue that the Healthy Realist movement be understood as a distinct body of films—different genres notwithstanding—that resisted the dominance of commercial cinema while being deeply influenced by it. Finally, by invoking the radical shift in 1970s international politics, I illustrate how the stylistic characteristics of Healthy Realism were swiftly transposed to policy films of that decade. The movement's aesthetic paradigm eventually reached an impasse between aesthetics and politics, leading to the next conception of film aesthetics with the emergence of Taiwan's New Cinema of the 1980s, which the rest of the book elaborates.

Several focal points will further help us to navigate through this muddied terrain. First of all, genre films still dominated Taiwan's commercial cinema, a strong current continuing from the golden age of Taiwanese-dialect films. The variety of genres in Lee's films attests to both shifting commercial demands and changing cultural policies. Furthermore, even though Lee works in many different genres, his filmic styles—camera work, editing, and narrative strategies—and his thematic concerns—family values, ethics, tradition, culture, and nation—are remarkably consistent through the decades. The cinema of Lee's (and his contemporaries') films, both stylistically and thematically, provided a paradigm with which the New Cinema filmmakers would contend. Last, but not least, whereas his generic diversity demonstrates flexibility under commercial pressures, his thematic concerns met the mandates of the government's shifting cultural policies, which, in turn, revealed the government's own changing notions of the nation. The metamorphoses of the "nation" thus imaged and imagined would finally be challenged cinematically. Aesthetics no longer functioned as form serving content, but, rather, became the core of a new politics of aesthetics explored by the New Cinema.

* * *

Policy in the Middle: The Ambiguous Field between National Culture and Nationalist Propaganda

Cultural policies in Taiwan were never meant only as state propaganda, nor were they merely some explicit form of censorship. According to Cheng Ming-Lee, the Nationalists' cultural policy began as a reaction to Mao Zedong's 1942 speech in Yan'an, in which he famously declared that all arts be created from social reality and in the service of class struggle.[9] To counter that claim, the top Nationalist propagandist, Zhang Dao-Fan, published "The Cultural Policy We Need" later that year.[10] Among the four major directives Zhang proposed, his emphasis on the question of nation is particularly worth noting. Expounding on Sun Yat-Sen's *The Three Principles of the People*, Zhang claimed the supremacy of nationalism. "While a private-property [which denotes both capitalist and feudal] society espouses individualism and a communist society class consciousness, a society following the Three Principles of the People produces an ideology that places the nation above all else."[11] In other words, nationalism here is no longer an ideology but is figured as the Chinese nation's true destiny against other socioeconomic systems such as feudalism, capitalism, and, most importantly, communism. The nation thus defined spells out clearly its historical specificity: the grueling antagonism between the Nationalist and the Communist regimes.

Zhang's politically orthodox notion of national culture may seem naive, but its efficacy is derived precisely from such simplicity. For he does not give any rigorous explanation of what distinguishes nationalism from its nemeses besides the empty rhetoric, stressing only what his nationalist agenda will eventually achieve. "Culture," national or otherwise, becomes an empty space that accommodates all aspects of public life and private thought through a filter of the *positive*. That is, besides those ostensibly negative things attributed to feudalism, capitalism, or communism, everything else can be, and indeed is, made to represent the positive manifestation of the nationalist ideology. How the transformation of all social ills and economic inequality into a utopian nation may be attained is never prescribed specifically.

After relocating to Taiwan in 1949, the Nationalist government was quick to establish a cultural policy of "militarist literature and arts" (*zhandou wenyi*) with explicit belligerence against the Chinese Communist Party at its core. Penned by none other than Chiang Kai-Shek himself, the single most important document is the "Two Supplementary Chapters" to Sun Yat-Sen's *The Three Principles of the People*. In his discussion of "National Fecundity, Social Welfare and Education" and "Health and Happiness," Chiang emphasizes, on the one hand, that the goal of education is to produce national subjects who "engage in productive work and dedicate themselves wholeheartedly to the promotion of social progress and national regeneration,"[12] and, on the other, that the "literary and artistic policy" is gauged "with particular reference to the influence that literature and art are likely to exert on the citizen's mental health and happiness."[13] Chiang goes so far as to commend, though not naming them specifically, some literary works, dramatic performances in the Taiwan dialect, and even some motion pictures, for their "intense national feelings" and "anti-Communist and anti-Russian slant."[14]

The overt partisan emphasis is understandable, and the subsequent flood of pledges of allegiance from either Chiang's avowed followers or fearful subordinates should come as no surprise. One striking example of this phenomenon was a particular pledge, billed as being from "all walks of the nation" (*quanguo gejie*), in support of Chiang's call for eradicating the "three perils" (*sanhai*)—red (communism), yellow (pornography), and black (tabloid journalism)—started less than a year after the publication of Chiang's "Supplements," which collected more than 2 million signatures within a month.[15] After 1954, many official and semi-official literary and artistic organizations and publications were formed, none of which strayed from a militant definition of the arts and their educational function as part of the state propaganda apparatus.

As we have seen in chapter 2, in terms of the film industry, profit had largely trumped any explicit "policy" while the commercial cinema remained a battleground for various genres. In the first two decades after Taiwan's return to the Nationalist government, state- or party-owned studios focused mainly on the production of newsreels and educational films, and were no competition against imports from Hollywood, Europe, Japan, and Hong Kong, or even against domestically made Taiwanese-dialect films. But that would change in 1963, when Gong Hong (aka Henry Kung) took the helm of the Central Motion Picture Corporation (CMPC) and worked hard to conceive a different kind of cinema that would be ideologically compliant as well as commercially viable.

* * *

The Golden Horse on the Strait

It is important to contextualize those changes that would soon occur in the film industry to understand why they transpired in certain ways. One of the early efforts by the Nationalist government to boost film culture was the establishment of the Golden Horse Awards in 1962. Often regarded as the most important film event for Chinese-language cinemas, the Golden Horse commenced its annual event under the auspices of the Government Information Office (GIO) of the Administrative Yuan. The name itself is of interest. *Jin-Ma*, which literally means "golden horse," is an auspicious symbol in Chinese. However, it is also derived from the names of two Nationalist military island outposts, *Jin-men* and *Ma-zu*. Right off of the coast of the Mainland's Fukien Province, these two islands have long been the front line in the Republic of China ("ROC") and People's Republic of China ("PRC") conflict. This naming of the most prominent cultural event to date on Taiwan sent an unequivocal political message, fully in keeping with the cultural policy of militarism.

However combative they may sound, the early years of the Golden Horse Awards followed a different script.[16] The first Best Feature Film winner in 1962 was a Hong Kong production, *Star, Moon, Sun*. A two-part, nearly four-hour-long epic, the film showcases the production conditions of Hong Kong's affluent film industry as well as its rich heritage from Shanghai filmmaking of the 1930s and 1940s. Shot with film stock imported from the United States and later color-printed in England, the lavish color cinematography brilliantly complements the film's sophisticated narrative, which spans the entire Sino-Japanese War period. Significantly, however, while China's victory over Japan is the final pivotal plot point and the film ends in Hong Kong some years later, the Communists' liberation of China is not mentioned at all. Most of the other awards went to the highly popular costume drama musicals, the Yellow Plum Melody films. One of the most successful films of this genre, *The Love Eterne* (aka *Butterfly Lovers*, 1963), another Hong Kong production by the Shaw Brothers Studio, would go on to win several major awards in the following year. This film tells the famous story of two ill-fated lovers with the lead female character in male drag for a good part of the film. The romantic intrigues play out with well-performed musical scenes and various elaborately choreographed comic and tragic sequences. Both films were crafted by masterful hands, ones that only an established industry could lend. Technical know-how and star power secured the success of these two films, which revealed to many, Gong Hong among them, that Taiwan sorely lacked the capability to produce such advanced films.

The provincial government-owned studio, the Taiwan Motion Pictures Studio, actually produced Taiwan's first color film in 1962. It was a collaborative project with Japan, directed by Bu Wancang, a prominent filmmaker in Shanghai during the 1930s and 1940s. According to some reports, however, the film was unsuccessful because of the lack of true collaboration among the different sectors of production.[17] The CMPC for their part had been sending technicians to Japan and the United States to learn color cinematography, but a color production completely independent of foreign, especially Japanese, technical support was not possible until 1963.[18] If the CMPC was to invest in color cinematography and to put forth productions that were able to both compete with other commercial films and comply with the state's cultural policy, they would have to conceive something different from the two Hong Kong films just mentioned. However well crafted and well received, for the CMPC, these two films' subject matters and their representation of Chinese history were not positive or specific enough. *Star*'s ambiguous relationship with the Communist mainland and *The Love Eterne*'s indulgence in fantasy and melodrama would certainly be inadequate. In other words, when CMPC was finally ready to launch a national cinema campaign, with technology in hand and talent in place, one last question remained: What kind of film would best represent a positive image of the Chinese nation in Taiwan?

* * *

Healthy Realism Is *Not* ...

I am completely convinced that a single work giving the sunny side of this wonderful world of sun and shade its due...would exert a deeper, warmer, more stimulating, more reformist influence than all these brilliant studies of putrefaction.

—*Paul Heyse, Nobel Prize Laureate in Literature, 1910*[19]

The Society for Chinese Cinema Studies in Taiwan held a roundtable in 1994, discussing "The Significance of 1960s Healthy Realist Film in Taiwan Cinema."[20] Participants included key Healthy Realist practitioners and film critics and historians. While director Lee Hsing commented on the lack of research on this movement, film critic Li Tian-duo questioned the political, economic, and sociohistorical context within which Healthy Realism emerged. In response to Li's query, veteran film critic Huang Ren spoke "from [his personal] memory" of many of Taiwan's filmmakers at that time who rejected Hollywood-style film production in favor of Italian Neorealism. He then singled out the new director of the CMPC, Gong Hong, as the key figure who promoted Healthy Realism as a priority. In Huang's account, Gong thought that, "Italian Neorealist films after World War Two were mostly about the dark side of society, for example, *Bicycle Thieves*." The same logic would extend, Huang continued with added emphasis, to another realism: 1930s Shanghai leftist cinema. Apparently, Gong Hong found that "the kind of realism flourishing in 1930s Shanghai was a means which the leftist camp employed to incite discontent against the government, posing a threat to the Nationalist government at the time." Consequently, "realism" became politically suspect for the authorities even after the government was relocated to Taiwan." In short, "realism" was less an aesthetic than a *political* category.

Even more important was how the term "realism" would continue to be politicized. Before Healthy Realism could be a feasible project, an acceptable framing of "realism" had first to be conceived. If Italian Neorealism was faulted for its dubious emphasis on exposing the darker side of the society, and if 1930s leftist cinema in Shanghai was deemed politically subversive for Taiwan's Nationalist government in transition, during its ostensibly temporary retreat to Taiwan, Healthy Realism could only be framed by what it was *not*: whatever it might be, it was not Italian Neorealism, nor was it Shanghai's leftist cinema. This *negative* definition of Healthy Realism would inform the initial period of conceptualization which helped define what realism would mean for Taiwan.

The screenwriter for many important Healthy Realist films, Zhang Yong-Xiang maintained that, "Healthy Realism derived its meaning from the times we lived in, full of hopes and stories under the sunshine. To tell stories that are healthy, bright, and lively means that 'healthy' [subject matters] can be realistic, too." Lee Hsing was the first to concur by saying that "under the constricting political circumstances at that time, we decided to produce films that could be made under the sunlight. That decision was definitely connected to the social environment of the time."[21] The political milieu, in this sense, became more than a context or limitation within which filmmakers created; rather, it positioned itself as an idealistic filter through which only selected elements could pass. The much-repeated metaphor of "sunlight" attests to the guarded nature of Healthy Realism since its conception.

* * *

Healthy Realism Is Like...but Not Quite...

To define Healthy Realism, film historian Liao Gene-Fon provides a comparison with Italian Neorealism by summarizing André Bazin's realist aesthetics. For him, Bazanian realism is characterized by "accidental events presented in a meandering narrative structure, non-professional actors, a semi-documentary style, black-and-white on location shooting, natural lighting, dialog in dialects when necessary, detailed attention to the surrounding environment, and psychological depiction of both primary and secondary characters." Healthy Realism, on the other hand, emphasizes "vividly plotted narrative structure, both studio and on-location shootings, star casting, color schemes that match the demand of color cinematography, special lighting arrangements, artificially created sets, unrealistic use of Mandarin or Mandarin speeches with a Taiwanese accent." To sum up, while Italian Neorealism is best understood through Bazinian realist aesthetics, Healthy Realism leans heavily on "the tradition of formalist aesthetics since Eisenstein and Arnheim."[22] This comparison follows a conventional realism/formalism dichotomy, which is helpful, but only in a limited way.

Both realism and formalism are aesthetic strategies and choices whose relationship with "reality" is always representational; whatever means is at the filmmaker's disposal is always formal. To say this is not to deny the different *tendencies* toward the "reality effects" between these two traditions.[23] However, any choice tends toward certain desired effects and those effects are always representations of that desire. It is with such a keen understanding of film aesthetics that André Bazin famously declared, "[Realism] in art can only be achieved in one way—through artifice."[24] In the case of Healthy Realism—whether it is described as realist, formalist, or otherwise—I want to focus on what that desire to represent is, instead of chasing the elusive "reality" that is always in excess of representation.[25] It may be more productive, as Liao himself would agree, to examine Healthy Realism not as a specific *genre,* but, rather, as a film *movement* inclusive of various genres. That is, Healthy Realism can be grasped as a collectivity whose discourse informs and is informed by the specific social and political context within which it operates, resulting in different sets of aesthetic techniques and traits traveling fluidly across genres.

* * *

Healthy Realism and Its Historical (Dis)Content

When investigating the significance of Healthy Realism, film historian Liu Xian-Cheng emphasizes the social and political context of this movement and paints a compelling picture of it by articulating the political and the economic with the cultural.[26] For Chen, Lee Hsing came onto the scene at the nexus where those forces intersected.[27] Already involved in a number of films, either as actor or assistant director, Lee directed one of the most popular Taiwanese-dialect films in 1958, *Brother Wang and Brother Liu Tour Taiwan,* which was discussed at length in chapter 2. After a few more years of struggle between directing commercially successful dialect films and making unsuccessful attempts to join the CMPC, Lee even ventured into documentary filmmaking for one of the state-owned studios before founding his own production company in 1961 to produce and direct a comedy. *Both Sides Are Happy* is a rather delightful film that brings to the fore the conflicts between Mandarin- and

Taiwanese-speaking communities and suggests how those differences may be resolved. After a few more dialect films, in 1963 Lee Hsing directed *Head of the Street, End of the Lane*, again produced by his own company. Yingjin Zhang praises the film because it "conveys not only the bitter pathos characteristic of Taiwanese-dialect films but is also reminiscent of the social realism of 1930s Shanghai.[28] The revisionist mention of Shanghai's leftist cinema notwithstanding, Zhang's appraisal may well explain why CMPC director Gong Hong believed that he had found the right person with whom to collaborate in making films that were "healthy," "real," and specific to Taiwan.

An immediate result was the first domestically produced color film, *Oyster Girl*. Halfway through the production, however, another film was conceived and Lee Hsing was pulled from the *Oyster Girl* project to direct *Beautiful Duckling*. The completion of both films marked the beginning of the first golden age of domestically produced Mandarin films in Taiwan.[29] *Duckling* is remarkable not only because it succeeds in employing realist filmic techniques to tell a riveting family melodrama, but also because it displays distinct filmic styles and thematic treatments which would continue to characterize Healthy Realism—across a wide variety of genres—in the next decade and a half.

Inspired by a famous painter's watercolors of Taiwan's rural landscape, duck farming in particular, *Beautiful Duckling* begins with the camera surveying one such painting, with a female voice-over intoning the film's intention to present to its audience the beautiful agricultural society of Taiwan. As the narrator announces the title, the film cuts abruptly to live footage of flocks of ducks in the water. To heighten the dramatic effect, orchestral music with discernable Taiwanese folksong motifs swells on cue. Even more striking is how the sequence punctuates each credit with a freeze frame of the lively fowl. In other words, the opening scene animates a static surface with movement—from watercolor stills to moving images—and rearticulates that movement with stills—from moving images to freeze frames. That is, the film begins by setting an unambiguous tone that explicitly foretells, verbosely through its voice-over narration, the *ideological* content of unchanging values as its *thematic* content—aesthetics in the service of politics, an *aesthetics of politics*. Furthermore, the articulation of plastic representation (watercolor paintings) with documentary (the cinematic capture of live action) sutures the constructed with the natural, further politicizing the visual field of representation.

This opening sequence bears a striking resemblance to the one in its immediate predecessor, *Oyster Girl*. The earlier film also begins with an off-screen voice commentary, this time over close-up images of the namesake shellfish before transitioning to live footage of oyster girls at work, while the bright red title dominates the entire screen. What follows, for both films, is also identical: long shots of the idyllic country landscape, oyster fields and duck farms respectively, accompanied by music heavily marked by Taiwanese folk music motifs. It is abundantly clear that the early efforts of Healthy Realism are focused on imagining an agricultural paradise where nature and culture harmoniously coexist. This coexistence gives an impression of timelessness. Indeed, as both narrators assert, duck and oyster farming are the ways of livelihood for those farmers since time immemorial; this is a Taiwan that has lived a rural lifestyle of unchanging tradition and diligent labor. As we shall see in the interlude, labor continues to figure centrally as a key trope for the ideal citizen, a state of work in progress, one may say, on which the modernizing nation depends but over which it gradually loses hold. In short, the *stasis* of realist aesthetics in the service of the Nationalist ideology of unchanging values and unified nationhood would eventually become incompatible with the inevitable *change* demanded by the rising pressures of nation-building by modernization. Healthy realism is finally this dynamic, paradoxical *stasis of change.*

* * *

The Parade of Ducks and the Landscape of Film Aesthetics

The notion of stasis is not immediately apparent in Healthy Realist films. For example, a positive message about the government's investment in improving the living standards in the fishing villages is embedded in the tragicomic romantic drama of *Oyster Girl*. Similarly in *Beautiful Duckling*, change, or, more specifically, progress through modernization, is posited as the manifest or official message. However, the emotional drama of *Beautiful Duckling*—the *other* message, concerning the importance of familial relationships and of social mores and work ethics—evolves around Mr. Lin, a duck farmer, and his adopted daughter, Hsiao-Yueh, who does not know about her adoptive status. Hsiao-Yueh's biological brother has been blackmailing Mr. Lin, threatening to disclose the fact to Hsiao-Yueh.

What ensues is a poignant melodrama about familial bonds, both biological and historical.

In many ways, Hsiao-Yueh is equated with what the ducks stand for—untouched innocence, earthy beauty, rurality as such—but something else as well. After the credit sequence, the film proceeds to show Hsiao-Yueh at work with the ducks. Her cheerful movements and playful birdcalls when feeding the livestock complement the natural landscape. Together, they create a total image of Taiwan in its full agrarian bliss. After swiftly establishing duck farming as an emblem of Taiwan's rural life, the film introduces the changes that will occur. Mr. Lin is shown in the following scene with two officials from the Farmers' Association, commissioning him to conduct an experiment; he is to raise a new hybrid breed of ducks, record their growth in detail, and mark each duckling with an identity tag. *Modernizing* duck farming is thus posited as a parallel line with the film's main narrative of family melodrama, and individual/familial development is intimately linked with national development.

For Chris Berry and Mary Farquhar, this parallel "endorses small-scale rural modernization as the backbone of modern society." From what they consider a fusion of "Confucian ethics" and the "spirit of capitalism" arises the constructed image of the nation that is the Republic of China on the island of Taiwan.[30] While agreeing with their general assessment of Healthy Realism's ideological functions, I want to go further and ask how the cinema peforms those functions before attempting to offer a fuller conceptualization of the modernity promoted in this cinematic movement. One way to start this inquiry is to look closely at how Healthy Realism constructs a cinematic space in which those heavily burdened themes—Confucian ethics, family values, the capitalist spirit—are staged.

The previous scene introduces one such salient feature of Healthy Realism's spatial construction: realistic sets as counterparts to actual locations. From the outdoor scene of Hsiao-Yueh tending her flock of ducks, the film cuts to a close-up of ducklings only to reveal with a slow and deliberate zoom out an elaborate set of two adjacent farmhouses on a soundstage, furnished with a footbridge over a tree-lined creek and hundreds of live ducks. The degree of attention to detail and the scale of meticulous construction were unprecedented in domestic production, rivaling the lavish sets associated with Hong Kong produced costume musicals or martial arts films. Different, of course, from those genre films' spectacle of fantasy is *Beautiful Duckling*'s relentless drive toward realism.

Years after making *Beautiful Duckling*, Lee Hsing reminisced about the conditions of production of the film. Gong Hong's interest in location shooting was so strong that he took the director with him to visit several actual duck farms. When decisions were made to shoot those scenes on a soundstage, no effort was spared to reproduce the actual location as faithfully as possible.[31] This drive to emulate reality would continue to characterize Lee's later films and set a high bar for other productions. It has great ramifications for film aesthetics as well. Unlike earlier domestic films with much lower budgets, *Beautiful Duckling* opened the door for extensive location shooting as well as realistic set constructions. With these two combined, lengthy montage sequences involving both in- and outdoor shooting are fashioned with such seamlessness that they achieve the Healthy Realist goal of representing the bright side of reality.

One sequence in *Beautiful Duckling* exemplifies just that. Halfway into the film, Mr. Lin and Xiao Yueh embark on their annual trip, bringing their ducks to a friend's rice fields at harvest time so that scattered grains can feed the ducks while the duck droppings fertilize the land for future crops. This strikingly beautiful sequence of the parade of ducks begins with the father-daughter team herding the flock from their farmhouse across the bridge. The mobile camera smoothly follows their movement before a cut to the next shot effortlessly links the two locations—soundstage and outdoor location—and merges them into a total effect of spatial continuity. Several long shots from various angles capture the beautiful scenery and the farmers' harmonious movement with their ducks across the rural landscape. It is not enough to suggest the fictional adjacency of those places by continuity editing; realist aesthetics must also convince the viewer, visually and stylistically, of such a spatial continuum.

It may seem unremarkable at first glance, for has it not been one of realist cinema's goals to create an illusion of spatial and temporal congruity and narrative contiguity through cinematic means? Extremely important, however, is this cinema's ability to construct a diegesis of compelling visual similitude at the ideological core of Healthy Realism. It is not simply a coincidence that Healthy Realism was conceived and put into practice when the CMPC became capable of color cinematography. Inevitably the new technology increased the effect of realism, but that realism served the ideological mission of representing Taiwan through an idealizing lens. The beauty of rural Taiwan captured in abundance in many long shots in this and many other films was deliberately distanced from the unclean, even backward, images of actual village life in close-ups. Because the long shots on location capture, in broad strokes and across a large canvas, a serenity of physical beauty at a distance, the camera can then zoom in on the more intimate drama staged on the meticulous sets. The success of such cinematic representation of healthy subject matter depends on this blurring of the boundaries between natural and constructed cinematic spaces.

Other films demonstrate this significant aesthetic function as well. A good example is another highly popular film, *He Never Gives Up*, directed by Lee in 1978. A meticulously constructed set of a city street where the two protagonists live was built on a soundstage. The set displays the loudness of a real urban street but not the noise, the bustling but not the chaos, and the crowd but not the mess. Both instances show how crucial it is for Healthy Realism to deploy all means at its disposal to construct a total image of Taiwan, cleansed of all undesirables and awash in brightness. In this way we come to understand how realist techniques are always already ideological tools. The rawness of Taiwanese-dialect films in the previous decade can then be appreciated in a different, perhaps more positive light. And, less than two decades later, Taiwan's new cinema in the 1980s must be understood as a *repoliticization* of realism. The latter cinema's insistence on raw reality represented with minimal stylization would come to be the signature of its aesthetic politics.

* * *

Close Encounters with Modernity of a Healthy Realist Kind

If we return to the parade of ducks in *Duckling*, one may wonder where modernity—change, progress, modernization—finds a place in this rural paradise. Playfully choreographed with cheerful music on the soundtrack, the band of farmers and ducks marches on in the beautiful landscape of rural Taiwan without even an electricity pole in sight. Suddenly, however, the ducks and their farmers come to a pasture where gigantic power plants loom ominously in the background. With no explanation, not even a pause as the music plays on, the parade of ducks moves past the plants under the same sun until it sets. Ducks and power plants, coexisting only for this brief moment in the film, make up an emblematic picture of 1960s Taiwan in the process of modernization. But, as abruptly as the power plants burst into the scene, they take leave of it; modernity has to find solace elsewhere.

Modernization, an ongoing process of change, is antithetical to stasis; therein lies the fundamental problem of Healthy Realism, what I have called a "stasis of change." In the leftist cinema of 1930s Shanghai, for instance, energy is directed toward change and the cinematic means of representation—narrative and framing—are organized to channel that energy for change.[32] In contrast, Healthy Realism insists on the notion of stasis—familial relationships, Confucian ethics, national culture, and so on—but it cannot address how modernization may bring inevitable changes to bear upon those supposedly unchanging values. One way to do so—and we see it over and over again in this period—is the repeated affirmation of those themes of the national by conflating aesthetics with politics. In short, realism becomes a vehicle for how the real can, and indeed should, be represented. To put it differently, Healthy Realism is a successful alternative to Taiwanese-dialect films because it approximates the epitome of what the dominant politics wishes to see. Along with other Healthy Realist films, *Beautiful Duckling* shows a utopian space where modernity can be housed in a place of the unchanged, but change turns out to be an unstoppable force even in the site of stasis that Healthy Realism has so painstakingly constituted.

To see this paradox, one has only to look at the representation of town and country in Healthy Realism. Early on in *Beautiful Duckling*, a character voices his suspicion of change represented by Mr. Lin's agreement to modernize the duck farm by participating in the experiment of hybridization. For this farmer, who has farmed the same type of duck all his life, improvement or progress is mere nonsense. He confronts Mr. Lin by invoking a simple and yet pointed question about change: "An improved duck is still a duck; can it become a goose?" Indeed, what exactly is to be changed?

Nothing. That nothing is fundamentally changed would be the first reasonable answer. Take a fixed moment, say, in 1964, when the first two Healthy Realist films were produced almost simultaneously. The notion of representing a harmonious life in either fishing or farming villages does not go very far from stereotyping rural life as happy, and of course healthy, under the ruling regime. Be it a promotion of "town and village self-governance" (*chengxiang di fang zizhi*) in *Oyster Girls*, or revitalizing duck farming by science and technology in *Beautiful Duckling*, the benign governmentality of the state is only assumed and never really represented, let alone scrutinized. What we see in the early years of Healthy Realism is an obscure, nearly invisible government; the state recedes into the shadow of other values such as family and tradition in its uneasy relationship to progress and modernization.

I use the concept of "governmentality" here advisedly. Judith Butler defines the Foucaultian notion of governmentality as "the ways in which political power manages and regulates populations and goods," the technique through which state power is not so much legitimated as "vitalized." Particularly relevant here is that, for Butler, govermentality *has* to vitalize state power, or else it "would fall into a state of decay."[33] The context in which she speaks is instructive: the United States in the ongoing war on terror and its struggle to legitimize the horrific violation of human rights and the arrogant disregard for international laws, all in the name of homeland security. That is a deployment of the mode of crisis *par excellence* when governmentality is vital for the state scrambling to legitimize its actions. In the case of Healthy Realism, we see a classic moment when state power safely remains invisible. At the same time, however, that obscurity would require a different kind of visibility by representing a civil society without government.

*   *   *

Unparalleled Tracks

It is peculiar that, especially with the Nationalist cultural policy of antagonism toward communism, Healthy Realism in its early years should opt for an almost clandestine style of representing the government's rule on the island. Particularly striking when the government was keen on improving the infrastructure in Taiwan—the completion of the Shihmen Reservoir in 1964 is a prime example—Healthy Realism's response to that effort seemed lacking at best. This would change, of course, with agitated urgency, when Nationalist Taiwan was forced out of the United Nations in 1971. Soon after that, in 1972, Japan also severed its diplomatic ties with Nationalist Taiwan. The rest of the 1970s continued to be a turbulent time, culminating in 1978 when the United States established official diplomatic relations with Communist China, further marginalizing Taiwan on the international stage.

Those harsh changes in international politics were reflected in the further diversification of film production in Taiwan. A trend of popular cinema that had competed against Healthy Realism since its inception became increasingly contentious in the 1970s. The differences between the two lie as much in their varied relationships to realism as in their representations of the power of the state, on the one hand, and national culture and tradition, on the other. For the sake of clarity, I will call the counterpart to Healthy Realist films a "trans(Chinese) national commercial cinema." The awkwardness of the term is deliberate, even necessary, because the phenomenon it names is anything but neat. To trace the two cinemas' contentious history, I turn again to the 1960s and to *Beautiful Duckling* and Lee Hsing.

The moment when the duck farmers and their flock come across the power plants expresses a paradoxical attitude toward agriculture and industry. If the looming structures behind them were to be deemed benign, and if rural life were to benefit from modernization (electricity in this case), the scene also belies that possibility. Serving as the segue to the next shot in this two-minute sequence, the brief encounter with modernity ends as abruptly as it begins, while the parade of ducks marches on, enveloped by the rural beauty of Taiwan. The sequence can thus be said to insist on the rural and suppress the modern, should the latter be seen as the antithesis of the former. After this crucial sequence—especially the pivotal shot of the power plants, which never appears again—the second half of the film unflinchingly returns to the unchanging rural scenery imagined and imaged as Taiwan.

If Taiwan in the mid 1960s could be identified with the stasis seen in *Beautiful Duckling*, change would come more forcefully to the fore in the 70s. As the international political climate worsened for Taiwan, and its economy rapidly developed, two films by Lee demonstrate how Healthy Realist films reflected these imposing changes in the late 1960s and the 70s. *The Road* (1968), for example, is a compelling melodrama which focuses on individuals, families, and village communities. The larger theme of national development remains obscure, much as in *Beautiful Duckling*. A marked difference is, however, that *The Road* devotes much more screen space, if not explicitly narrative significance, to explicit visualization of modernization. For instance, the film opens with a stark sequence of a highway construction crew working heavy equipment. The scene alternates mechanically between close-ups and long shots, accompanied by deafening noises of trucks and machinery on the soundtrack. In other words, there is no music to assign extradiegetic significance as in both *Oyster Girls'* and *Beautiful Duckling*'s openings on Taiwan's rural beauty, or, if we go further back, the song sequences in Taiwanese-dialect melodramas. It is almost as if road construction were less than desirable, a point driven home even more strongly when the crew finishes the day's work to drive home in a truck along a tranquil rural road, puffing exhaust fumes as it passes a goat herder and his flock. The beauty of a rural paradise in previous films is now, quite simply, polluted. What we learn from this opening sequence is not the advancement of Taiwan's infrastructural development, but, rather, in a straightforward manner, that the main character is a construction worker. Brother Guo is not only a capable and diligent laborer but also well liked and respected by his colleagues and neighbors. The other road Guo paves is for his only son, Chang-Ying, to finish college, and, then, either to get a good job and marry a nice woman, or to go abroad for further education. While each goal will meet obstacles along the way, the film's formal quality remains consistent with the depoliticized aesthetics which has characterized the earlier Healthy Realist works. The twists and turns of the plot eventually enact only the stasis of its aesthetic paradigm, the very form of the Nationalist nation in transition.

I am not suggesting that Healthy Realism is antiprogress; nor do I consider it to be antithetical to Berry and Farquhar's assessment, in line with China's Socialist Realism of the same period, as "[conveying] a faith that the present is the road to national utopia through the metaphor of the reconstructed family and rediscovered home."[34] However, the progress and change in what they call the "proto-national reunion or *datuanyuan*: 'coming home' to Taiwan," plays out only on the narrative level, and, even there, with great ambivalence. In other words, although Healthy Realist films do often end with reunions or homecomings, they do so not by a coming together of narrative and aesthetics, content and form, but by conforming to and aligning with the larger ideological, nationalist mandates. The "homecoming," or, better put, *becoming a nation*, is not possible until a firm sense of belonging to the land is established, for the mainlander and the native Taiwanese alike. Another major film by Lee in the late 1970s shows us just that.

One of Lee Hsing's later films, *He Never Gives Up*, was an adaptation of an immensely popular autobiography. It tells the story of a young man who, despite a birth deformity in both legs and an impoverished family background, finishes a law degree, returns to his hometown, dedicates himself to education, and finally dies of cancer in his prime. The film was released just months before the United States severed its official ties with Taiwan and established diplomatic relations with the PRC on the Mainland. In such turbulent times, the film became the most appropriate metaphor for the island: a small boat adrift on the massive and hostile ocean, which is the literal meaning of the title. The sense of national crisis felt by the people in 1970s Taiwan is not hard to imagine, and the film responded to that sense of abandonment with abundant inspirational scenes that emphasized the virtue and, indeed, the necessity of never giving up crucial to Taiwan's survival.

One such scene takes place when a storm hits the poultry farm tended by the young hero. The elaborate set recalls the farmhouses in *Beautiful Duckling*. However, if the earlier film showcases the rustic beauty of an agricultural village, this film puts it right in the path of the formidable destructive forces of the elements. The realistic set and masterful mise-en-scène produce a powerful identification with the hero struggling to keep the fowls safe by putting himself at risk of drowning. His feeble yet persistent struggle to stay afloat in the raging flood is intercut with an imminent rescue by his mother and older brother. The suspense is not so much whether he will survive, as the audience knows well that he will, since the emotional weight of the entire film lies heavily in the final scenes when he does die, a knowledge that every viewer has before coming to the theater.

The last scenes of the film are about the hero as he lies dying. Various important characters from throughout the film come to bid him goodbye. As the final moment slowly approaches, another sequence of intercutting extends the affect of finality to an almost excruciating degree. From the hero's deathbed, the film cuts steadily to documentary footage of a religious ceremony that takes place at the village temple. The temporal simultaneity of these two events is undercut, however, by the visual discrepancy between the two locales (soundstage and location shots), which makes the sequence awkward at best. The indoor scene displays a kind of craftsmanship now mature after 15 years of production. The outdoor scenes, on the other hand, teeter between the rawness of documentary footage and an obviously staged collective prayer for the hero's health. Inside, the familiar faces of real actors earnestly portray a grief-laden scene of imminent loss; outside, however, countless extras go about their usual religious activities only to kneel in concert, doubtlessly choreographed for the film's benefit. The seamlessness between soundstage and live location in earlier films such as *Beautiful Duckling* is no longer in existence. And the reasons for that failure cannot be simply technical or stylistic.

The problem lies in the actors on the screen and the failure to incorporate them into the constructed space of cinematic realism. It is not unusual for films in the 1960s and 1970s to include scenes shot on location involving a number of real-life extras on scene. *Beautiful Duckling* can move from soundstage sets to real locations in a single breath because the significance of those locations is derived from their shared state of stasis. *He Never Gives Up* carries with it, however, an immediate sense of the current social and political urgency, a level of realism that the Healthy Realist aesthetics of politics, which can by now be understood as a politics of the imaginary nation failing to take root, can no longer achieve.

*   *   *

My main argument has been that the paradigm of Healthy Realism's politics cuts across generic boundaries and eventually becomes an aesthetic of politics. By imagining a Chinese nation on Taiwan with rigidified styles and generic conventions, however explicitly support-ive of the State's nationalist ideology, mainstream Taiwan cinema in these two decades ends up obscuring the multiplicity of possible faces of a nation and losing its hold on the real. This leaves an opening for a clearer picture of the nation, a new face that would only slowly come into view through New Taiwan Cinema filmmakers' politics of aesthetics starting in the early 1980s. Chapter 4 emphasizes how New Taiwan Cinema since the early 1980s re-politicizes realist aesthetics by a progressive reinvention of film aesthetics inherited from Healthy Realism. By focusing on two leading filmmakers, Hou Hsiao-Hsien and Edward Yang, and their early works between 1982 and 1986, I hope to demonstrate a decisive shift in film realism driven by renewed concerns with cinematic time and space related to nation and moder-nity, both of which will continue to inform chapters 5 and 6 on 1990s Taiwan cinema. But even that shift is not an easy one, especially the intriguing moment of transition between these two realisms that is discussed in the Interlude.

Interlude

Hou Hsiao-Hsien before Hou Hsiao-Hsien: Film Aesthetics in Transition, 1980–1982

In Hou Hsiao-Hsien's 1986 masterpiece, *Dust in the Wind*, a memorable scene takes place in a mining village in the hills. Two young lovers making a meager living in Taipei return home for a visit. As part of an ancestral offering, an outdoor movie screening is set up for the evening. There in the dark, country folks, both young and old, sitting on benches and stools, watch a film projected on a big white screen slightly fluttering in the wind. What is shown is none other than the parade of ducks from Lee Hsing's *Beautiful Duckling* (Figure 1).

Made more than 20 years later, *Dust* looks lovingly at the older film only to cut away to a group of young men and women. As the cheerful music for the marching ducks chirps on the soundtrack, one of the youngsters recounts the physical abuse he has suffered at his workplace in Taipei. When the camera returns to the screen, the moving images on the screen within the screen come to a sudden halt due to a power outage. Without complaints or chaos, the audience hangs on with great patience and the scene ends on a comic note when an old man mistakes a firecracker for a candle in the dark. Even at its most dramatic, the film remains quiet and reserved. An utterly different realism in 1986, New Taiwan Cinema at its peak pays homage to its Healthy Realist predecessors.

Much happened between the end of Healthy Realism and the height of New Taiwan Cinema, as the former dominant mode of cinematic representation made way for the latter. This statement implies, of course, a linear relationship between the two realisms, while the notion of the "new" suggests a break separating them; the Interlude

Figure 1 *Dust in the Wind*, Hou Hsiao-Hsien, 1986.

looks precisely at this historical problem. Before fully engaging with New Taiwan Cinema, I am compelled to examine this short period of transition. Instead of subscribing to a common fantasy scenario in which Taiwan's New Cinema simply bursts forth and takes the global art cinema by storm, I take the notion of transition dialectically. Transition here does not mean a mid-point in a linear history, a passageway for history to move from one stage to the next, as if by design or destiny. Rather, the transition is one of dynamic tension that shows historical transformation as struggle and negotiation, and, in the case of Taiwan cinema, as a resistance to previous paradigmatic structure as well as an emergence of a new aesthetic sensitivity in contention with the sociopolitical reality it cannot but inherit.

Long before becoming a director himself, Hou worked extensively between 1973 and 1980 on some 20 films as screenwriter and assistant director to luminaries such as Lee Hsing. Notably, at the very beginning of his filmic career, he served as Lee's assistant director for *Heart with a Million Knots* (1973), a highly successful adaptation of a Qiong Yao romantic novel. James Udden has called this period Hou's "strange apprenticeship," during which the future master learned the nitty-gritty of his trade in commercial cinema and eventually emerged as a "leading director of the Taiwanese New Cinema in 1983."[1] It may not be surprising that, according to Shigehiko Hasumi,

Hou himself does not consider his first three feature films—*Lovable You* (aka *Cute Girl*, 1980), and the other two films that soon followed, *Play While You Play* (aka *Cheerful Winds*, 1981), and *Green, Green Grass of Home* (1982)—as part of his directorial career. He was paying his dues, as it were, for the greater creative freedom those profitable productions would afford him.[2] These three popular films, made between 1980 and 1982, were often dubbed his "commercial trilogy." The year 1982, to be sure, marked the beginning of a very different era in Taiwan's cinematic history, entangled with shifts of cultural policies and changes in social forces, of which Hou was and continues to be a prominent figure.

As we have seen in the previous chapters, there has been very little English-language scholarship on Taiwan cinema before the New Cinema.[3] Udden's "Taiwanese Popular Cinema and the Strange Apprenticeship of Hou Hsiao-Hsien" is a rare exception. For Udden, certain techniques, such as the quick zoom, out-of-focus objects in the foreground, inattention to lighting, and unusually numerous camera setups for a single scene, are the aesthetic norms of 1970s commercial cinema in Taiwan; Hou's early films are no exceptions. Therefore, Udden concludes, "the style of [Hou's] commercial trilogy…is not entirely distinguishable from other films of this time."[4]

I disagree. Even though Hou's first three films are indebted to the existing mode of production, they also challenge the commercial cinema paradigm. If Udden is right that Hou's apprenticeship has allowed the future master to learn his trade, the transition period had greater significance in the history of Taiwan cinema, I believe, than what Udden allows.[5] And if an aesthetic *stasis of change* in the form of generic proliferation characterizes Healthy Realism, a careful examination of this aesthetics in transition between 1980 and 1982 prepares us for the next set of questions regarding cinematic style in Taiwan's contested national cinema.

* * *

Lovable Enough, Not Real Enough

Hou Hsiao-Hsien's directorial debut is something of a curiosity. Unlike the prolific body of work widely known and revered in international art cinema circles for more than two decades, *Lovable You* is a lighthearted romantic comedy, served up with even a few musical sequences. Feng Fei-Fei, a Taiwan pop music diva, stars alongside

Kenny Bee, a popular singer from Hong Kong and lead actor of Lee Hsing's last two Healthy Realist films, *Story of a Small Town* (1979) and *Good Morning, Taipei* (1980). The story is simple. A young woman from a rich family residing in Taipei escapes to her hometown in the countryside before an arranged marriage. A young engineer visits the same town as a member of a highway construction crew. They meet and fall in love. The woman is then summoned back to Taipei to meet with her father's chosen son-in-law-to-be, but the engineer does not give up pursuing her, which results in a few comic sequences before the lovers reunite. There is yet a final obstacle for the young couple: the woman's father insists that she be betrothed to someone with a comparable family background, which means, of course, equal social status and financial affluence. Without much prior hint, the young man's father is revealed in the last minute to be no less wealthy than the woman's.

All problems thus solved, the final scene shows the couple, the wife now pregnant, back in the countryside by the giant tree where they first professed their love. In an extreme long shot, the couple embraces under the tree with the lush rice fields stretching into a mountain range in the distance. A bright red title appears to address the audience directly by wishing them a happy Chinese New Year, an ending befitting the *raison d'être* of the film: an entertaining piece produced for the holiday season[6] (Figure 2).

The film was a box office success, profitable enough to allow for Hou to direct two more similarly commercial films before making his breakthrough in 1983 with *Boys from Fengkuei*, immediately preceded by *His Son's Big Doll* earlier in the same year.

I want to stay with this final shot a little longer, and, indeed, the film itself stays with it for several seconds more. As the happy couple slowly makes their way out of frame, the red title also disappears. What remains is the beautifully composed image, a still as it were, without human subjects or extradiegetic titles, of Taiwan's rural landscape (Figure 3).

It is a familiar scene; we have seen variations of this image in many films before 1980 and will see many more later. Healthy Realism in the previous two decades established a cinematic space within which a diversity of genres on screen displayed a stunningly consistent set of dialectical relationships: sociopolitically, between city and country; thematically, between family and nation; and aesthetically, between on-location depictions of physical reality and soundstage reconstructions that combine different degrees of physicality into a total effect

Figure 2　*Lovable You*, Hou Hsiao-Hsien, 1980.

Figure 3　*Lovable You*, Hou Hsiao-Hsien, 1980.

of a cinematically constructed reality. However, although Healthy Realist films, particularly in the late 1970s, mastered realist techniques of outdoor locations and indoor sets, they were confronted by increasing difficulties in representing human subjects, as seen, for example, in the final scenes of *He Never Gives Up* which I discussed. Such incongruity is particularly stark between high-profile stars and faceless social actors. I call the latter "social actors" advisedly. Rather than mere "extras" whose presence serves as backdrop or accessory, those people occupy the cinematic space *as* themselves, appearing real, perhaps too real, and belying all the artifice that is the only truth of film realism.[7]

In *Lovable You* we encounter precisely this representational problem, but with a subtle and yet significant difference. The two leads' star quality has no doubt contributed to the commercial success of the film, but their physical presence is out of place at best. In Lee Hsing's *He Never Gives Up*, the villagers in the last few scenes appear awkward within Healthy Realism's constructed visual field. In *Lovable You*, however, a crucial change begins to take shape: it is now the stars' hyper-presence that seems misplaced, with their high fashion and overly made-up faces, not to mention the musical-song sequences mandated by the star-singers' package deals. This shift of the weight of the human figure—star versus real peasant, for one example, and child actors versus real children, for another—provides us an opportunity to observe how Hou, even if intimately connected to Healthy Realism and other earlier commercial cinematic paradigms, and his budding aesthetics of realism contend with and transform the aesthetic field woven by its many predecessors.[8] It is as if the stars were but a facade, and very close to being exposed as such; the background—the heretofore faceless country folks and schoolchildren embedded in the voiceless landscape rich with hidden histories and untold stories—is now on the verge of becoming the *real stuff* of an emerging cinematic space.

In the following I locate a few critical moments in Hou Hsiao-Hsien's commercial trilogy. By bringing to light Hou's still only partially visible aesthetic traits during this transitional period, I hope to open up in chapter 4 a much fuller discussion of the New Cinema between 1982 and 1986, a dynamic period when Taiwan leapt onto the center stage of global international art cinema. New Taiwan Cinema would soon mark, perhaps for the first time, a critical moment for a potential "national cinema" of Taiwan to come into view, one that is decidedly different from any previous official representation dominated by the Nationalist ideology of a Chinese nation.

* * *

Men at Work, Children at Play

The representation of labor has often been a tacit requirement of Healthy Realism. The hardworking highway construction crew in *The Road* and the diligent duck farmers in *Beautiful Duckling* are but two examples that showcase the act of working. The physical performance of labor on screen guarantees the subject's status as a productive citizen. By contrast, play is a rare occasion permitted mostly to children, normally brief and always tucked into some insignificant narrative pockets. In Hou's first three films, however, child's play comes in prominently. *Lovable You* features a group of young children whose omnipresence on screen is striking. Even during the scenes of the young lovers' courtship, a narrative space formerly reserved only for heterosexual romance, particularly in Qiong Yao's melodramas, the children in *Lovable You* are their oddly inseparable companions.

Hou's next film, *Play While You Play*, further emphasizes child's play, albeit with an interesting twist. Again starring Feng Fei-Fei and Kenny Bee, the film begins with the former walking around a seaside village, apparently as a tourist who photographs the fishing village and its fishermen at work. Several other characters, also visitors from the city, are introduced, whose presence is again not explained. As the credits roll, we see one character urinating on the wall of an old military guard station by the beach, now deserted (Figure 4).

Feng slowly makes her way toward the man, who quickly finishes his business, just in time before Feng joins him, and together they walk off frame. What remains on screen is but a sign stating, "Photography Prohibited" (Figure 5).

Almost like an inside joke or a sight gag, this sequence references and pokes fun at the prohibited practice of photographing the coastline in the name of national security. It does so precisely by having the area photographed twice: by the diegetic characters and, before that and always already, by the cinematic apparatus. We may here recall the final image of *Lovable You* when the screen is cleared of human subjects and the cinematic image becomes enriched with a material rawness previously hidden, or at least obscured or distracted, by the actors' presence. Different and particularly noteworthy in this

Figure 4   *Play While You Play*, Hou Hsiao-Hsien, 1981.

Figure 5   *Play While You Play*, Hou Hsiao-Hsien, 1981.

instance in *Play* is the marked presence of state interdiction, even though it has already been ridiculed by the yet unknown man's excretion, a crude but highly effective tactic.

Immediately after the opening credit sequence, the film cuts to a long shot of a group of children playing with firecrackers. As if the urinary playfulness were not enough body humor, this second sequence details how these children discover a perfectly formed cowpie in the middle of the country road. The children conspire to stick a firecracker in it and time its explosion to coincide with a grown man passing by (Figure 6).

Unfortunately their improvised explosive device turns out to be a dud, allowing the unwitting man a safe passage. Disappointed, the children gather around their makeshift weapon when it suddenly goes off and turns the pranksters into the butts of their own joke. Just as surprising as the dung explosion, a sharp call of "Cut!" interrupts the comic scene of child's play. The entire sequence is, in fact, a film within a film—the nonphotographable now doubly double-photographed—and child's play is not play but work after all (Figure 7).

It turns out that Feng and company is a production crew filming a laundry detergent commercial. To make matters worse—or, better—the perfectly shaped cowpie is in fact made of flour, a fake produced for the sake of realistic effects. Running out of flour to make another

Figure 6 *Play While You Play*, Hou Hsiao-Hsien, 1981.

Figure 7   *Play While You Play*, Hou Hsiao-Hsien, 1981.

perfect dung, the frustrated director asks the prop master to "find the real stuff," which in turn occasions a comic scene when the reluctant production team member chases after and pleads with a cow, aiming a bucket at its rear. Play, scatological or otherwise, is thus transformed into work, and playfulness into a commodity for consumption, thereby self-reflexively unraveling previous realist films' concealment of artifice. One may say, therefore, the playful opening of *Play While You Play* exposes that aesthetics—style, artifice, film, and filmmaking—to be the *real stuff* of cinematic realism; the cinema is not the reality captured and presented, but rather, always and first and foremost, representation through and through.

Film style is a key element which would eventually take center stage as soon as the New Taiwan Cinema movement commenced. Critics often comment on Hou's exquisite use of long takes. Udden, too, notes the prominence of child's play in Hou's early films as the result of the director's conscious effort to enhance the child actors' performance by allowing them to improvise; that is, to do their work by playing. This practice results, Udden continues, first directly in the necessity of longer takes and then indirectly in Hou's other privileged stylistic choices in his later films.[9] That granted, I nevertheless see far greater implications in the turn toward an aesthetics driven by the relentless desire to document not only what unfolds in front of the camera with as little human intervention as possible, but also by doing so through a substantial period of time and at a considerable distance. Recall here how Healthy Realism works so painstakingly to present a narrative embedded within the nation-building project. The more Taiwan cinema tries to capture the present political and cultural reality, most clearly in policy films in the 1970s, the more the cinematic representation loses its hold on the real.[10]

What we see in Hou's early films, then, is a restrategizing of the ever-elusive chase after the real. I will have more to say in chapter 4 about how important members of the New Cinema, such as Hou and Edward Yang, bring film style to bear upon the difficult question of nation and national identity in a time of increasing transnational pressure. For now, it is important to understand clearly what the representational impulse is and what it means in this transitional period of Taiwan cinema. Even more than the previous two films, Hou's third film before his artistic breakthrough prepares us for just that. *Green, Green Grass of Home* oscillates dynamically between the commercial mandate of a film star's presence (the ubiquitous Kenny Bee) and the desire to stay with children at play. But what of long shots and long takes that insist on looking from a distance, over time? What specific effects are created by that aesthetic choice and how do they work?

* * *

Durée at a Distance: Long Shot and Long Take

Commentators on Taiwan's New Cinema have long noted, if only briefly and in passing, that Hou's first three films forecast an imminent new aesthetics. Veteran film critic Li You-Xin, for one, characterizes Hou's early works as showing, first, a "strong anarchistic tendency," which includes the obsession with the irreverent or even unhygienic portrayal of seemingly random activities;[11] second, a "longing for fields and nature," that is, a continuing interest in the dialectics between town and country and between control and spontaneity; and, finally, his "masterfully directed mise-en-scène of children at play," a surprising shift from the thematics of films to his direction and style.[12] According to Li, another veteran film critic, Liu Sen-Yao, also praises Hou's refreshing "directing and shaping of child actors" as a key reason for *Green*'s success.[13]

Udden's insight into Hou's direction of child actors that leads to a film style privileging improvisation will prove productive here. In the first three minutes of *Green*, Hou deftly introduces the child actors who are not marginal or merely functional, but central to the film. During a typical school day, scores of children make their way to the daily morning flag-raising ceremony. Many inventive and spontaneous activities take place; in one case, a group of kids races a train as it comes out of a tunnel, and, in another, a boy twirls his water bottle on a bridge only to lose hold and send it into the river while his older sister watches disapprovingly in the background. Most strikingly, when the school bell tolls, a medium shot shows a child—by now a familiar face, as he is the main child actor in *He Never Gives up*, *Lovable You*, and *Play While You Play*—hastily wolfing down breakfast. The scene cuts to a medium long shot when the kid rushes out of the house to the insistent ringing of the bell. The child runs toward the camera, making his way down some stairs, and, instead of a cut, the camera pans as he runs down even more stairs, and slowly recomposes into a long shot of the school's athletic field, where many students have already gathered in formation. As the child runs off the frame quickly, the visual field suddenly shifts its visual weight to what was previously its background, all within one take: from a medium shot of the single child to an extreme long shot of the entire school field, only to be rejoined by the child appearing from the lower left corner as he rushes to make it to the required, patriotic ritual that starts a normal school day (Figures 8–11).

Figure 8   *Green, Green Grass of Home*, Hou Hsiao-Hsien, 1982.

Figure 9   *Green, Green Grass of Home*, Hou Hsiao-Hsien, 1982.

Figure 10   *Green, Green Grass of Home*, Hou Hsiao-Hsien, 1982.

Figure 11   *Green, Green Grass of Home*, Hou Hsiao-Hsien, 1982.

This scene, particularly that brisk and efficient long-take sequence shot, is remarkable in several ways. First, different from the previous two films where the setup in the opening sequences situates the star at the center, *Green* immerses its star, the lead female character, among many schoolchildren without letting her stand out. Even though her stiff posture and thick makeup are incongruous with the rest of the frame—though less conspicuous, of course, than her predecessor's many ostentatious hats—the long-shot composition works to contain her as part of the scene, rather than making the scene the background in front of which the star appears. Similarly, the privileged long shot creates a space for mise-en-scène in depth.

The depth of field is further elaborated in subsequent scenes throughout *Green*. One striking example brings the two thematics of work and play into a dynamic interplay. Halfway into the narrative, two children are playing by some rice paddies as farmers work the fields. Often in the same frame in long or extreme long shots, the carefree child's play and the rewarding labor of abundant harvest complemented by a cheerful soundtrack suggest a harmony of rural bliss, rivaling Healthy Realism's optimism at its best (Figure 12).

If the scene strikes a balance between work and play, it is soon disrupted when the stars enter the frame. In an extreme long shot, Kenny Bee and his cohort rush down a windy country road on their

Figure 12   *Green, Green Grass of Home*, Hou Hsiao-Hsien, 1982.

shiny bikes in fashionable casual wear en route to a picnic by the river. In accordance with its commercial mandates, the camera dutifully follows its stars. Very soon both children and farmers disappear; the play and work space for the villagers is transformed into a stage for the stars on display (Figures 13–14).

Interestingly, what immediately follows and performs a recuperation of sorts is a scene when the farmers take a lunch break and one of them joins the children in play. Such subtle staging is made dynamic by the use of long shots and depth of field. As is well known by now, both of these traits will become part of Hou's signature realist aesthetic. And it is clear by now that Hou's visual style is developed in the context of working within *and* against the commercial cinema paradigm.

The average length of a shot in Hou's early work is indeed notably longer than in that of his contemporaries. The average shot length of Taiwan's commercial cinema in the early 1980s is at slightly above eight seconds, while that in Hou's first three films is almost 50% longer, at eleven to twelve seconds per shot. However, Udden himself admits the limitations of such empiricist, quantitative study that only gives us a "crude measurement." "There are shots," he continues, "that are much shorter than [eleven to twelve seconds], and a few that can reach almost a minute in length."[14] What this signals then

Figure 13   *Green, Green Grass of Home*, Hou Hsiao-Hsien, 1982.

Figure 14   *Green, Green Grass of Home*, Hou Hsiao-Hsien, 1982.

is Hou's observable tendency toward longer takes instead of quicker editing. Here we see a classical, manufactured tension between a formalism emphasizing the creative and analytic potential of montage and a realism favoring the faithful and accurate representation of reality. What Hou's early films exemplify is, finally, how film style is intimately linked to its historical context, the limits and limitations of its production and consumption, and not purely an aesthetic exercise.

One can go further still with this stylistic shift and what it tells us. Along with other long-shot and long-take scenes already prevalent in Hou's early films, which are often free of drama and without clearly defined plot motivation, the opening sequence of *Green, Green Grass of Home* anticipates the arrival of an emerging realism in Taiwan cinema. In its quiet insistence on observing its profilmic physical environment and physical persons, coupled with a respect for action and its temporal integrity, this new realism is distinctly different from its predecessor not only in its aesthetic style but, much more significantly, in the orientation toward a *point of view*. This notion of the point of view is not, of course, tied to any diegetic character's perspective. Rather, as will be elaborated in chapter 4 and continued throughout the rest of the book, New Taiwan Cinema collectively offers a new way to look at Taiwan's past and present, a point of view that is at once historical and historiographic.

II

Style

4

A Time to Live, a Time to Die: New Taiwan Cinema and Its Vicissitudes, 1982–1986

En Route to the Here and Now

In Our Time (1982), a four-part omnibus film featuring four new directors, presents a sort of time travel. The film leaps back in time to the early 1960s before taking the audience forward to the present; segment by segment, it moves through grammar school, middle school, college, and finally to adult life in contemporary Taipei City. Clearly a national allegory, *In Our Time* traces Taiwan's development through the 1960s and 1970s, using audio-visual technologies as its distinctive temporal markers. The first episode, "Little Dragonhead" by Tao De-Chen, depicts the transitional period from gramophone and radio to television in a disintegrating neighborhood and situates technology on the borders of class divisions: the haves eventually relocate to the United States and leave their electronic devices, and the have-nots must stay behind, inheriting those appliances secondhand. The second, "Expectations," Edward Yang's directorial debut in Taiwan, places television right in the heart of a middle-class household and emphasizes how it serves as a portal for transnational influences, in this case, the Beatles and the Vietnam War, that shape the young's budding sexuality as well as their worldview. The third, "Jumping Frog" by Ke Yi-Zheng, depicts television as ubiquitous, always broadcasting international sports in a semicommunal rental unit for college students and young professionals, its drama climaxing in an outdoor athletic competition between local and international college students.

The first three segments of *In Our Time* also suggest a spatial transformation through time. Many scenes in "Little Dragonhead" portray families and friends sitting around a radio or gramophone and later in front of a television, making domestic space the center of individual, family, and social life regardless of the different technologies. In "Expectations," the constant intrusion of external information—be it Western popular culture or world news—begins to blur the boundary between private and public spaces: a girl in her late teens who watches TV all the time at home and sneaks out at night to dance clubs whenever possible personifies this shift in domestic life. When television becomes a common fixture of any shared living space in "Jumping Frog," the lead character is obsessed with winning an athletic competition against foreign students, because the latter's presence and pressure, now inside Taiwan's physical space, is far more keenly registered than that on the television screen just a decade ago.

But what about the here and now? The *present* is at the core of metropolitan Taipei in the fourth and final segment, "Say Your Name," by Zhang Yi. Like the other three, this episode begins in domestic space, this time a young married couple's first morning in their newly rented apartment. On a mattress on the floor, amidst stacked up furniture and unopened boxes, the husband and wife reluctantly arise to another workday; this domestic space is one of transition. The cramped space is soon abandoned once the wife has left to report to a new job and the husband has accidentally locked himself out, wearing only a bath towel and a pair of boxers underneath. The rest of "Say Your Name" is a physical comedy of the half-naked man's various unsuccessful attempts to return to his domestic space. All the while, however, his utterly private state of undress is fully exposed to the public, relentlessly recorded and placed on display by the cinematic apparatus. Time and again, long shots of the vulnerable antihero walking on the rush-hour streets of Taipei highlight the jarring spatial displacement of a near-naked man in public incapable of returning to his private space. On location with actual social actors going about their daily business, those scenes are shot either from a high angle, such as a bird's-eye view, or with a telephoto lens from a distance. Those vantage points create a visual field that accentuates the man's distress as firmly lodged in the here and now. It is precisely the kind of documentary impulse that I have termed in the Interlude New Taiwan Cinema's historiographic point of view: an aesthetics that calls attention to its own stylistics by positing itself as a historical presence within the cinematic frame.

* * *

Befitting its status as the film that inaugurated Taiwan's New Cinema, *In Our Time* opens up new possibilities for filmmaking in Taiwan, as well as providing a new understanding of Taiwan's cinema in the decades to come. My brief analysis of the film suggests at least the following. To begin, the central filmic endeavors of Taiwanese-dialect films and Healthy Realism in the previous decades—the proliferation and vernacularization of genres for the former and the rationalization of nationalism for the latter—have now shifted from the stories being told to how they are told, to *style*. These temporal and spatial questions so deftly cinematized in those four segments mark a swift departure from the generic mandates, showing emergent aesthetic traits already evident in Hou's first three films during the transition period. In *In Our Time*, film style, perhaps best demonstrated in "Say Your Name," is driven by a desire to represent "reality" not only as what it is or should be, but also as what has created it and how it is represented; reality is no longer static, as in Healthy Realism, but as sets of dynamic conditions of which the cinema is a crucial part and an active agent. Without providing any easy answers, New Cinema poses questions about Taiwan's history and its cinematic representation. If New Cinema is to be regarded as "new," we must ask: What is new about it?

* * *

What is New? New "Nation"

As I noted in the Introduction, if somewhat begrudgingly, Kristin Thompson and David Bordwell have marveled at how, "In 1982, Taiwan was an unlikely source of innovative filmmaking.... Yet by 1986 Taiwanese cinema had become one of the most exciting areas of international film culture."[1] To the delight and surprise of fans and pundits alike, Taiwan arrived at the center stage of international art cinema in the early 1980s and still seems determined to stay. Even after New Cinema's supposed end in the same decade, local scholars and critics continued their attempt to make sense of this short-lived phenomenon, its quick success and sudden demise. More than two decades afterward and even when we may well be confident that the legacy of New Taiwan Cinema has indeed survived, it bears asking once more what the movement meant to Taiwan's cinema and how New Taiwan Cinema contributed to, if also complicated and troubled, the notion of Taiwan's national cinema. The quest for a Taiwan nation inevitably implies and, as we shall see in the remainder of the book, requires a double movement: *temporal retrospection* and *spatial displacement*, both of which are already evident *In Our Time*.

But, I ask again, What exactly is new about New Cinema? For Chiao Hsiung-Ping, New Taiwan Cinema was "new" in four important ways.[2] First, New Cinema, like new literature or theater, played an important role in helping to develop and reexamine Taiwan's culture. Second, with its continuous success in various international film festivals, New Cinema broke diplomatic barriers and became one of the most powerful vehicles to promote Taiwan's image. Third, New Cinema reestablished confidence in its local audiences, making them aware of the artistic, historical, and cultural significance that cinema is capable of conveying. And, finally, a new film critic system was instituted that rejected being a mere agent for the dominant Western culture, but stood firm in creating and advancing a distinct cultural identity.

These four areas of achievement beg further scrutiny. To begin, according to Chiao, cinema and its social and cultural function center around two major concerns. Externally, New Cinema has become a cultural ambassador of sorts, bringing Taiwan back onto the international stage with a new image after its expulsion from the United Nations in 1971 and other subsequent diplomatic defeats. Films invited to various international film festivals helped Taiwan gain recognition from and promote a new national profile in the global arena. Internally, New Cinema was the site of a cultural identity in the making, by means of reinforcing a set of collective values and resisting foreign dominance. Implicit in Chiao's assessment is that the independent entity that is Taiwan was thus made recognizable, if yet to be politically recognized, through the New Cinema and its international success: in short, New Cinema created a new image, which was different from the Taiwan previously known and unjustly marginalized.

But a nagging question remains: What exactly is this "new" image of Taiwan? As Chiao suggests, the success stories of New Cinema films in various international film festivals, at least implicitly, fulfill a diplomatic agenda of promoting that image. Perhaps then the most glaring omission in Chiao's cultural, social, and political assessment is what exactly has made Bordwell, Thompson, and others excited: New Cinema in Taiwan offered to an unsuspecting world "innovative filmmaking," in no matter how "unlikely" a location. In this particular regard, June Yip's account seems more satisfying. While acknowledging the "international" tendency, at least as the Government Information Office would have it, Yip focuses on New Cinema's style as a dynamic result of the tensions between cinema's aesthetic potential and its industrial limitations, between nationalist ideology and nativist consciousness, and between domestic stagnation and international competition.[3] In other words, even in retrospect, Taiwan's New Cinema in the 1980s may still shed light on the island's continuing efforts, borrowing the apt title of Yip's book, to "envision" itself.

Instead of treating this New Cinema as a collection of works on Taiwan history or an encyclopedic entry on global cinema, I focus in this chapter on the questions of its aesthetic innovation and what that new realism has to tell us about a renewed, but no less contentious, relationship between cinema and nation in 1980s Taiwan. I will begin with a brief mapping of the development of the New Cinema in order to establish a framework within which to situate its two key figures, Hou Hsiao-Hsien and Edward Yang. I then demonstrate how a productive rereading of two well-known New Cinema films, Hou's *Dust in the Wind* and Yang's *Terrorizers* (both 1986), yields new insight.

* * *

Policy, Industry, Language: New Cinema, New Questions

Post-1945 Taiwan cinema prior to New Cinema was comprised of genre films, according to June Yip, "at two extremes: anticommunist and anti-Japanese propaganda...and films of pure escapism," notable among the latter being martial arts films and Qiong Yao romantic melodramas.[4] As we have seen, Healthy Realism came between these two poles and influenced both camps with its paradigmatic realist aesthetics across genres, best exemplified by Lee Hsing's prolific career over three decades. The cultural policies during those decades mandated only the positive images of the nation be represented, resulting in a stagnation of film creativity despite a proliferation of realist style. After the 1960s, a decade often dubbed as Taiwan cinema's "golden age," the conditions for the domestic film industry rapidly deteriorated.[5]

The reasons for the decline were social and political as well as commercial and international. By the late 1970s, the conflicts between new and old, between political demands made by the rising middle class and authoritarian state control, reached a critical impasse, in which there was no clear, emergent social structure while the old one was collapsing. In terms of movie-going, frustrated audiences from all walks of life, particularly college-educated citizenry, practically stopped paying to see domestic films. With the growing accessibility of illegal videotapes, the last few years of the 1970's saw a great depression of the local film industry. It was commonly cited that "college students don't watch national films."[6] This phenomenon was further aggravated by the impact of the Hong Kong New Wave, which emerged, according to some accounts, "with the establishment of the Hong Kong Film Festival (1977), serious magazines, and college courses."[7] Those New Wave films were both commercially successful and artistically superior, and they took Taiwan's Chinese-language film market by storm.

Both internal and external impact precipitated a strong desire for a breakthrough in Taiwan Cinema, creating in the late 1970s and early 1980s a go-for-broke momentum. Modeling on Hong Kong's success, Taiwan's National Film Archive was founded in 1979, and an annual film festival began showcasing new and notable works three years later in 1982. Film periodicals began circulation and European classics were screened in universities, small art house theaters, and private cinephile clubs.[8] James Soong, then Director of the Government Information Office, himself a film buff, introduced a number of directives that aimed to "rebuild the financially beleaguered industry."[9] Among them were: reorganizing the national film awards (the Golden Horse Awards), to honor artistic innovation rather than thematic content, and to be judged by film professionals and not government representatives; creating the Golden Horse International Film Festival to bring in award-winning films that would raise local standards; encouraging Taiwan films to enter international competitions; updating the infrastructure of film law to lift the medium to a higher cultural level; and, finally, engineering tax reductions on ticket sales and providing tax shelters for producers.[10]

Soong's axiom for a new Taiwan film industry—"professional, international, and artistic"—summed up what this highly charged campaign was up against. First of all, the national film awards had been controlled by government representatives, and their judgment had been based on "thematic content," which reaffirmed a tension already in existence during the Healthy Realism period. Propagandistic and lowbrow entertainment films resulted in low box-office returns for domestic film productions. When the government stepped in, the policy change stressed a realist tendency that would reflect its citizens' everyday lives. Likewise, one of the solutions to ease the recession of the film industry in the late 1970s and early 1980s was to loosen state censorship in order to encourage free, or at least freer, artistic expression.

A key difference, however, was that, coupled with the propensity for internationalization (evinced in the expansion of the local film festival and active attempts to enter international ones), this new era of Taiwan's filmmaking was destined to be more explosive politically and less constrained by state control than ever. That tension would finally erupt at the critical point when productions financed by government subsidies or produced by government-owned studios could no longer be kept in check with the increasing degree of creative freedom, desired by filmmakers and critics alike. As early as 1983, an episode of *His Son's Big Doll*, "The Taste of Apples," by Wan Jen, criticized the U.S. presence in Taiwan, causing the state censor to demand the filmmaker re-edit the whole segment. Fervent debates stirred strong controversy, dubbed the "Apple-Paring Incident," referring to the government's order to cut off parts of the film critical to the authorities or the United States. And it was out of those heated discussions regarding film arts and politics that the term *New Taiwan Cinema* was coined and adopted.[11]

Mass media, particularly newspapers, were from the beginning active participants, even strong advocates, in this trend to sustain a new cinema. Almost simultaneously, the two largest newspaper corporations in Taiwan, *China Times* and *United News*, launched regular film columns and invited film critics (most of them Western-educated) to review films. Thanks to their daily circulation in the millions, these newspapers succeeded in exciting the public, especially the discontented intelligentsia. An immediate effect was that people were exposed to a serious and critical attitude toward film. An understanding of the correlation between cinema and culture was slowly built, as was an increased consciousness of "national identity." The concept of film appreciation or film criticism was raised to an unprecedented level. This was perhaps not exactly as Soong had intended, for he was, after all, a high-ranking Nationalist government official who, two decades later, became a fervent but unsuccessful contender for Taiwan's presidential post representing a pro-unification stance.

By the early 1980's, Taiwan had reached a point where the status quo could no longer assuage the widespread discontent felt by its citizenry. A "new" cinema was poised to emerge. As it had done regarding Healthy Realism in the 1960s, the government-run studio, the Central Motion Picture Corporation (CMPC), initiated the first move. A few points are worth noting here. First of all, New Cinema's "newness" was relative, and only in terms of its content and style, and it did not involve any major infrastructural changes. The CMPC, under state control, was still the leading studio; existing modes of production remained intact. For example, as producer Jen Hong-Zhi has pointed out, production crews would often refuse to take directions from those "new" directors during the making of *In Our Time*.[12] Different filmmaking concepts and practices clashed while no corresponding adjustment to the system was in place. New Cinema posed a challenge, in Jen's words, "not so much to the industrial infrastructure as to the dramaturgy and critic system."[13]

Second, the so-called New Cinema was not an organized movement with clear-cut objectives; it emerged only retrospectively. In contrast to romantic melodrama, martial arts films, lowbrow comedies, and propagandistic historical films, New Cinema was at once an experiment in storytelling and an exploration of realistic subject matter. New Cinema could be understood as a distinct collective of films or filmmakers only later. For instance, at the beginning of 1984, film critic Edmund K. Y. Wong could only speak of three "new" films, and his use of the term "New Taiwan Cinema" was made in reference to the Hong Kong New Wave.[14] This is a temporal disjuncture that continues to raise historiographical questions about periodization in Taiwan cinema.

Third, Taiwan's film market has always been a territory wherein domestic, Hong Kong, and Hollywood productions were mixed. "*Guopian*," which can be interpreted as "domestic," "Mandarin-speaking," or, most ambiguously, "national film," is itself an arbitrary term. Hong Kong films, made in Cantonese and later dubbed into Mandarin, were regarded as *guopian* by the government. They competed in the Golden Horse Awards as domestic films and enjoyed the same distribution privileges and exhibition rights. Hollywood films, on the other hand, were regulated according to a quota system with eight major U.S.-based distribution companies dominating the market. The case of Japanese films was even more extreme. After several short periods of openness throughout the 1950s and 1960s, Japanese films were banned after the diplomatic fallout between

Taiwan and Japan in 1972, and the door was not opened again until 1983, even then under strict regulations. A complete reopening for Japanese film imports would have to wait another decade, until 1994.[15]

The government's treatment of both Hollywood and Japanese films was fairly blatant, but the case of Hong Kong was intriguing. It is easy to see the relationship between Taiwan and Mainland China as rivalry; the place Hong Kong occupies is far more delicate. The distinction between Cantonese- and Mandarin-dialect films produced in Hong Kong is an interesting case in point. While the former was "Westernized as little as possible," the latter stemmed "from the emerging modern national consciousness [and tended] to be produced in sophisticated urban surroundings...by culturally cosmopolitan Chinese and to treat stories and use the movie medium in a way that comes to some kind of terms with progress and the modern world."[16] The use of language is thus closely related to the question of national identity. Films in Cantonese dialect were prominent in the Hong Kong New Wave attempt to create an identity by locality, with the linguistic as the most distinctive marker. Likewise, films made in the Taiwanese dialect were a common practice in New Cinema. In this context, Mandarin, the official language, came to represent a central power that the marginalized, in both colonial Hong Kong and postcolonial Taiwan alike, would seek to contend.

The traffic between Taiwan and Hong Kong, no matter how frequent and intimate, cannot justify any gross generalization that the two were of the same "culture" or shared a unified "cultural identity." Despite all the similarities—both are capitalistic societies, their people ethnically Chinese, and so on—on a deeper level, Taiwan had yet to resolve its own problems in terms of history, politics, and culture, much as Hong Kong had faced its challenges and opportunities in its postcolonial aftermath. The ambiguity of the term "culture," and "cultural identity" by extension, was exactly what urgently needed sorting out. Therefore, the anxiety felt by Taiwan's film industry toward Hong Kong, particularly after the New Wave, manifested itself in an intense reaction against any "foreign" cultural influence and the need to create its own identity.

James Clifford speaks of the concept of the West as a "force," one that is "technological, economic, political—no longer radiating in any simple way from a discrete geographical or cultural center."[17] What he suggests is an uncertainty about targeting a source from which "cultural imperialism" can be identified, an insight still relevant today. Indeed, the forging of cultural identity should be thought of "not as organically unified or traditionally continuous but rather as negotiated, present processes."[18] In the following, I map the development of New Taiwan Cinema. I do not intend to recount all the films made, people involved, or significant events that have transpired. I offer, instead, an interpretive engagement with the trajectories of this movement and the issues it raised and then left unresolved. My recapitulation of New Taiwan Cinema's vicissitudes between 1982 and 1986 provides the framework for my detailed analysis of Hou Hsiao-Hsien's and Edward Yang's films, whose *repoliticization of film aesthetics* had long been anticipated by Healthy Realism of the previous decades.

*   *   *

The Life and Death of New Taiwan Cinema

Regarded as the first to employ nontraditional filmmaking methods, *In Our Time* marks the beginning of New Taiwan Cinema. Jen Hong-Zhi calls it a film with "no stars, no established directors, no complete story, and no generic conventions,"[19] an assessment immediately calling attention to the importance of genres in the previous decades. This four-episode omnibus was a testing ground for the four new directors. The film's modest box-office success, combined with high critical acclaim, made possible another anthology film, *His Son's Big Doll* (aka *The Sandwich Man*, 1983). This three-part movie introduced another three directors, Zeng Zhuang-Xiang, Wan Jen, and, most remarkably, Hou Hsiao-Hsien.[20] Produced by the CMPC under the new guidelines set by the Government Information Office, both films represent the first waves of efforts to foster innovative filmmaking begun in 1982, whose distinctive characteristics can be found in two major areas: style and content.[21]

I will have much more to say about New Cinema's style in this chapter. In terms of content, however, I highlight here but one propensity of what Vivian Huang calls "Taiwan's social realism."[22] While town and country development, familial relationships and values, and individual and collective experiences are still common themes, the attitude toward those issues and their representation are drastically different from Healthy Realism. *In Our Time* depicts Taiwan through a developmental narrative. Each of the four parts corresponds to a significant phase in a person's life. From childhood, adolescence, early adulthood, to full adulthood, the film serves as an allegory of Taiwan's development. For example, *Reunion* (whose Chinese title literally means "we all grew up this way," Ke Yi-Zheng, 1985) takes the analogy of personal history to a broad, overarching, and collective level. The eponymous "reunion" provides an occasion for a large cast of characters to reminisce on their shared experiences of growing up in Taiwan's rapidly transforming society. They do not celebrate the progress made but, rather, bemoan the innocence lost in Taiwan's modernizing processes.

Jettisoning the conceived tactics of escapism popular in earlier films (Qiong Yao's romantic melodrama comes readily to mind), New Cinema is said to not only represent reality but also to actively expose the underlying problems in that reality. That is, realism serves as a lens through which more than the positive passes. Wan Jen's *Super Citizens* (1985), for example, can be seen as an unrelenting exposé about the morbidity of modern Taipei. The social ills and moral corruption coming with economic growth depicted in this film may now seem prophetic. No less realistic in style than Healthy Realism was in earlier decades, the content of New Cinema's "reality" is no doubt not quite as healthy as the government would like to see portrayed.

Not every film, however, was fortunate enough to enjoy box office success or international recognition. By the end of 1985, Chiao Hsiung-Ping was delighted by the heightening quality of New Cinema but could not help admitting that New Cinema's poor box office records might eventually be detrimental to its future.[23] Only one New Cinema film made it to that year's top-ten list, Zhang Yi's *How I Lived My Life* (1985). Even there, media attention surrounding the making of the film (such as the extramarital liaison between the director and the leading actress who put on over 30 kilograms of weight to play a pregnant woman, the CMPC's intervention in the production, and so on) might have contributed more to its commercial success than the general audience's recognition of the film's artistic accomplishment.

In such troubled times, the never-ceasing debate between commercial versus artistic values reached a new height. Yingjin Zhang summarizes, "The rise of New Taiwan Cinema fundamentally changed the image of Taiwan cinema, but its critics were eager to blame its inherent experimental quality for the decline of Taiwan filmmaking."[24] What had previously propelled the development of New Cinema now acted against this creative movement. Indeed, in the beginning the two major newspaper systems played a very supportive role of New

Cinema, but that attitude changed abruptly toward the end of 1985. New Cinema was now called "box office poison" in light of its alarmingly frequent commercial flops. Its persistent explorations of social reality were also subjected to criticism of self-indulgence. Even more unsettling was the charge against New Cinema films shown in international festivals as nothing more than promoting a "negative" image of Taiwan.[25]

On some levels, the appearance of the so-called "negative" image of Taiwan may have been a necessary phase in a social and political negotiation, especially after those two decades of Healthy Realism which focused only on the "positive." However, socially conscious films, such as Wan Jen's *Super Citizens*, were often accused of corrupting national morale and being subjected to enemy exploitation[26]—communist China, on the one hand, and the emerging domestic opposition party with its Taiwan independent slant, on the other. This highly politicized charge was joined by an economic indictment of New Cinema films for causing Taiwan to lose its overseas markets, mainly in Southeast Asian countries. Political privileges and commercial profits created some backlash against a more substantial infrastructural change, which would require a *re*distribution of exactly such privileges and profits.

What about the government? Since the CMPC had up to this point played the leading role in Taiwan's film industry, its continuous support would have been key to New Cinema's fate. With the tremendous pressure from the media against the New Cinema, the CMPC began to show signs of retreating from this controversy. In her annual report about Taiwan cinema in 1986, Chiao Hsiung-Ping made some interesting observations.[27] First of all, there was not even one locally made film that had reached the top-ten *guopian* box office list; all were from Hong Kong. An overwhelming tendency was to point the finger at New Cinema, indicating that the recurring recession of the local film industry was a result of its anticommercialism in the face of the dominant Hong Kong cinema. It was suicidal, some commentators would opine, to keep indulging in the illusion of cinema's artistic values but neglecting its economic failure.

This seemingly convincing assertion was in fact ungrounded, as was pointed out by Chiao herself. Her insight that New Cinema was but a scapegoat for more general industry weaknesses touched more than some nerves. But actual numbers speak louder than words. In 1986, the Nationalist Party subsidized the production of *Dr. Sun Yat-Sen* with a budget of 90 million NT (New Taiwan) dollars. Hou

Hsiao-Hsien's *Dust in the Wind* from the same year cost only about eight million to make. To blame the red ink in the annual balance sheet on New Cinema was misleading at best. Chiao's argument also highlighted a fatal problem that New Cinema has never been able to address, that is, government policy. If the CMPC's financing, and, more broadly speaking, the government's subsidization, was the bread and butter for New Cinema, its future was foreordained to be limited, especially with the lack of a stable film industrial infrastructure.

New Cinema was able to flourish with support from the media and the government. But when the tide turned, and it surely did, New Cinema's days were numbered; efforts had to be directed elsewhere. As a result, less than a handful of New Cinema directors were able to produce films in 1987; namely, Hou Hsiao-Hsien's *Daughters of the Nile,* Wong Tong's *Scarecrow,* Chen Kung-Ho's *Osmanthus Lane,* and Wan Jen's *The Seashore of Goodbye.* Some of the New Cinema directors would not get another chance until as late as 1989, while others completely disappeared from the filmmaking scene. New Taiwan Cinema practically ended by 1986, albeit on a high note with films like Hou's *Dust in the Wind* and Yang's *Terrorizers.*

*   *   *

Parallel Tracks

The opening of Edward Yang's "Expectations" segment in *In Our Time* is a high-angle traveling shot gliding along the top of a wall; the smooth horizontal movement offers the viewer only a partial glimpse of the house behind it. A Chopin nocturne softly plays on the soundtrack. A schoolgirl appears in the house and the camera slowly lowers itself to eye level in anticipation of the teenager opening the bright red door from which she eventually emerges, looking both ways before quickly walking out of the frame. Fade out.

Later that year, Hou Hsiao-Hsien directed "The Sandwich Man" portion of *His Son's Big Doll,* another CMPC anthology film with three parts.[28] The segment opens with the eponymous character dressed as a clown, fully done up in a long gown, ragged wig, red nose, and pointed hat. The sandwich man walks toward the camera but the telephoto shot flattens him into the background amidst a sea of street signs. He is but another such sign, only an outdated one. A cut to a close-up of the sandwich man, the background blurs into a haze, highlighting the crudely made-up face of the clown whose tight-knit eyebrows and dripping sweat become painfully visible over the thick face paint. Two more quick cuts show various town folks coping with the sweltering heat. There is no music, only the quiet but oppressive hum of a hot summer afternoon in a small town. Cut.

In the short years of New Taiwan Cinema, Hou Hsiao-Hsien and Edward Yang produced more impressive and coherent bodies of work than any other directors. Graduating from the omnibus setup in 1982, both went on to very active careers in the next few years. Before *Terrorizers* in 1986, Yang directed *That Day, on the Beach* (1983) and *Taipei Story* (1985). Hou, on the other hand, put forth *Boys from Fengkuei* (1983), *A Summer at Grandpa's* (1984), and *A Time to Live, A Time to Die* (1985) before *Dust in the Wind*, also in 1986.

The reasons why I chose Hou and Yang as my primary examples are based on two significant sets of contrasts between their works.[29] First, Hou and Yang represent two distinct subgroups in New Taiwanese Cinema. Hou's filmic career corresponded closely to the local filmmaking history as evinced by his connection with Healthy Realism. Having received formal film training at the University of Southern California, on the other hand, Yang represents another group of mostly Western-trained filmmakers who brought foreign influences to Taiwan's cinema.

Hou's and Yang's respective styles and contents characterize the other pair of major themes explored in New Cinema films. Yang is keen on contemporary urban Taiwan, its emerging middle-class culture and their many crises. For example, *That Day, on the Beach* traces the lives of two women whose individual experiences parallel Taiwan's economic development, while *Taipei Story* tells the story of two lovers growing apart in an increasingly alienating metropolitan Taipei. Often considered a humanist filmmaker, on the other hand, Hou portrays Taiwan's transition from an agricultural to an industrial society, focusing on the rural past.[30] *Boys from Fengkuei* follows a group of young men before military conscription who visit Kaohsiung (Taiwan's second largest city in the south) from a remote island and chronicles their gradual loss of innocence. *A Summer at Grandpa's* portrays the city-and-country differences from the opposite angle by showing two Taipei elementary schoolchildren's summer vacation in the countryside, in a gentle story nonetheless haunted by dark undercurrents of rape, murder, and betrayal. Finally, as a semi-autobiographical piece, *A Time to Live, a Time to Die* returns to a time when immigrants from the

Mainland after 1949 slowly lose hope for a homecoming and begin to take root in Taiwan.

Despite these apparent differences, both Hou's and Yang's works display similarly a remarkable energy in their repoliticizing of film realism. The rest of this chapter is devoted to the legacy of New Taiwan Cinema in its exploratory years. Despite the emphases on their differences—country and city, past and present, traditional and Western—I hope to suggest that Hou and Yang in fact share in their efforts to envision anew a Taiwan nation: Hou's temporal retrospection travels deep into the past, while Yang maps the spatial present of Taiwan. Cinematic time and space, in short, mark the coordinates of a reconfigured relationship between cinema and nation.

*   *   *

Dust In the Wind of Change

Veteran film critic for the *Village Voice* Godfrey Cheshire describes the Taiwan portrayed in Hou's cinema as "an island nation and an island not yet a nation locked in the fraught embrace of caring master and dutiful servant." The complex colonial history of Taiwan results in a peculiar bond between the former colonized and its colonizer. "That bond would soon be sundered," Godfrey continues, "leaving the two cultures eyeing each other with a mix—so familiar in the postcolonial age—of wary antagonism and repressed nostalgia."[31] The need to resolve tensions of this sort indeed makes up a large and yet often latent part of Hou's cinema. Taiwanese identity—after waves of colonizations, from the Dutch, Spanish, Japanese, to "Chiang Kai-shek's displaced Nationalists"—is one of "indeterminacy: people, places, and eras caught always in the flux of becoming something else."[32] Indeed, the notions of "indeterminacy" and "becoming something else" characterized the great transition at stake. The cinematic manifestation of the condition of 1980s Taiwan is nowhere clearer than in film aesthetics as demonstrated by *Dust in the Wind* and *Terrorizers*.

Hou Hsiao-Hsien's *Dust in the Wind* tells the story of a "love mutiny" (*bingbian*), a term designating common cases in Taiwan when young lovers end their relationships during the boy's term of military conscription. In this film, a young boy and girl grow up together in a mining village under dire financial circumstances without the required means to continue their education. After middle school, first the boy and then the girl relocate to Taipei City where they learn a trade, hoping for a better living than the mining jobs their fathers have had to endure. However humble, theirs and their hometown cohorts' dreams are thwarted by the rapid economic transition for which they are not prepared. Soon the boy is drafted to serve in the military on a small island off Taiwan. The girl promises to write him every day but ends up marrying the mailman who delivers their daily correspondence. The heartbroken boy is finally discharged from the military and the film ends when he returns to the village and has a brief conversation with his grandfather by their sweet potato fields. Rain is scarce that year, the grandfather complains, portending a poor crop, and the film ends as they quietly smoke cigarettes.

Contemplative in mood and reserved in tone, *Dust in the Wind* opens with a long shot from a moving train's viewpoint, a visual metaphor of traveling in space as well as in time. As the train snakes its way in and out of darkened tunnels, we are introduced to the boy, named Ah-Yuan, and the girl, Ah-Yun, commuting from school to their mining village. This scene brings to light the central issues the film addresses: the distance between urban and rural settings and the imminent transition facing the characters, symbolized by the train as the connecting device. Fredric Jameson observes the image of the train in *Dust*, "The image of these small suburban trains... becomes a virtual new wave logo... in which the empty station and the sound of the train in the distance end up articulating the narrative and standing as signs or shorthand for mutations in the Event."[33] Larger than all the characters, the Event is the unstoppable change in the modernizing world far beyond their immediate temporal and spatial frame. The image of a moving train connecting places not only visualizes transition as a world in motion, but also disrupts the tranquil scenery of the countryside visualized not from any specific character's perspective, but from that of the moving train itself. By opening *Dust* with this image, the film leads us into a world situated within the larger context of a Taiwan already deep in the process of modernization.

Getting off the train, Ah-Yuan and Ah-Yun walk home along the track. The owner of a small grocery store tells Ah-Yun to bring home a bag of rice to her mother. They come across the preparation for an outdoor movie screening right next to an abandoned track presumably for mining carts (and we soon learn that the miners have been on a long-term strike). A quiet, village life and its major economic and social activities are close-knit along the railway. The next shot frames a hillside trail which the characters climb to get home. This whole sequence sets up a mood in which we are led *backward*, both temporally and spatially, into an older way of living, while the railway constantly reminds us of Taipei and its modernity on the other end of the track, the direction toward which the younger generation inevitably heads.

To prepare us for the change of locus, *Dust* utilizes another sequence at the train station. After being hospitalized due to an accident in the mines, Ah-Yuan's father comes home on a train. Grandpa, himself almost a part of the scenery, waits patiently on the platform for the train to arrive, unaffected by the commotion. A stirring anticipation, however, is expressed through Ah-Yuan's anxious search when the train does arrive. A subliminal relationship with the train, one of moving and transition, is captured by this medium long shot in one long take. Soon Ah Yuan himself will board the train to Taipei and pursue a wished-for better life. What the train brings is the modern convenience of mass transportation and, at the same time, it takes away stability, threatening to diminish the borderlines between modernized and traditional lifestyles. Before we know it, Ah-Yuan has left home and gone to Taipei.

The train station as the site of shifting borderlines between human relationships is meticulously articulated in Ah-Yun's first appearance at Taipei Main Train Station. Her expressionless face is a most eloquent portrait of a youngster's first sight of the capital city. Waiting for Ah-Yuan to come and pick her up, she unwittingly allows a (potential) con man to take her luggage and lead her away. Ah-Yuan arrives just in time to prevent the unthinkable consequences of Ah-Yun's naive trust of strangers in the city. We see from a distance, along with Ah-Yun, the two men fighting on the interwoven tracks, their bodies entwined in a physical struggle. As visually depicted by the complicated rails and power cables that line the space, human relationships in their rural village are sharply differentiated from those in a big city.

During the struggle with the stranger at the train station, a spilled lunch box is shown but not explained, nor is Ah-Yuan's being late in the first place. In the following scene, at his workplace, we see a schoolteacher bringing the boss's son home, informing the parents that the boy has fainted during his physical education class. The mother inquires anxiously only to find out that her son did not have lunch. She immediately turns and shouts at Ah-Yuan, demanding to see the lunch box in question. The authoritative tone she adopts and the demeaning words she throws at Ah-Yuan reveal quickly that

Ah-Yuan has not been treated well by his employer. In other words, if the first part of *Dust* establishes human relationships as communal and intimate, within minutes of arriving in Taipei, they are redefined in economic and hierarchical terms.

* * *

My analysis so far shows that transition is a movement at once spatial and temporal; the gap between town and country must be measured in both terms. If the opening of *Dust* is a temporal and spatial backward movement, the modern lifestyle thrusts upon the characters not only spatial displacement (physical relocation or migration) but also temporal reconfiguration (new timeline, new schedule, new speed). The open space of their mining village and quiet living at an unhurried pace are nowhere to be found in the squalor of their cramped living space and controlled schedules as menial laborers in the city. If the new temporal and spatial conditions represent irreversible progress that a modernizing region such as Taiwan cannot prevent, how does the cinema register this unstable state of transition?

* * *

During the lunch box incident, there is a curious cutaway from the boss's wife's fierce reprimand, to her son's somewhat mischievous expression half hidden behind a door. Using this as a transition, the next shot cuts back to Ah-Yuan showing the infuriated mother the broken lunch box in a long shot, whose specific point of view remains ambiguous. Not only does the duration of the entire event test the audience's patience and ability to sort out the causal relationships among minute details, but the distance of the camera from the action defies conventional expectations of a dramatic scene as, say, in Lee Hsing's Healthy Realist films such as *Beautiful Duckling* or any Qiong Yao romantic melodrama.[34] Hou's de-emphasis of the dramatic content of a scene gestures toward a very different film aesthetics from the melodramatic.

Ellipses rather than dramatic conflicts and ambiguity instead of narrative coherence define this aesthetics. The scene when Ah-Yuan's motorcycle is stolen is exemplary. Starting with a long shot of the shopping center next to the railway, the sequence establishes its locale. The deep focus enables the viewer to observe the whole surroundings: shabby urban buildings, wandering street people, crosscutting traffic, and rows of motorcycles parked on the roadside. Ah-Yuan and Ah-Yun walk into the frame amidst the chaos. As soon as he finds out his motorcycle is gone, they walk closer to the foreground, lost in a frenzy of futile searching. The character-environment relationship is powerfully conveyed through an objective correlative suggestion that is faithful to both spatial and temporal realism.

Dust allows us a few more seconds to take in the whole situation before it cuts to an elderly man puffing out a cloud of smoke on the roadside while looking indifferently at a man on a motorcycle riding out of the frame. This curiously long cutaway (about 12 seconds in length) brings additional dimensions to the whole sequence. First of all, this shot serves as a transition; it leads to the subsequent shot of Ah-Yuan and Ah-Yun's continuing search for the motorcycle. This shot also fills in certain possible gaps in the narrative's intentionally ambiguous unfolding. It can be read either as a flashback or a flashforward. Could the man on the motorcycle be the thief? Or, could the sequence be a time-compressing device linking the previous shot and the one that ensues? This cutaway shot is then a detail of the larger picture of which the whole social milieu is the canvas, and humans and their activities in a given time and space the true subject matter: the social environment in a time and space of transition.

Narrative ellipses and stylistic ambiguity carry *Dust* forward, and its style poses a fundamental challenge to the conventional dramaturgy before the New Cinema. The disclosure of Ah-Yun's marriage to the mailman is a case in point. The scene exemplifies a radically different treatment of dramatic conflicts.[35] The beginning of this sequence shows Ah-Yuan in an army barrack, reading a letter from his younger brother. The latter's voiceover narration brings the scene back home to the front stairs of Ah-Yuan's family home, on which sit Grandpa and his younger siblings, staring off screen in apparent puzzlement. The next shot shows Ah-Yuan's mother trying to pacify Ah-Yun's while the families sit in the background. Not until after this shot do we see Ah-Yun sobbing quietly with the embarrassed mailman husband by her side. This whole sequence is structured to divulge the most dramatic conflict of the entire film but that plot point is presented in a nondramatic way. "In the era of 'the old cinema,'" Jen Hong-zhi comments on this specific moment, "no directors would give up the chance to exploit a conflict scene to its fullest extent; they believe that that is the sole source of *drama*."[36] Instead, this scene is done mostly in medium and long shots and the inherent drama is only implied, even removed from a direct representation in both temporal and spatial terms.

Understood this way, the so-called "narrative ellipses and stylistic ambiguity" are in fact very specifically about the temporal arrangement of events, deliberately out of chronological order, to give space its meaning through time. A specific scene, or, better, a repeated mise-en-scène, illustrates this significant dynamism in Hou's static long shots. The scene of Ah-Yuan picking up father at the train station is followed by an extreme long shot of the Jians walking along the railway. As our eyes wander around the screen, permitted by the duration of this shot, a host of meanings reveal themselves through juxtaposed elements, derived from our understanding of this particular character-environment relationship: family, tradition, community, and what is changing and what other changes are yet to come.

Similar to the composition of the opening sequence, the houses sitting on the hillside in the background serve as a backdrop in front of which human activities are recorded. The train tracks remain a poignant symbol of transition by their prominent physical presence. The direction in which the human characters are heading is the same as in the beginning sequence and in several subsequent visits of the ill-fated lovers and other young people from their village. We are being constantly reminded of the imminent and repeated departure of the young.[37] A reverse movement is therefore all the more jarring in the scene when Ah-Yuan is leaving the village to report to his military draft, foreshadowing his homeward-bound return at the end of the film. The repeated mise-en-scène takes on a dense temporal dimension beyond the physical reality it records by way of the many variations of that environment throughout the film's narrative. At the core of Hou's film aesthetics, exemplified by long shots and long takes— *durée at a distance*—is precisely this intensified cinematic configuration of the temporal-spatial relationship between the characters and their environment.

* * *

Terrorizers, or a Never-Ending Urban Nightmare

If Hou's films between 1982 and 1986 foreground the temporal-spatial relationship between characters and their environment, particularly in the mode of retrospection and a style of further elaborated *durée* at a distance, Edward Yang's works map the modernizing urban Taiwan, specifically Taipei City, according to their spatial-temporal coordinates. We may begin to understand the spatial dimension of Yang's works through his creative genealogy. Talking about Hou Hsiao-Hsien's reputation Godfrey Cheshire emphasizes that, "[Hou] (unlike such contemporaries as Edward Yang) was largely untouched by foreign films, has never lived abroad and dislikes travel."[38] This contrast implies a division among the New Cinema filmmakers, one group as local and the other foreign-influenced. Indeed, Edward Yang received a year of film education at the University of Southern California and worked as a computer engineer for seven years in the United States.[39] His first feature, *That Day, on the Beach*, incorporated much of the Western art cinema tradition. *Beach*'s open-ended narrative structure and well-to-do but alienated characters recall Antonioni's modernist *L'Aventurra*. *Taipei Story*, furthermore, is akin to an adult version of Godard's *Masculine Feminine* in which the Paul and Madeleine characters have grown into an existential void after Coca-Cola's complete triumph over Karl Marx.[40]

Such generalizations lead to stylistic comparisons as well. Edmund K. Y. Wong categorizes Yang's films up to *Taipei Story* as works of a "bourgeois aesthetics," characterized by their fragmented delineation of urban settings.[41] Chiao Hsiung-Ping, on the other hand, considers Yang's style as European, displaying an outlook on an increasing modern alienation that expresses itself in tightly controlled compositions captured in stark and cold cinematography.[42] Even though his focus is clearly on the industrialized urban Taiwan, Yang's style is overwhelmingly considered Western. "Bourgeois" and "Western" film style is thus designated as (middle-) class specific; its national origin, however, remains elusive.[43]

Fredric Jameson addresses this debate over "whether [Edward Yang] has sold out to essentially Westernized methods of style." His observations are of special interest here.

> [In] the great debates...over nativism and Westernization, modernization versus traditional ideals and values, fighting the imperialist with his own weapons and his own science or reviving an authentic national (and cultural-national) spirit, the West connotes the modern as such in a way that it no longer can when the modernization process is tendentially far more complete and no longer particularly marked as Western.[44]

In other words, the modernization process, toward the end of the twentieth century, has to be regarded in global terms. However,

Jameson's view risks conflating internal with external influences; nor does it specify the needs or means for a developing country to survive in this increasingly globalizing world. Therefore, when talking about a problematized "putative Taiwanese identity," Jameson dismisses a cultural link by saying that "the opposite of Westernization...cannot be China itself." He goes on to propose that Yang's focus be seen as an "example of some generally late capitalist urbanization...of a now-classic proliferation of the urban fabric that one finds in the First and Third Worlds *everywhere alike* [italics mine]."[45]

Jameson's argument is extremely powerful, even more so two decades after *Terrorizers*' release. The key to the postmodern notion of "neoethnicity"[46] is a self-reaffirmation about and practices of a chosen identity above and away from regional coordinates, which implies in effect an all-consuming power of globalization. That process, *pace* Jameson, cannot be uniform as it occurs in various contexts. That is to say, even with intensifying international traffic and communications, social and cultural facets of a particular nation/entity do not lose their attributes but, on the contrary, contend even more strongly in the age of globalization. The frame of the "national" is, in short, not going to be abandoned any time soon. Seen this way, Jameson's argument may have disregarded certain nuances in this film in order to keep its theoretical framework intact and thus risked ignoring significant points that might illuminate the specific context of Taiwan. My concern in analyzing *Terrorizers* is how it can be understood with respect to this particular "putative Taiwanese identity" in the making. After all, cinema does not exist without a context.

A highly complex narrative, set in contemporary Taipei, *Terrorizers* introduces multiple seemingly unrelated storylines only to weave them together into an explosive conclusion—or, better, several nonconclusive endings. A young man waiting for his military conscription notice is obsessed with photographing the city. By chance he captures an image of a teenage Eurasian girl, White Chick, as she flees a police raid when her boyfriend is arrested for an unspecified crime. Grounded by her mother who still longs for the American lover who fathered the girl, White Chick begins making random prank calls, either making fake suicide claims or telling made-up stories to wives about illicit relationships with their husbands. One such couple is Li Li-Chung, a medical laboratory researcher awaiting an imminent promotion, and Chou Yu-Fen, a novelist frustrated by a writer's block before a literary award deadline. The phone call triggers a series of events that leads eventually to the disintegration of Li and Chou's already unstable marriage. When Li fails to get the promotion he has so desired, he sets out to hunt down White Chick. The plot spirals out at a vertiginously accelerated pace until the film closes abruptly by leaving several radically different endings unresolved.

If Hou Hsiao-Hsien's primary concerns are with time and cinema, Edward Yang focuses on space. The two main female characters' states of imprisonment shed some light. To begin with Chou Yu-Fen's prize-winning novella—or, rather, for most of the film, the painstaking process of her attempt at writing it—not only serves as a driving force for the narrative but also symbolizes the problem of women's place in modernizing Taipei. Jameson has called this composite character of a woman and a writer an "old-fashion reflexivity." He argues that, "the aesthetically ambitious now want to become great filmmakers, not great novelists." "This anachronism of literature and its once-interesting reflexive paradoxes is," Jameson continues, "what...makes [*Terrorizers*] relatively conspicuous within contemporary Third-World production, where there are plenty of intellectuals and even writers, but perhaps somewhat less 'modernism' in the Western sense."[47] There is, at least for Jameson, a discrepancy between "modernism" as an aesthetic movement and its practitioners' inevitable entrapment within their global geopolitical locations. Chou represents, in short, the impasse or entrapment of a Third-World artist in the global symbolic order.

There is a simple question that needs answering: What is the place for modernism in 1980s Taiwan? First of all, "modernism" was initially articulated within a Western context; criteria based upon and signs indicated by that example do not necessarily apply to situations in other contexts. That is, what might be distinctive manifestations of modernism, such as Expressionism, Surrealism, and atonal music in the 1920s and 1930s, *pace* Jameson, do not explain artistic and literary trends in so-called Third World countries in the 1980s or 1990s. More importantly, contrary to the anachronism Jameson sees, in Taiwan writing has continued to be a commercially profitable and socially respectable vocation till this day. With the establishment of the Golden Stone bookstore franchise in the early 1980s, the framework within which *Terrorizers* must be situated, writers even began to occupy an increasingly prominent space in cultural activities and became crucial players in the market of popular culture. That the Eslite bookstore chain has been one of the most influential cultural agents since the 1990s further attests to this phenomenon.

Within this context, the writer character in *Terrorizers* is not at all far-fetched and not the least outdated. Chou Yu-Fen's writing crisis expresses a crucial aspect of the middle-class life the film scrutinizes. On the one hand, Chou represents a relatively new middle class composed of young and well-educated people (Chou has gone to the top-ranked National Taiwan University). Chou's character also allows an explanation of gender norms, in particular women's confinement in Taipei's fast-developing urban environment. What is then this spatial confinement imposed on female characters in *Terrorizers*? It seems unclear at first when we are informed that Chou has in fact chosen to stay home and write. Without children, Chou is a woman engaging in a very different kind of productivity than, say, the duck farming Xiao-Yue in *Beautiful Duckling* or the self-sacrificing wife in *He Never Gives Up*. On a more personal level, Chou's confinement is not imposed nor is she incapable of participating in the workplace and gaining financial independence. Hers is a self-confinement. For a woman with education and a gainfully employed husband, she is free *not* to work. Only four years earlier, the representation of this urban class was different, for example, from that in the "Say Your Name" segment of *In Our Time* when the couple can barely maintain a middle-class lifestyle with double incomes. We shall see later how domestic and public spaces for this newly affluent class bear upon their cinematic representation.

White Chick's case may bring further insight into the question of women's confinement. The Eurasian girl embodies the residual history of the American military presence in the previous decade. Her unknown father is only tacitly mentioned once in the film, when her mother takes her home from the hospital after the girl has broken her ankle while fleeing the police. Mother is extremely upset and starts hitting White Chick with whatever object is at hand. "Are you not wanted or disciplined by anybody?" the mother yells. "If you are so capable, why don't you just leave, like your father, and never come back?" White Chick's problem then appears to have begun with her fatherlessness. On an allegorical level, however, her predicament extends further into a state of rootlessness. White Chick's hybrid background renders it nearly impossible for her to belong to any specific locality.

Caught between her less than respectable mother and unknown American father, White Chick is confined within a paradoxical world of material wealth and psychological impoverishment. The only place for her is on the margins of the city she roams. As soon as she is rid of the cast on her injured foot, White Chick runs away from home—from her mother and all the shame associated with her background, and resumes a wanton life, using her body for money. She even stabs an abusive john, whose fate remains unknown, with a knife she carries in a hidden pocket of her jeans. There is no future, no aspiration, and no hope for White Chick, or so it seems. A shocking resemblance emerges between the mother and her adolescent daughter: while the former used to prostitute herself for the pleasure of those economically superior American military servicemen in Taiwan and ended up with nothing but an illegitimate daughter, the latter plunges into the concrete jungle of Taipei City not caring what tomorrow may bring.

White Chick's existence is on an immediate level, one may say, escaping a past she cannot discard and having no real future to pursue—a condition I call the "impossible Now" which will be explicated more fully in chapter 6. All her maneuvers and actions in the city are strictly on a moment-to-moment, step-by-step basis. Chou Yu-Fen's repeated protests of "You don't understand," to both her husband and later her lover, show her inability to comprehend her unhappiness vis-à-vis middle-class values, best represented by her desperate desire for cultural capital by becoming a prize-winning writer. By contrast, White Chick's silence eloquently articulates the disappearance of values in urban life. These two women share a condition of physical confinement: White Chick's ankle is broken and she is then locked up by her mother, whereas Chou Yu-Fen is imprisoned by her aspiration to write, by her desire for cultural capital through writing. They also share another significant condition: their existential dilemma lingers, to quote Jameson once again, "because they are urban, and even more because they are articulated within this particular city."[48] Here we finally arrive at the thematic and aesthetic core of *Terrorizers*: the city and the cinematic representation of urban space.

*   *   *

If *Dust in the Wind* provides a temporal contemplation of Taiwan in the recent past and, more importantly, a nation in transition, *Terrorizers* looks unflinchingly at the spatial disconnect and isolation beneath the glitter of the urban splendor. My analyses of Chou Yu-Fen and White Chick have suggested as much. Further indications can be seen in the parallel between Li Li-Chung, the writer's husband, and the lumpen photographer from a wealthy family. The photographer's random phototaking is not that different from Li's detachment from the world outside his single-minded concern for his promotion. Both display the same apathy that epitomizes urban alienation. For example, in an extensive scene we see the photographer on a pedestrian bridge randomly taking pictures of passersby with a telephoto lens. The final shot of this scene is of his camera dangling, with the busy traffic underneath, utterly unaffected by his presence. In like manner, Li Li-Chung drives by White Chick and then the police car and ambulance after the shoot-out in the opening sequence. It is very probable that Li's childhood friend, the police detective at the crime scene, and Li have just passed each other by unknowingly. Li's, as well as the photographer's, self-absorbed indifference to the outside world shows that, even though the two male characters are seemingly more mobile than the women, they are equally devoid of true connection with their physical environment.

Li and Chou's marriage serves as another example of the pervasive condition of isolation shared by all characters in *Terrorizers*. Li's obsession with the promotion and oblivion toward his wife's frustration make him a no less alienated person than the photographer. The dire detachment from his surroundings will eventually cause his total breakdown when he loses the promotion and his marriage fails, both of which he has taken for granted. The first time the husband and wife are introduced shows the unbridgeable gap between them. In a medium shot, we see Chou waking up in the morning. The next shot shows her sitting on the edge of the bed as the camera begins to pan slowly left. Before showing Li doing calisthenics on the balcony, the camera pans across a thick wall, the weight of whose darkness dominates the screen and marks the separation of the two spaces. The pan continues by following Li to the front door and, as he sits down to put on his shoes, it dollies in and frames him in a medium shot. Quite unexpectedly, Li looks at and speaks directly to the camera before a quick cut to Chou sitting in a chair staring off frame. A final reverse shot back to Li ends this scene, efficiently showing their estranged relationship cinematically.

The shot/reverse shot pattern persists throughout the film, but not to suture the two halves of the diegetic world into a whole. Indeed, as the narrative progresses, the gap between the couple only widens. The formal device succeeds in physically separating Li and Chou throughout the film, and it creates a stunning sense of even greater alienation when they do share the same frame. That only happens four times in the film. The first takes place right after Chou has committed adultery with her ex-lover and Li has betrayed his coworker in order to secure the promotion. The second and third times bracket the scene when Chou is getting ready to move out of the house and, finally, the last shows Li's desperate attempt to get Chou back, even physically grabbing her arms in public, ending up utterly rejected and humiliated. This notion of spatial separation manifests itself in urban alienation. Exemplified especially in Li's public outburst at the failed connection, it takes on an ominous presence, gesturing toward a state of unrest, even potential destruction. The ubiquitous gas tanks situated in the middle of Taipei City serve as a constant reminder of the compromised security of urban living, a startling symbol of imminent disaster. Besides the broken marriage between Li and Chou, there are other physical signs of potential crises. Chen Ru-Shuo comments on the scene when Chou Yu-Fen goes to visit her ex-lover, Hsiao Hsen, in a high-rise office building. After reminiscing about their past, Chou steps up to a window and pushes it open. A reflection of two window washers hanging onto a platform from the outside suddenly comes into view. This shot offers an insight into the reticular structure that undercuts the seemingly prosperous society, and, according to Chen, "a dialectic contrast between inside/outside, middle class/working class, and beautiful memories/cruel reality, is captured."[49] Such an unbalanced social and economic distribution of wealth and resources among classes and individuals eventually leads to the explosive eruption of rage at the film's nightmarish end.

* * *

At one point or another, each of the main characters of *Terrorizers* wakes up from sleep, looking either startled or disturbed. One such rude awakening opens the final, perhaps most compelling sequence, while another closes the film with vertiginous multiple endings like a nightmare from which no one awakes. After a night of drinking and telling delusional lies about having received the promotion and having gotten over Chou's departure, Li sleeps on the couch in his police detective friend's dormitory. The detective snores slightly as the dawn light leaks through the mosquito nets. Li Li-Chung sits motionlessly, tears streaming down his face, as an old-fashioned electric fan hums next to him. Following a cut to a schoolchild swiftly running by Li's boss, the first shock comes with a loud gunshot and his fallen body in final spasm by the car in the next shot. After the cold-blooded killing of his boss, Li proceeds to find Chou and her boyfriend. He shoots Hsiao Hsen twice, leaving their apartment after firing another shot that shatters a mirror while Chou sits terror stricken right next to it. Next—but is it after the double murders?—Li is wandering on the street, unsuspected by any of the passersby. His finding of White Chick is shown in highly grainy shots that elicit a documentary and yet surreal feel. The film reaches its climax when the door to the hotel room with Li and White Chick inside is kicked open while another gunshot is fired. A quick cut shows blood splattering across a wall. We are left with the expectation that Li has completed his vengeful mission, but, instead, find out that he has committed suicide in a communal bath at the police quarters of his detective friend.

More disorientation ensues when the film then cuts to Chou Yu-Fen suddenly waking up from her sleep, followed by Li's body being found in the detective's bathroom, with the blood and brain tissue still dripping from the wall. Is it all a dream, or multiple dreams? Whose dream is it? Is it Li who, unable to act on any physical aggression, avenges himself in fantasy before putting a bullet through his own head? Is it the police detective's nightmare foretold by his friend's strange behavior the night before? Or, perhaps, is it a reenactment of Chou Yu-Fen's award-winning novella in her own nightmare? This disturbing confusion would seem a deliberate design—not simply to confuse the audience, but to make a final, arguably most important, statement, as anticipated by the film's poignant title.

All of the characters are potential terrorizers and have, indeed, terrorized others as well as been victimized themselves. Their intertwining fates in this urban hell allow no escape. Starting with the photographer's voyeuristic impulse to invade others' lives with his photographic apparatus, the film time and time again reminds us of the destructive undercurrent in all of the characters' actions and interactions. The photographer can leave his girlfriend for an unfounded obsession, and she, in turn, not only trashes the former's belongings but also slashes her own wrists. Hsiao Hsen takes advantage of Chou's confession of her life problems to get her back into his life after his own divorce. Incapable of reconciling with her apparent mediocrity as a writer, Chou puts all the blame on her oblivious husband. Finally, White Chick lashes out through random irresponsible actions directed at others, disregarding the consequences. Even her mother can only resort to physical violence against her own daughter and imprisons her and herself within an all-consuming nostalgia for an irretrievable past. In our guessing game of whodunit, trying to figure out who the eponymous terrorizer is, a final awareness strikes as soon as everything goes awry: anybody and everybody can indeed be the aggressor and victim at the same time. Ultimately, Taipei is the terrorizer for all the inhabitants trapped in its entangling web of human alienation and spatial disconnect. When all the city dwellers are an integral and yet segregated part of the suffocating entrapment and random violence therein, which will be destroyed first, the city or the people in it?

*   *   *

Unlike Hou Hsiao-Hsien, Edward Yang does not employ long shots extensively; the camera distance he favors is the medium shot. Often combined with the use of a telephoto lens, this stylistic choice evokes a sense of fragmentation and surveillance. Examples of this technique abound. The scenes in which White Chick wanders through the commercial areas or when Li Li-Chung walks on a bridge in search of his attempted murder victim are but two striking examples. The look of those scenes seems to follow the Neorealist tradition and, by extension, European art cinema and the French New Wave, with characteristics such as on-location shooting, jarring and non-polished camera work, and so on. But what about the specific physical environment spatialized in this film's cinematization, especially when we now understand the grim urban conditions which are the film's main message?

A series of scenes helps depict further the cinematic spatial configuration of Taipei. First of all, Chou Yu-Fen's rendezvous with Hsiao Hsen in a park is one of the only two instances (the other being the suburban villa of the photographer's wealthy family) when we see some "nature" in this film. The first shot is peculiar in that Chou is standing on the far left side of the frame and facing left as well. The intricate lines formed by the trees in the background and her posture in this composition seem to indicate that Hsiao Hsen is out of frame to the right. After the relatively long take of her monologue, the next shot disorients the viewer by showing that Hsiao Hsen is in fact standing next to her, to her left. Another example comes near the end when Li Li-Chung is wandering on the street, presumably searching for White Chick. We first see him among the crowd, with a cut to White Chick's pimp/boyfriend, and then White Chick herself. These three are all high-angle, telephoto shots. The out-of-focus background does not render clear reference to their being in the same area. The fourth shot back to Li, however, orients us by not only explicating a logical spatial relationship among the three characters, but also by accentuating the intertwining fate within the web of Taipei's urban environment. The next shot shows the pimp/boyfriend in a hotel corridor, discovering, to his great dismay, that the door on which White

Chick has left a piece of gum as signal is not unlocked according to plans. Narrative vagueness is not risked because such a time lapse in fact prioritizes a spatial simultaneity that, with Taipei as an abstract and all-inclusive location, minimizes the relevance of linear causality. That is, the relationship and interaction between characters and their environment are, ultimately, about their coexistence in simultaneous spatial displacement.

*   *   *

The Death of New Taiwan Cinema

A formation of F-16 fighter jets zips across the sky. Underneath them a multigenerational group gathers for a photo session. On the sound-track, intoned by one of the most popular singers at that time, Su Ruei, is a song whose refrain, "All for Tomorrow" (*yiqie wei ming-tian*), is a catchy one. Produced by Hou Hsiao-Hsien, in collaboration with other prominent New Cinema filmmakers such as Chen Kuo-Fu and Wu Nien-Zhen, this music video was played on television as well as in movie theaters after the national anthem. Commissioned by the Ministry of Defence for armed forces recruitment, this short propaganda film was launched in October 1987.[50] Critics were quick to denounce it as unabashedly selling out to the Nationalist government's ideology. The participants refuted such charges, either citing "the complex circumstances of Taiwan's film industry" (Wu and Chiao Hsiung-Ping) or flat out denying any "ideological" implication (Hou).

By arguing that *All for Tomorrow* marks the death of the New Cinema, film critic Mi Zhou advances three charges: first, the film represents " a reactionary current packaged by commercialism;" second, the filmmakers produce a "false memory" of Taiwan's past; and third, the progressive aesthetics today (which New Cinema has symbolized) may become conservative "tomorrow."[51] In retrospect, Mi Zhou's criticisms highlight New Cinema's complex dialectics, which later films would continue to explore: the film industry between art and commercialism, cinema between art and politics, and, most importantly, film between history and memory.

This chapter has been centered on the works of Hou Hsiao-Hsien and Edward Yang in the 1980s, demonstrating the New Cinema's aesthetics both in temporal and spatial terms. From Hou's temporal retrospection to Yang's spatial displacement, it is clear that Taiwan cinema in this period casts an inward look at the island itself. Even though it may seem at first glance that the transnational forces informing the filmic scene in the previous decades have become less visible, it would be a mistake to ignore the stylistic and thematic exploration by the New Cinema in an international context. The short-lived movement's legacy in the following years would demonstrate vividly how Taiwan cinema continues to inquire into its identity. This is done in national terms that contend with, on the one hand, the colonial history and subsequent rule of the Nationalist government from the Mainland, and, on the other, the globalizing forces encroaching and imposing upon its cinematic construction of local space. The next two chapters extend my analysis in both temporal and spatial terms into the 1990s and beyond.

5

Island of No Return: Cinematic Narration as Retrospection in Wang Tong's Taiwan Trilogy and Beyond

Memory, or the Ambiguity of Cinematic Narration

Wang Tong's *Banana Paradise* (1989) is a melodrama about Chinese Nationalist soldiers' forced migration to Taiwan, a story of broken families and lost identity that spans 40 years, from 1949 to 1989. The main character, Men-Shuan, has for four decades adopted a false identity, as Li Chi-Ling, holding Li's job at various government posts and raising Li's family in his stead. The political division between Communist China and Nationalist Taiwan has prevented millions, Men-Shuan among them, from reconnecting with their loved ones, up until the lifting of martial law and the gradual reopening of the passage across the Taiwan Strait beginning in the late 1980s. Epic in scope, this film ends in a particularly intriguing final scene. The night before, Men-Shuan spoke to Li's father over the phone, a complex and emotional event during which Men-Shuan and his adopted identity, Li, finally merge as one; he sobs and wails, begging for the father's forgiveness for having left him behind in China. Clearly, he cries not only for Li but also for himself and, perhaps, for all who have suffered the same fate. The scene cuts to the following day at work. Men-Shuan/Li stares blankly into the air while a coworker pokes fun at him for presenting a fake diploma in an effort to petition for postponed retirement. Other coworkers gather around his desk. Their chatter slowly fades as the camera dollies in, fixes on his face, flanked by two darkened figures in the foreground, and eventually comes to a freeze frame.

But that is not the last image of this film. As the main theme song begins to play subtly on the soundtrack, the closeup of Men-Shuan/ Li's face is suddenly replaced by yet another still image. And it is that image which lingers over the final moment of the film. In a nearly monochromatic darkish green, the image shows a high angle shot of the back of a man and a woman walking away from the viewer, down into an underground tunnel with darkened stairways prominently in the foreground, graphically matching the closeup of Men-Shuan/Li's face a moment ago. What is curious about this last image is that it is not derived from any of the previous scenes. A *non-diegetic* image, it precipitates a reconsideration of the entire diegetic narrative that precedes it.

Starting with the Nationalist army retreating to Taiwan, the film tells the story of the characters' forced migration, and, though slow and painful in coming, subsequent settlement in Taiwan. A series of mishaps have caused one character to lose his mind, but, by the film's closing, Men-Shuan/Li's family has become a typical middle-class household in late 1980s Taiwan. At first viewing, therefore, *Banana Paradise* is an apparently conventional act of storytelling whereby events unfold chronologically. However, the final image as described above opens up possibilities for a rather different kind of analysis. First, pensive and melancholic, the pause on Men-Shuan/Li's face that comes so close to the end of the film encourages a reading of all the previous scenes as an extensive flashback in his mind. However, this can at best be only partially true because the film shows events far from likely to be seen from his point of view; for example, the entire narrative line when Men-Shuan/Li and his comrade are separated for years before their reunion. Furthermore, the actual final image of the unspecified couple in the tunnel calls the entire narrative into question. Who are they? Where are they going? Where have they been? The narrative thus becomes destabilized and the seemingly transparent narration is troubled by that hitherto unknown narrational source. Most significantly, the forward trajectory that has been established from the first to the penultimate image of the film is suddenly reversed and becomes a *backward* movement, be it by way of Men-Shuan/Li's flashback or the implied narrative mediation of some unknown agent. In short, *Banana Paradise* cannot be other than a return to a historical past recounted here by the still ambiguous narrator.

It is naive, of course, to think that any filmic discourse is not produced, in the first and last instances, by the filmmakers specifically and by the cinematic apparatus in general. Indeed, before *Banana Paradise*'s end credits start rolling, a title is inserted which verbosely, as well as retrospectively, explains what the whole film was about. The title describes how the economic value of Taiwan's banana production began its decline in 1973 and how overproduction in the ensuing decade culminated in 1987 when 8,500 tons of bananas were dumped into the ocean. The title laments, "From that point on, the golden age of this unique sub-tropical fruit was buried in history." Things in the past, therefore, lie at the core of this film's narrative, and the passage of that era is cast in the context of international economy of which Taiwan cannot but be a part. This revisitation of the past reveals a desire to come to terms with the state to which things have turned. Indeed, the title ends with a rather clichéd and awkward sentence. More reluctant than affirmative, it reads, "Chinese people, who are used to suffering with forbearance, continue to face toward a future when everything will be better." The underlying sense of dissatisfaction with the present is, however, only barely masked under a projected future that promises a better life: we have understood how we have come to be but a good life, a *better* life, still lies in a wished-for future.

* * *

Such temporal tensions prefigure the central argument of this chapter. By discussing Wang Tong's dramas about Taiwan's colonial past and memories of modernization, I argue that the backward temporal movement in his films is a defining feature in Taiwan cinema's representation of modernity. Because of the complicated colonial pasts in Taiwan's still troubling "national" history, the quest for some clarity that might make sense of the present must take the form of *retrospection*. Modernity for contemporary Taiwan cinema must register this complex set of temporalities in its narrative processes of construction and imagination. Wang's Taiwan Trilogy—all three were originally conceived as one large project—includes *Strawman* (1987), *Banana Paradise*, and *Hill of No Return* (1992). Three years after the completion of this trilogy, Wang Tong made a highly autobiographical film, *Red Persimmons* (1995), whose interwoven personal memories and national histories remain intimately connected to the three earlier films. These works provide an impressive corpus, a careful analysis of which will have much to tell us about how Taiwan cinema represents modernity in the postcolonial context through various and yet consistent narrative strategies and formal devices. These narrative movements foreground the problems of a postcolonial subject and its intricate historical positionalities; they reveal equally thorny questions about Taiwan cinema as a national cinema still trying to make sense of its colonial histories while facing the intensifying pressures of globalization.

In the following, I provide a revised account of the historical background of New Taiwan Cinema from a different angle than that in chapter 4. Through a review of the changing notions and practices of film historiographies, I establish that the tension between public history and private memory is the predominant trope in the earlier part of this cinematic movement. The tension between public and private is further complicated when various identificatory positions become available and are subsequently articulated with divergent contested and negotiated public vis-à-vis personal histories. And it is at this juncture of historical tensions that I place director Wang Tong's Taiwan dramas at the center of my discussion of cinematic narration as retrospection.

* * *

Historiographies of the New

Many film critics and historians of New Taiwan Cinema see a common characteristic in films made in the early years of this movement. Take, for example, Xiao Ye, one of the initiators of New Cinema and a critic and screenwriter for several important films, including the 1986 *Terrorizers*. He posits, "The ways in which those new films return to the past in order to sort through the Taiwan experience [*Taiwan jinyan*] are intimately connected with the filmmakers' own personal background of growing up." He even goes on to prophesy that New Cinema filmmakers would eventually expand their filmic representation to cover "the larger and more complex experience of all Chinese people."[1] What this statement implies is that cinema reflects collective history in its representation of personal experience. Commonalities among these new films are, therefore, a direct result of the filmmakers' similarity in age and background. Situated between the personal and the collective, "coming-of-age" [*chengzhang*] becomes a prominent thematic in 1980s Taiwanese cinema.[2]

Chiao Hsiung-Ping also notes specifically the New Cinema film-makers' "personal development" as synchronic with "Taiwan's rapid transformation."

As a result, their collective characteristics tend toward reflection and nostalgia for the old life. At the same time, they share certain dissatisfaction with contemporary life and modernization.... Only by understanding this creative obsession can we appreciate why so many films, even those about contemporary society, pursue the past and memory. In this regard, voice-over narration often works to bring out subjective memory, and...has become an almost indispensable technique.[3]

Chiao here spells out a relationship between the thematic concern of coming-of-age and its corresponding filmic styles. For her, "voice-over narration" cinematically performs active remembering and, in so doing, brings the historical past to the cinematic present, that is, the state of being narrated. This cinematic device is "indispensable," furthermore, because there exists little creative space to narrate the present due to the political milieu of the time when martial law was still in effect and political taboos abounded.

The political context has a profound impact on how the personal is brought into the public domain in cinematic representation, as well as how critical discourses make sense of that representation as a reflection of the collective. For instance, in his discussion of Hou Hsiao-Hsien's films in the 1980s, William Tay terms the theme of coming-of-age as an "ideology of initiation." His main argument is that Hou's "realization of this theme is subtly contextualized so that the collective memory of growing up in and with Taiwan as it progressed from an agricultural society to a newly industrialized economy is quietly reconstituted."[4] Subtly and quietly: it is as though this project, the discursive practice of recounting Taiwan's growing up, had to be done in a whisper. Put differently, the specific effects that Hou's stylistics produce are seen here, circularly and redundantly, as symptoms of the very political context in which his films are discursively placed.

From Xiao Ye, to Chia and then Tay, a running undercurrent is the deep anxiety over how to read political influence into 1980s New Cinema's theme of personal coming-of-age, and how to endow personal memory with historical significance. The rather suppressed critical tone changed, however, when martial law was lifted in 1987 and, particularly, after Hou Hsiao-Hsien's *A City of Sadness* was released in 1989. June Yip is correct in pointing out that this film marks the emergence of a new historiography. In her discussion of Hou's Taiwan Trilogy (of which *A City of Sadness* is the first film), Yip adopts a postmodernist view that sees history as a constellation constituted of "a mass of millions of insignificant and serious little stories." *A City of Sadness* performs one such little history by bringing together "a dialogue between...conventional historiography...and those that are normally excluded."[5] That is, the emerging historiography attends to previously unrepresented histories by pitting them against the official history—in this case, the Nationalist government's history, the "one China" grand history long before and beyond *The Descendants of the Yellow Emperor* in the 1950s. Cast in this light, New Taiwan Cinema as a whole has "contributed toward the definition of a distinctly Taiwanese 'nation' through its groundbreaking attempts to construct historical representation of the 'Taiwan experience'...on film, to claim cinematic space for Taiwanese 'popular memory.'"[6] Hou's films, in particular, represent a new historiography, for Yip, because "[they] have greatly contributed to the reexamination of Taiwanese history from which has emerged an entirely new picture of the Taiwanese 'nation,' one that challenges the Nationalist myth of Chinese consanguinity by revealing the complex multiplicity of heritages that make up contemporary Taiwanese identity."[7]

Yip's enthusiasm is unmistakable, and it is stunning to see the eagerness with which she attributes to filmic representation the formation of a new national identity in the larger nation-building project. However, a problem with such rhetoric is that it in effect substitutes one grand narrative—"Chinese consanguinity"—with another—a "distinctly Taiwanese identity." Even though Yip does include the Nationalist government's rule as a part of Taiwan's multiple heritage, the focus is decidedly shifted to how the newfound voices from the inside (an implied "real" Taiwanese) reclaim historical authority and authenticity from the old, oppressive ones from the outside (the Mainland Chinese).

In this context, coming-of-age or personal memory becomes a pretext, a textual plane onto which the social, cultural, and political can now be rewritten as alternative histories. For Wu Chi-Yan, however, the trope of the personal is at once New Taiwan Cinema's most salient feature and, precisely because of that, its greatest limitation. New Cinema's representation of history in the 1980s, for Wu, is largely told from the "popular memory" (*renmin jiyi*) of the "commoners" (*shumin*) in opposition to Taiwan's hegemony (the Nationalist government); Yip's writing is an example of this. Such a dichotomy results

in special attention to different representative groups of underprivi-
leged people (for example, laborers, Nationalist soldiers and veter-
ans, "Taiwanese"), but neglects a proper "collectivity" (*zhengtixing*),
understood conceptually as that which is all-inclusive of Taiwan's
numerous and complex groups and communities with intersecting
backgrounds and a shared future. Wu contends further that, because
of the overemphasis on the personal experience of coming-of-age, collectivity is "reduced, even omitted in the process of representation"
and it eventually "disappears from the viewer's consciousness."[8] That
is, the "Taiwan" experience is only a reduced version of its totality
because certain filmmakers' personal memories, especially those
countering the Nationalist official history, are afforded a privileged
place in the realm of cinematic representation; a reverse discrimina-
tion of sorts in the age of opposition.

The push and pull between the collective and the personal are
particularly intriguing here for two reasons. Historically speak
ing, the change in critical attitude as delineated above does
reflect the change of the political milieu in Taiwan (Xiao Ye, Chiao,
Tay). The possibility of an explicitly critical analysis of film comes
with the loosening of the gridlock of government censorship (Chiao,
Luo). Historiographically speaking, on the other hand, the privileging of popular memory as personal coming-of-age stories or of historical narrative embedded in private familial history, has enabled
some initial efforts to resist the official story. That historiography,
however, will eventually become obsolete because it is still a privileged viewpoint with limited representation (Wu).

To get out of such a dilemma, Chen Kuan-Hsing proposes a pro-
vocative framework with which to analyze the historical complexity
and historiographical thorniness in New Taiwan Cinema. In his essay
"Why Is 'Great Reconciliation' Im/Possible?" Chen discusses two
films, Wu Nien-Jen's *A Borrowed Life* (1994) and *Banana Paradise*,
and argues that the prevalent dichotomous categories of "native
Taiwanese" (*benshengren*) versus "emigrant Mainlanders" (*waishen-
gren*) are historically meaningful *only* when the different "structures
of feeling" they each represent are considered. Cold War politics is at
the core of the Mainlanders' historical experience after World War
II, Chen maintains, just as colonialism is for the Taiwanese natives.
Chen has this to say:

> Because [emigrant Mainlanders and native Taiwanese] live in different
> structures [of feeling], cold war and colonialism become two different

axes along which different historical experiences are produced. These structural experiences, identifications and subjectivities are in turn constructed differently on different emotional levels.[9]

This parallelism highlights at least three sets of contending yet interconnected factors in Taiwan's contemporary history and its process of modernization: identity as Taiwanese or as Mainland Chinese, Japan as former colonizer or as invader, and, finally, Cold War politics as anti-communist or pro-nationalist. To be sure, Chen's is a much more nuanced view of the Taiwan experience than a dichotomy between the personal and the collective within which previous discussion has been trapped.

Not surprisingly, Chen's view was met with much contention; a productive debate, in my mind, that helps open up further possibilities for understanding the so- called "Taiwan experience." The same issue of the *Taiwan* journal where Chen's polemical essay appears also includes five articles which respond directly to Chen. Each of these essays brings added layers of complexity to the questions of Taiwan's history and modernity. For example, Chiu Kuei-fen insists on paying close attention to differences within the categories of Taiwanese and Mainlanders. She argues that, while the notion of "China" that the Nationalist government has propagated affects all who were born after World War II, these younger generations do not necessarily share the same view of Japanese colonialism or Cold War politics as the older generations, be they Taiwanese or Mainlanders, especially as such divisions have become increasingly thin.[10] Chu Tien-Hsin, on the other hand, calls attention to her own background with a Taiwanese mother and a Mainlander father,[11] and Zheng Hong-Sheng discusses his complicated familial history from his grandparents' migration to Taiwan in the late Ching dynasty, to his parents' experience under Japanese colonization, and, finally, to his own with Nationalist modern American-style education.[12]

All the identificatory positions are historically valid, if also muddied. The negotiation and contestation of those positionalities reveal how unstable labels such as "native Taiwanese" or "emigrant Mainlanders" are. For each carries with it multiple historical pasts and intersected meanings. That is, each identity-category represents a unique history, a temporal trajectory as well, and its interrelation with other identities makes up the complex web of Taiwan's history, one that a unified notion of "nation" does not suffice to explain. An analysis of Taiwan's colonial history must thus attend to the complexity of the critical as well as historical language applied to New Taiwan Cinema. My discussion of Wang's films is situated at a juncture where Taiwan's histories of modernity and coloniality must be understood as representational and historiographical sets of questions. In other words, I not only describe what the filmic narration narrates—the stories, content—but also investigate how that narrational act is performed—its narrative functions, procedures, and effects.

The ensuing passages focus on director Wang Tong, whose works have to date received relatively little critical attention in English-language scholarship. To bring him into the critical discursive field greatly expands what existing literature on this cinematic entity has been heretofore preoccupied with. And I hope to go beyond an easily accessible and identifiable ideological framework, such as alternative narratives as resistance to an oppressive Master History. By introducing a wide range of viewpoints, especially those of the local Taiwan film critics' circle, I aim to enrich the study of Taiwan cinema and contribute to a broader understanding of the cinematic registering of history through a rigorous historiographic lens.

*   *   *

The Two-Way Street of History

Wang Tong was born in China in 1942. His family relocated to Taiwan in 1949 when his father, an army general, retreated with the Nationalist government. His special place among New Cinema filmmakers is not, however, merely because of this mixed personal background which places him between the dichotomous categories of native Taiwanese and emigrant Mainlanders. Critics of his films often describe him as a "realist" and "humanist" and his style as "smooth," "non-aggressive," and even "traditional." Edmund K. Y. Wong, for instance, sees Wang as different from other New Cinema filmmakers who are "iconoclasts with an aggressive attitude," whereas Chiao Hsiung-Ping distinguishes Wang from others whose "empty and pretentious content is flawed by their overly formalized and self-conscious style."[13] In short, even when considered a member of this cinematic movement, Wang is often categorized as a softer and less radical filmmaker.

Chen Feibao, a film scholar in China, describes Wang's filmic style in great detail in his book on directors in Taiwan, a collaborative effort with the Film Directors' Guild of Taiwan. The subtle, almost ambiguous, rhetoric he uses in the section on Wang Tong signals some reciprocity, if in the form of a slippage, between Taiwan and China, which is particularly telling about Wang's oft-noted in-between position. Chen explicitly states that Wang is different from his peers, including Hou Hsiao-Hsien, Edward Yang, and Wan Jen, to name but a few, because

> [Wang's] artistic exploration is based on a Chinese cultural self-awareness that expresses a selfless care for humanity at large. Furthermore, he is attentive to the local and the traditional Chinese film aesthetics that address the Taiwanese audience's psychological needs and viewing habits while establishing a narrative style without alienating the audiences on the Mainland.[14]

Here Chen hints at a possible difference between a Taiwanese audience and its Mainland counterpart, but he carefully places both under the larger umbrella of "Chinese culture" as if it were a self-evident category. That is, while acknowledging Taiwan's distinctive locality, Chen conjures an aesthetic meeting ground—"Chinese culture" at large—where a commonality can be forged to map Taiwan's locality within the general cultural landscape of a uniform and unquestionable "China." Wang's work is thus made into a channel, a passage, through which an assumed Chinese cultural reception of his films travels both ways. Taiwan's history is not apart from, but, rather, a part of China's history.

Although I disagree with Chen's historiographic sleight of hand that appropriates Wang's films into the all too obvious political agenda of One China, what he calls attention to—narrative, narration, cinematography—are indeed crucial to an analysis of his filmic representation of Taiwan's history. I will begin with *Red Persimmons* for two reasons. For one, the film's backward narrative movement registers an anxiety over Taiwan's processes of modernization since the late 1940s in broad strokes and, for the other, the debate over its historical representation brings to light the problems of identity politics in Taiwan's 1990s. *Red Persimmons* serves, in short, as a nexus at which the major trajectories of Wang's filmic discourses meet and from which further discussions can be expanded. Specifically, I will discuss two prevalent problematics in Wang's work: the cinematic narrator and narration, and the representation of modernity and its narrative containment. By placing these two sets of problematics together, I argue that the unique backward temporal movement of the narrative and narration best elucidates postcolonial modernity in Taiwan cinema.

* * *

Narration and Retrospection: History as Cinematic Remembrance

Like *Banana Paradise*, *Red Persimmons* opens in a clearly denoted past; specifically, near the very end of the civil war between the Nationalist and the Communist regimes in 1949. General Wang of the Nationalist army relocates his family to Taiwan, reportedly only temporarily, before they can return home after the war. They leave but never come back. Highly autobiographical, the film tells the story of the family's life in Taiwan, spanning the period between 1949 and 1965 by chronicling the Wangs' family history. This is a story often told and, at first glance, also a story similar to many others in terms of what it is being told. *How* it is told, however, tells a different story.

Almost completely in a monochromatic gray, the opening sequence of *Red Persimmons* shows General Wang's brief return home and the ensuing relocation of the family to Taiwan. While General Wang is in battle somewhere inland, the entire family—led by Mrs. Wang and her mother and accompanied by a nanny, a cook, and the General's aide-de-camp—boards a ship from the port of Shanghai to Keelung, a harbor just north of Taipei in Taiwan. A shot of the waves the ship makes as it sails across the Taiwan Strait dissolves into another of a military truck speeding toward the light at the end of a tunnel. Fifteen minutes or so into the film, full color images finally appear on screen with a long shot of the truck exiting the tunnel onto a road amidst lushly green rice paddies. A title announces that it is now "Taipei, 1949." All that has taken place in Mainland China is locked in the past with its dreamy and archaic black-and-white imaging, while the narrative now flaunts its state of being present, being narrated as the Now, in vibrant colors which saturate the entire screen.

Seemingly straightforward in this temporal framing by means of a color versus monochromatic division, the black-and-white segment has but one significant exception. In the middle of the sequence, at the defining moment when the Wangs gather in the courtyard before departing for Shanghai, a craning shot gradually pulls up and away as the family exits through the front gate. As the camera rests in an

extreme high-angle long shot, this stunning long take shows prominently in the center of the frame the eponymous persimmon tree, on
which a broken white kite dangles and ripe fruits ooze blood red,
spilling over the branches and onto the ground below.

This imagery is especially striking because of the deliberate manner in which it solicits multiple readings.[15] Based on Wang Tong's
comment on red persimmon as "the symbol of the family's emotional
center," Hsiang-chun Chu proposes that the use of red be read as
signaling the "aura" of the filmic represented objects.[16] Similarly,
Chia-chin Tsai sees the blunt image of the red persimmon tree in the
black-and-white sequence as the "center of the familial memory,"
a past that refuses to be forgotten and a recurring visual "motif"
that demands active remembering both from the diegetic characters
and from the spectator.[17] Chaoyang Liao, on the other hand, sees the
insertion of the color red into the monochromatic treatment of this
sequence not as a "forced revisitation of a traumatic memory" but,
rather, as a result of the symbolization of that trauma "reflecting back
onto the past by such imagistic creation."[18] All three writers focus on
the meaning of the image—"symbol," "aura," "trauma"—but do not
go further to provide an analysis of how those meanings are produced
cinematically, especially in terms of the narrative structure and narrational construction of the film.

I am concerned less with affixing a deep meaning onto the image
than with what role that image plays in the film's narrational procedure and what temporal problems it reveals in that narration. If the
monochromatic opening sequence is a cliché that signals a past, the
blatant use of the color red is doubly clichéd: it not only reiterates
the sequence as a piece of memory but also calls attention to itself as
an act of remembering. Not surprisingly in bright red, the film's title
appears right after the image of red persimmons. The monochromatic
visual treatment continues, however, for a few more minutes and is
only transitioned into the more transparently realist representation in
color *after* the Wangs have arrived in Taiwan. In fact, after the film's
main title comes a shot with a caption, "Shanghai, 1949," which symmetrically corresponds with the first shot in color that reads "Taipei,
1949."

Here, the textual and the visual framings of the film seem to run
their separate courses according to different logic. Textually, the film
title appears to mark the beginning of the narrative proper.[19] Visually
still in the monochromatic mode, however, the appearance of the main
title does not yet offer any anchorage for the viewer to experience the

film's narration within clearly demarcated diegetic parameters; that is, to understand that the film has indeed begun and its narrative will follow a certain temporal and spatial trajectory until it reaches its conclusion at its closure.

A more detailed analysis is called for. As I indicated earlier, the textual and visual lines of narration do converge after the Wang family finally arrives in Taiwan. The on-screen text, "Taipei, 1949," coincides with the moment when the full spectrum of color is restored to the visual field. If the monochromatic sequence is set in a past *prior* to the act of remembering that the color sequences will now perform, there are at least three modes of retrospection embedded in *Red Persimmons'* filmic narration of the past: from the diegetic present (the time of the story, between 1949 and 1965), from the extra-diegetic present (the time of the film's making and its exhibition, in 1995 and whenever the film is viewed subsequently), and from what I will call a *meta-diegetic* present—the historiographic Now—that oversees the general backward narrative movement.

The first two modes of retrospection designate a pair of clearly positioned vantage points from which history and memory, and their respective modes of representation are seen as parallel to one another. To begin, the diegetic mode of retrospection is comprised of the filmic representation itself, the material and materialized content of that representation as visual and aural text. That is, it is what the act of looking back sees and offers to be seen, perceptually and representationally. The extra-diegetic mode splits off, however, into a multitude of viewing positions whose proliferation is the very process whereby the film's making, exhibition, and critical reception form their endless loop of production and reproduction. When a film is produced, the production immediately involves the makers and the cinematic apparatus. Both productive agents come together and perform a collective act of looking back through cinematic manifestations of sight and sound. The visual and aural product, the film itself, is then sent into the exhibition circuit whose reception sets forth yet another chain of looking back at the film text's looking back at the past. This procedure can be, and, indeed, is repeated in an endless cycle; every spinning off spawns a new web of looking and reading, each with its particular context and limitations. Specific elements of the diegetic can be placed with those of the extra-diegetic in order to reveal the desire of the stylistics, the historiography of the historical representation, and, in this case, the general *looking back* of the temporal movement; that is, the prevalent theme of representing Taiwan's history in New Cinema.

To explain the last mode of retrospection, I need to return to the image of the colored persimmon tree, this time at the end of the film when the image of the fruit in red is shown again. The film is ending after a span of nearly two decades, and the grandmother has just passed away. We are shown a full screen of granny's fiery red burial gown fluttering in the wind. The camera pans to the right, revealing Mrs. Wang's profile next to the gown as she quietly sobs. The soundtrack underscores the mood of sadness and crescendos to its highest volume when the visual track cuts to the persimmon tree, the same red fruit with the same white kite. This imagery retrospectively determines, and *over*-determines, the entire narrative, bracketed by the twice-repeated images, beckoning to one another on each end of the narrative.

What is different cinematically between these two shots is of great significance. The shot in the beginning is a high-angle craning shot seen from the perspective of an omniscient observer, fully enabled and literally propped up by the cinematic apparatus. The second visual return to the tree, however, is a low-angle shot that suggests an embodied point of view, a subjective perspective. The question is, whose point of view is this? Chia-chin Tsai, for one, notices this subtle change in composition and suggests that this shot implies a "homecoming,"[20] or, at least, a desire for that return. Indeed, as a semi-autobiographical film, it could be easily assumed that here the writer-director's viewpoint is finally materialized in the form of the camera's perspective. This is a possible explanation but not entirely satisfying.

My discussion of film historiography in the earlier years of the New Cinema shows a tension between the personal and the collective; more specifically, an anxiety over how the personal theme of growing up can match, or at least parallel, the so-called Taiwan experience. Now in the mid-1990s, what *Red Persimmons* offers is ambivalent at best. A personal narrative is performed, a past remembered, but then what? The last shot of the film shows the grandmother's funeral procession passing by a line of Nationalist army soldiers marching in the opposite direction. After less than two decades in Taiwan, the familial and the national rub shoulders only to part ways, each indifferent to the other. Such apathy is a comment made, however, not about the 1960s, the time frame in which the narrative is set, but, rather, about the 1990s when the film was made. It is utter ambivalence about the past that reveals the discontent of the present. The revisitation of the past serves as a means to pose questions of what the present has become and is ultimately forward-looking. It is finally this meta-diegetic retrospection that brings the past to the present, cinematic representation of history firmly lodged in the Now.

* * *

Wang's other films share interesting similarities in the ways in which their narratives are structured and framed, a discussion of which brings us to a broader understanding of the historiography of representing the colonial past in Taiwan cinema. Of all of Wang's films discussed in this chapter, *Banana Paradise* is the only one that does not have an immediately identifiable narrator. Even *Red Persimmons*, with its well-established autobiographical nature and particularly overtly self-conscious opening sequence, makes its narrational act quite conspicuous from the start. However, my earlier analysis of the last few images of *Banana Paradise* pointed out an awkward gesture that attempted to assign the narrative a specific historical significance (the decline of banana production in 1980s Taiwan). One is tempted to say that, for a cinema dealing with historical crisis, it is hardly possible to construct a narrative without a culturally, historically, and politically charged narration. For all New Cinema films then, a highly pronounced self-conscious realism symptomatizes the impossibility of the sort of transparency that defines a more secure cinema like the so-called classical Hollywood paradigm.

* * *

Narrator Staged, Narration Framed

Set in the time of Japanese colonial rule, *Strawman* and *Hill of No Return* move toward an even more explicit use of a narratorial structure with clearly positioned narrators placed within the diegesis, even though each is done with its peculiar intrigues. A story of two peasant brothers in 1940s Taiwan during World War II, *Strawman* is narrated by the eponymous scarecrow guarding the rice and yam paddies they till. The film opens with a Japanese military marching band delivering urns of ashes of Taiwanese draftees who have died in the war Japan wages in Southeast Asia. An urn, a Japanese national flag, and a certificate of honor are presented to the family of each soldier, now dead and cremated. When the villagers in rags and the army representatives in clean and stiff uniforms part ways, each group blasts its own musical instruments in cacophony. Amidst this aural and visual chaos between the colonizer and the colonized a piercingly loud voice is heard. As the title credits roll, the Strawman yells greetings in Japanese ("Long Live the Heavenly Emperor of Japan!"). He explains, "Everybody, don't be scared. At that time, that was how we greeted each other." After a medium shot of the Strawman limp and propped upon a stick in the rice field, an introduction of the two brothers and their family ensues while a series of flashbacks is organized corresponding to the Strawman's narration.

This narration is a seemingly conventional one; it sets up the story and introduces key characters. When the opening sequence ends and the narrative proper begins, however, that is also the last time we hear from the Strawman. The omniscient and embodied narrator in the beginning turns silent and inanimate throughout the remainder of the film. Indeed, when the brothers' fields are invaded by flocks of sparrows right before harvest, the lead character can only scream at the useless and motionless scarecrow whose mute presence has by then become a parodied figure of the utterly powerless peasants.

What the Strawman stands for is ultimately an inability to speak in the present tense for a past history. Time and again we see the scarecrow in the field, slumped on a stick, indifferent to the toiling and suffering around it. At the end of the film, the recounting of events is performed by the diegetic characters who reclaim, as it were, their own voices, instead of being spoken for. This ambivalence between having a diegetic narrator and then rendering it impotent says two things: for one, the historical drama in Wang's films has to be situated specifically as such—a past, a piece of history; for the other, the narrator's address is at once direct (at the film viewer) and reluctant (about the history it speaks by its circuitous narrativization process).

Hill of No Return offers yet another interesting example of how Taiwan's colonial past is narrated. *Hill* opens with an older man telling the legend of Golden Toad Hill to a group of younger farmhands. A myth or a fable, this tale of fortune and success lures two brothers into running away from the farm before their contract is fulfilled. The film's narrative thus begins with the two brothers' search for Golden Toad Hill. All the intriguing and complex events there notwithstanding, it is particularly important to note how the film ends. After all the shattered dreams and broken hearts, the film returns to exactly the same setting as in the beginning, only this time the narrator appears much older as he narrates the end of the two brothers' story.

The diegetic narrator functions as an embodied storyteller. His appearance at the beginning and the end of the film works to frame the story into a coherent narrative. The particular ways in which the film's narration is addressed are interesting. First of all, in the first telling of the legend, the narrator is shown in a deliberately theatrical setup (recalling here the operatic mise-en-scène in earlier films such as *The Descendants of the Yellow Emperor* in the 1950s). Golden light beams on the narrator's face while darkened figures sit quietly in the shadows. A stage is set, figuratively and visually, on which the narrator performs with great vigor. A sudden cut to the two brothers clearly distinguishes them from other farmhands and, in so doing, transports them onto the narrator's stage. The older brother asks a question and the ensuing point-of-view shot of the narrator shows a direct address. This is thus a story told to the brothers. By the end of the film, however, the narration becomes a story told *about* them; the addressees become the content of the address. The narrator is now shown partly obscured, and no clearly discernible listeners are in sight.

Hill's narrative begins with a diegetically contained narration—from one character to others within the film. It then shifts to an ending where the address lingers ambiguously within the diegesis while gesturing toward the film audience as the narrator does indeed turn and face the camera at the last moment. Lights dim and the film ends. This film has, in fact, had the film viewer as its addressee from the start. The listeners within the film are only surrogates for the film audience. This spectatorial identification is structured in such a way that the story told is eventually about those who are listening; the film's address locks, though circuitously, back onto what it addresses.

This film thus narrated reveals grave uncertainty of Taiwan's history by situating modernity insistently in a narrative past. To stay with *Hill*, the film's narrative is structured around the two brothers' dream of getting rich by mining gold for the Japanese colonizers. Chaoyang Liao comments on this narrative's focus in relation to the narratorial structure of the film. Initially, the old man's tale is nothing more than a legend. However, because of the actual recruitment of the gold mine, Liao observes,

> [The] old man's story suddenly transforms into a legitimate hope that can be realized. When dream becomes a legitimate hope, that is, the two brothers step closer and closer into the trap of the desire resulting from "greed" and, to some extent, look to identify with the role of modern exploiters Japanese colonizers represent.[21]

The emphasis here is a complex dynamics of the desire of the colonized to benefit from the position of the modern on which only the colonizer can lay claim. While the colonized inevitably aspires to identify with the colonizer's position, the desire for the modern becomes inseparable from the colonial desire from which it derives. What I have been suggesting here is that *Hill* and other films about Taiwan's colonial past exhibit an utterly ambivalent attitude toward the modern and the colonial because of the interpenetrated relationship between the two. This ambivalence is seen most vividly in how the modern—technologies of the New as the primary trope—is contained by the narrative construction and restaging of the colonial situation.

What was modern and, in other words, what was new, is placed within a cinematically constructed space of the past and the cinematic apparatus emphatically affirms the pastness of that space. A scene in *Hill* illustrates this point. The Japanese mine director is introduced in a masterfully executed sequence shot. It begins with a lingering pan along the wall, surveying some half-obscured photographs, presumably of the mine director's family in Japan. The camera then sweeps across the room to the carefully landscaped garden and, in the process, shows both the back and front of the director, sitting pensively on a chair. Finally, the camera approaches and then casts its gaze caressingly on the gramophone that has all along been playing a piece of Western classical music. It is striking how dense and complex this apparently smooth and quiet shot actually is. This sequence, shot cinematically, performs spatial congruity among at least the following four elements: the natural (the sequence is immediately preceded by an extreme long shot of the eponymous hill of the film); the cultural (architecture, classical music, landscaped gardens, printed books); the technological (the gramophone and the photographs); and, finally, the personal (memory, pleasure, longing, desire). In short, what the scene represents historically is a sense of *loss* by way of overloading the space with an abundance of references to the past, and doing so with rich historical details. It is a meticulously reconstructed colonial space of nostalgia—both diegetically for the mine director's longing for home and extra-diegetically for 1990s Taiwanese viewers' remembering of the past: the *meta-diegesis* that is the historiographic Now.

What can be said further about the aspect of the technological is how this highly self-conscious long take with its sweeping camera movement calls attention to itself as a cinematic construction, by making the spectator fully aware of the viewing Now. And the meta-diegetic ambivalence is finally revealed in the secured and yet overloaded significance of the narrative reconstruction of the colonial modern. What is framed within the narrative as the new is here an object of nostalgia represented precisely as such. It is then not a coincidence that, when the mine director is brutally murdered later in the film, he is again posed in front of the gramophone, only this time the previously modern/new technology—now seen emphatically as outmoded and old—fails as the needle skips and scratches the record it plays.

Similarly, the diegetic narrator in *Hill of No Return* performs, with great theatrics, an act of telling that addresses the film audience by way of an initial address of the diegetic characters. Structurally speaking, these two segments serve as brackets, or better yet, *quotation marks* that demarcate the beginning and the end of the narrative as such, a story in the past. This narrative involves at once all three levels of retrospection. The extra-diegetic film audience's retrospection is addressed by the diegetic narrator and, with an almost circular movement, the two modes intertwine into a meta-diegetic retrospection that sees modernity together with coloniality. The reluctance to arrive at the present shows, finally, the problematic conditions of postcolonial modernity in Taiwan. Compared with the insistent pursuit of the New in 1930s Shanghai which projects itself onto an infinite future of the "will-have-been,"[22] this New Cinema's representation of modernity places the New in its historical past and evades the present of what that New has now become. The multiple identificatory positions with their complex histories and the intricate negotiation between the personal and the collective in filmic narrative and narration, are defining features of New Taiwan Cinema in its efforts to come to terms with those temporal conflicts and historical problems.

* * *

Film historian Lu Feii laments, "Cinema has documented the hard times in Taiwan since after the war and it has also accompanied our generation as we grew up and became strong. Collectively speaking, cinema is the nation's visual history; personally speaking, on the other hand, films are the colorful memories belonging to each and every one of us."[23] Positioned between the collective and the personal, and again floating between history and memory, Lu's historical narrative shares the same sentiment and dilemma with filmic narrative by filmmakers such as Wang Tong. The last words of Lu's *Taiwan Cinema* read, "We are sure that these memories will follow us into the next century, but we cannot be sure if Taiwan cinema will continue on forward with us."[24] It is, to be sure, a historical past recounted while the future remains utterly uncertain. To write history, to represent history, is finally a desire for a future hidden under the backward temporal movement of cinematic retrospection that has been, from the beginning, casting its longing gaze forward.

6

Anywhere but Here: The Postcolonial City in Tsai Ming-Liang's Taipei Trilogy

This chapter considers questions of cinematic space in the seemingly deterritorialized contemporary Taiwan cinema. I focus on Tsai Ming-Liang and his Taipei Trilogy—*Rebels of the Neon God* (1991), *Vive L'Amour* (1994), and *The River* (1995). As figured in those extraordinary films, Taipei is a city devoid of historical specificities and depleted of spatial immediacy. Often described as "counterdramatic" or "antimelodramatic," Tsai's films cinematize the impossibility of the Now which best characterizes the postcolonial conditions of Taiwan. Compared also with the retrospective narrative forms of Wang Tong's films discussed in chapter 5, this peculiar *ahistoricity* in Tsai's cinematic representation of Taipei begins to gesture toward some possible ways of understanding the impact of globalization in Taiwan's cultural landscape near the end of the twentieth century.

My discussion of Tsai's Taipei Trilogy seeks to elucidate two particular spatial features of 1990s Taipei, most aptly described as *homelessness at home* and *connectedness by separation*. These two conditions shed light on the problems of failed reciprocity and the impossibility of human relationship through spatial proximity, and they characterize the dialectics of the local and the global with even greater urgency than Edward Yang's works in the 1980s. First of all, the breakdown of the traditional family in Tsai's films is at once the cause and the effect of urban living, emphatically portraying family life as being away from home. Furthermore, in depicting Taipei as a modernizing city, Tsai's films capture new urban spaces at moments of transition. Whereas the urbanization process figures in Tsai's films as endless construction, the state of building new roads, new parks, and new apartments is shown as always incomplete and the coexisting old always in disrepair. The spatial quality of this transitional realm is marked by the characaters' connection to as well as separation from one another; a spatial paradox that is reflected in their movement within those spaces. In short, the urban space in 1990s Taipei in Tsai's films is marked by the breakdown of spatial meaning which calls attention to the impossible Now that is finally the condition of national cinema in the global age.

*   *   *

Rebels of the Postcolonial City

Rebels of the Neon God (1992) is Tsai Ming-Liang's filmic directorial debut. Although Tsai was already well known for his work in television, theater, and screenwriting, this film received an immediately enthusiastic reception.[1] Critics were quick to point out that, with this film, Tsai began to demonstrate very different sensibilities from those of his New Cinema predecessors. For example, during the deliberation for 1992's *China Evening News* Film Festival Awards, Chiao Hsiung-Ping summed up as follows the jurors' comparison of *Rebels* with Wang Tong's *Hill of No Return* of the same year:

> They are films of two different times made by filmmakers of two different generations and they show different notions of the values and directions of the cinema.... Wang's creation operates within a "closed" paradigm...and therefore demonstrates his usual classical dramaturgical patterns with this film. With ever increasing subtlety, Wang continues to elaborate his concerns for Taiwan's history....*Rebels*, on the other hand, is an "open" text....The vote we are to cast today is a choice between "I'm voting for what I have always believed in the cinema" and "I'm voting to show that I'm pleased to see changes in Taiwan's film style."[2]

The result of the vote was an affirmation of change; *Rebels* won out over *Hill of No Return* and was named by the jury the best film of the year.[3]

What precisely was the nature of the change that these critics saw in Tsai's film? One juror, New Cinema veteran Xiao Ye, emphasizes the "heavy" or "solemn" sense of history in Wang's *Hill*. While he basically concurs with that view, another juror, film historian Lu Feii, goes further and states that "*Rebels* is completely different [from *Hill*] in that it is non-historical and non-moralistic . . . its narrative style is non-linear and non-classical."[4] In short, *Rebels* is characterized in a *negative* register vis-à-vis the established paradigm. Compared to New Cinema films of the 1980s—Lu specifically mentions both Hou Hsiao-Hsien and Edward Yang—*Rebels* signals a change toward a different representation of history, a different historiography that focuses on the Now and departs from the "nostalgic and historical" retrospection of past experiences.[5]

What the Now encounters here is a cinematic evacuation of historicity in the representation of Taipei as a postcolonial city. The breakdown of history takes the forms of the collapse of domestic space, and the alienation and paradoxical conflation of the public and the private. Author of a comprehensive book devoted to Tsai's films to date, Wen Tian-Xiang, sums up this tendency in terms of the personal and the collective that was at the core of Taiwan cinema in the previous decade.

> In contrast to New Taiwan Cinema in the 1980s that either rewrites Taiwan's history from a macro-historical perspective or reconstructs Taiwan's past from a micro-historical point of view, collective memory is *the* common thematic of the cinema. Tsai Ming-Liang's films, digging deeply into modern subjectivity almost without any sense of historicity, undoubtedly surpass their predecessors' frameworks and are open to a different kind of cinematic reflective gaze.[6]

Once again, a salient feature of Tsai's cinematic representation is highlighted as its *ahistoricity*. But what does that mean and how is it represented cinematically?

As Tsai's first feature film, *Rebels* shows distinctive traits—both thematic and stylistic—which he continues to explore and expand in his later films. To begin, *Rebels* is first and foremost a film about Taipei. The city is not simply the locale for the narrative, the setting in which the story unfolds. More importantly, Taipei the city is figured as a problem around which the narrative is constructed and with which the film is ultimately concerned. For many critics of Tsai's impressive body of work in the past decade, one distinctive feature is found in the *cinematization* of the urban space. For example, in a special issue of *Modern Chinese Literature and Culture* on Taiwan cinema, several contributors see Tsai's films in the light of a city caught between construction and destruction. Yomi Braester focuses on the breakdown of public and private spatial division and the "loss of Taipei's old spatial semiotics...construed as tantamount to the destruction of collective memory."[7] Carlos Rojas, on the other hand, locates the loss of spatial meaning in Tsai's formal treatment of "the themes of water and fluidity" to symbolize "the concurrent dissolution of existing physical boundaries, together with the suturing of otherwise unconnected lives."[8] For both, Tsai's cinematization of Taipei is most emphatically the *disappearance* of spatial markings on which personal memory as well as collective history hinge.

The notion of disappearance deserves further comment, especially in relation to how it elucidates the general conditions of Taipei as a postcolonial city. In his discussion of Hong Kong, particularly in the years leading up to the 1997 handover, Ackbar Abbas has called the city's physical place and cultural territory a "space of disappearance"; a space whose core problematic is its very location, or, better, its dislocation. Between "the local and the global," Abbas insists, the boundaries are so blurred and the spatial (as well as temporal) demarcations so troubled that "[the] difficulty with the local...is in locating it."[9] The challenge is, in other words, to see space as tidy, as homogenous. To see space as disappearance is, instead, to break free, invoking Walter Benjamin, from the "homogenous, empty" space, conceived as a discrete spatial unit in terms of both its knowability and locateability.[10]

Specifically in reference to the cinematic space of disappearance in Wong Kar-wai's films, Abbas proposes one particularly intriguing way of envisaging those seemingly oxymoronic concepts, such as the space of non-locality and the presence of disappearance. For him, Wong's films materialize the conditions of "proximity without reciprocity" among his characters and their urban environment; the defining characteristic of Hong Kong's postcoloniality. Compared with the loaded spatial significance arising from the physical proximity of characters in 1930s Shanghai urban melodrama, the Hong Kong that Abbas describes can be understood as its Shanghai counterpart's inverse, *negative* manifestation. Disappearance is, finally, not a state of absence but, rather, a "'lived' experience of the *negative*" [my emphasis]. This peculiar visuality of disappearance—the negative form of appearance—can be extended to a discussion of Tsai Ming-Liang's Taipei Trilogy.

*   *   *

To analyze *Rebels of the Neon God*, Carlos Rojas begins by introducing a documentary Tsai Ming-Liang makes four years later on his friendship with several persons living with AIDS in Taiwan, *My New Friends* (1995).[11] The linkage between this film and *Rebels* is more than the appearance of four letters—AIDS—in an act of vandalism in the earlier film. In one of the climactic scenes in *Rebels*, one teenager, Xiao-Kang, vandalizes the motorcycle of another teenager, Ah-Tse, in an apparent act of vengeance. Before he is through with wrecking it, however, Xiao-Kang spray paints "AIDS" on the bike. And that is the only reference to the disease in the entire film.[12] Taken "abstractly," for Rojas, AIDS is not so much a "specific disease" as "a figure for random encounters and flows of contagion that effectively challenge the firm spatial and social boundaries upon which identity may be imagined to be grounded." He continues, "The figure of AIDS in *Rebels* resonates with themes of fluidity and mediation, suggesting a vision of identity that is not based on specific spatial or libidinal loci, but rather is the product of more delocalized processes of transference and displacement."[13]

It would be interesting to entertain, if one were to push further Rojas' figurative use of AIDS, how the viral phantom of HIV at the millennial juncture comes to stand in for the nineteenth century flâneur who travels on the global map with no origin nor destination. Even more productive, perhaps, would be to focus closely on the notions of fluidity and flow, especially in terms of negativity and disappearance, and tease out their cinematic manifestations in *Rebels*. In other words, rather than proposing a global view based on a global generality—the case here being the prevalence of AIDS as a global pandemic both literally and figuratively—it would be necessary to locate first how the local is connected to the global. The "abstraction" of fluidity, for example, can indeed be better understood as the breakdown of domestic space that admits the in and out of its flow or, as Rojas seems to prefer, its contagion in flux as a breach of boundaries, an uninvited and uncontrollable movement.

To turn to the film itself, *Rebels* opens with a Taipei drenched in torrential rain. The very first image is an extremely claustrophobic interior shot of a public phone booth with raindrops splattering on its glass panels and passing vehicles' distorted contours exaggerated by their own meandering headlights. Two teenage boys, Ah-Tse and Ah-Bin, rush into the booth from the rain and, after lighting some cigarettes, they proceed to force open the coin box of the pay phone with an electric drill. The sequence then cuts to a low-angle shot of yet another teenager, Xiao-Kang, sitting at a desk staring out of the window with his back to the camera. Those intercuts between the two plot lines continue until Xiao-Kang accidentally breaks the window glass and cuts himself. A close-up in extreme proximity shows Xiao Kang's blood dripping onto a geography textbook on the desk, open to a page on which several maps of the island of Taiwan are shown.[14] The opening sequence ends with a long shot of Xiao-Kang rushing to the bathroom, while his parents, who are shown sitting in the dining/ living room area, notice the disturbance, and join in the commotion caused by the incident.

The first few minutes of *Rebels* establish several common themes that Tsai continues to explore in his later films, such as the theme of recurring "confined spatial areas" as well as those of "water and fluidity" which Rojas notes.[15] The contrast between Xiao-Kang's confinement and the free roaming of Ah-Tse and Ah-Bin is clear. The ubiquity of water and fluid also warrants close attention. Jean Ma, for example, sees the many "forms of watery excess" as a "textual inscription" which has far more profound "existential or even metaphysical significance" across the entire body of Tsai's films.[16] Instead of water and flow, however, Wen Tian-Xiang homes in on the more concrete and prevalent thematic: home. With the indoor/outdoor parallel, Wen sees a stark contrast between two types of family: "one family [Ah-Ze's] without a parent and another [Kang's], even though both parents are present, with an utterly alienated familial relationship.... In either case, having a home is like having no home at all."[17] The ultimate condition for the characters in *Rebels* and other films by Tsai is precisely this notion of *homelessness at home*.

The dialectics of containment and fluidity can thus be understood in terms of home and homelessness. The "home" without parents in *Rebels* symptomizes this problem. Ah-Tse lives with his older brother, whose face is never shown. Their apartment does not even have the pretense of a home—barely furnished, dirty dishes piled in the sink, and mattresses without bed frames. Most strikingly, due to a clogged water drain in the kitchen that neither of the two brothers puts any effort into cleaning, backed up water gradually floods the entire apartment. Just like the spoiled milk Ah-Tse finds in the refrigerator, the deterioration of the home space from the inside is complemented by the invasion of wastewater regurgitated back up through the drainage from the outside. It is a "home"—if one can still call it that—that has lost its function as a shelter that divides the public from the private space. The sense of "fluidity" here is a troubling one, as the film constantly emphasizes by showing the rippling reflection of light and shadow upon its characters' forlorn faces.

As homes lose their binding power, characters in *Rebels* are much more often seen in public places—streets, video arcades, and, significantly, hotels. Indeed the anonymity of cheap hotel rooms and corridors are a constant reminder of Tsai's characters' state of being away from home. The fourth major teenage character and the only girl, Ah-Kuei, is particularly intimately linked with the alienation and anonymity of the hotel space. After an apparent one-night stand with Ah-Tse's faceless brother, Ah-Kuei awakes to yet another morning having no idea of her whereabouts. We soon find out that this is not an exceptional occurrence. In a later scene, after all-night merrymaking with Ah-Tse and Ah-Bin, she passes out on the bed of a cheap hotel room, unaware of the porn film flickering on the TV screen. A highly disturbing long shot shows the three teenagers sprawled about the room. In only her undergarments, Ah-Kuei is spread in front of the camera as the TV screen in the far corner relentlessly emits skittish green light across her scantily clad body and the two teenage boys' youthful, if also lustful, faces. It is all the more chilling when she calls Ah-Tse the morning after, demanding to know where she is and whether they have taken sexual advantage of her in her drunken state.

These three teenagers are mostly associated with the nonfamilial space; their homelessness takes place away from home, on the streets, in the video arcades, or the ice-skating rink. Xiao-Kang, on the other hand, is portrayed as slipping away from a family life in the process of coming unglued toward its eventual breakdown. After a chance encounter at an intersection where Ah-Tse, the motorbike-riding teenager, smashes the side-view mirror of the taxicab his father drives, Xiao-Kang begins an obsessive search around Taipei, stalking Ah-Tse and his cohorts. After he successfully vandalizes Ah-Tse's bike by painting "AIDS" on it, Xiao-Kang continues to follow Ah-Tse as he pushes the vandalized motorcycle along the endless roadside construction sites to a repair shop. In a telephoto long shot, Xiao-Kang, on his moped, slowly approaches Ah-Tse from behind and makes his first and only move toward an interaction. Xiao-Kang's offer to help is met by Ah-Tse's violent rejection. As Ah-Tse curses at Xiao-Kang and continues to push his bike toward the camera, Xiao-Kang is left alone with the blurry cityscape in utter chaos and disrepair.

The notion of "fluidity," therefore, does not sufficiently explain the different kinds of flow as seen in *Rebels of the Neon God*. If the characters' movement seems fluid, that is because of a lack of anchorage and shelter. Put differently, the fluidity of movement is in fact a result of the loss of spatial boundaries; instead of flow, with its common association with freedom or lightness, what *Rebels* shows is a Taipei full of leaks and holes, an urban maze wherein the youngsters roam with no direction and no destination. Indeed, at the final moment of the film, Ah-Kuei asks Ah-Tse to leave Taipei with her. When the question of "Where to?" is raised, the answer is not surprisingly "I don't know." There is no place from which one may take leave and no place to which one can return.

* * *

A Borrowed Home, Almost a Love Story

Tsai Ming-Liang's next film, *Vive L'Amour*, pushes the notion of homelessness to an greater degree of intensity. Through the story of two homeless young men and a woman realtor, *Vive* tells an impossible love story of unbearable loneliness and longing taking place in an empty apartment unit in Taipei. Now a salesperson of cremation storage units for a columbarium, Xiao-Kang returns in this film as a loner who has stolen the key to a luxurious apartment in order to commit suicide there. In the meantime, the woman real estate agent for this apartment comes in with another man, Ah-Rong, for a one-night stand. The noise of their lovemaking interrupts Xiao-Kang in the middle of his suicide attempt. Soon it is revealed that Ah-Rong, a street merchant selling women's clothes and accessories he purchases and brings back from overseas, has also stolen a copy of the key to the apartment from the realtor. The bizarre, concealed, and conccited interactions among these three urbanites in and around this borrowed space ensue for the remainder of the film.

Edmund K. Y. Wong calls this new breed of Taipei residents a "nomadic tribe" [*piaoyou qunzu*][18] whose homelessness is most excruciatingly felt in their desperate search for belonging. The futility of that search is depicted in a darkly comic scene between the two men. No more than a pair of squatters, Xiao-Kang and Ah-Rong each occupy a bedroom. The film emphasizes this strange cohabitation by foregrounding the hallways and doors that connect as well as separate their respective spaces. These two young men first become aware of each other's simultaneous existence in the apartment through an intricately choreographed sequence of physical comedy. The elaborate scene dramatizes the peculiar borrowed living space they share as partaking in a condition of *connectedness by separation*. Having just returned from one of his overseas trips, Ah-Rong goes back to inspect the supposedly vacant apartment. After making sure that it is clear, he moves his belongings from his car into the apartment. While he is taking a hot bath, however, the other illegitimate occupant, Xiao-Kang, returns with a watermelon. Ah-Rong grabs his clothes and begins a hide-and-seek dance with Xiao-Kang, unbeknownst to the latter. From the room where he sleeps, Xiao-Kang walks all the way across the hallway into the room that Ah-Rong uses. The camera slowly pans, following him as he strides from one room to the other, until, with a dramatic and exaggerated movement, he rolls the watermelon-cum-bowling ball along the hallway until it smashes against the far wall and breaks into juicy pieces.

All the while Ah-Rong is shown ducking under the bed, crawling through glass doors to the balcony, climbing through windows between rooms, and hiding under the bed, all in a strenuous effort to evade Xiao-Kang's detection. However, when Xiao-Kang finally realizes that he is not alone—a fact betrayed to him by the last bit of the bath water being sucked down the drain as he urinates—he in turn assumes the role of an intruder and begins to run and hide as well. The hide-and-not-seek chase becomes a mouse-and-mouse game, one in which there is no pursuer, only the pursued. Hallways, doors, and window frames, all become multilayered blockades and veils that are mobilized to turn the emptiness of the apartment into a venue for the performance of a particularly ironic space of presence and disappearance.

It is a space over which neither of the two men has legitimate claim, a space that both can occupy, temporarily at best, as their borrowed home. Xiao-Kang and Ah-Rong continue to interact with each other further until one morning the realtor's surprise visit forces both to sneak away together. Homeless but not without means of transportation, the two young men take a trip to the columbarium where Xiao-Kang works as a salesperson. The seemingly endless rows of container spaces in different sizes recall the nameless corridors of hotel rooms for nightly rental in *Rebels* as well as the high-rises and apartment buildings for sale in *Vive L'Amour*. The connection is drawn through the explicit commercialization of spaces—for the dead and the living alike.

What the film emphasizes, ultimately, is not living space offered up for occupation. Instead, the commercial effort of selling places is constantly shown as a futile act. The meticulously portrayed daily routine of the woman realtor is a case in point. Always fashionably dressed and zooming around in her small white car, the realtor is often shown jaywalking and climbing atop her car to put up for-sale signs. Several times when she is speaking to potential buyers, either in person or over the phone, she is the only one who is shown talking on screen: never a word in return, never any communication nor reciprocation. A good example is a scene when she holds an open house for a ground-floor unit; the visual representation of the space she sells is stunning but also typical in its striking barrenness.

The sequence begins with the woman realtor putting up bright-red signs on trees and utility poles in various public locations near the unit for sale. After placing one large sign on her car, she is shown in a long shot entering an empty ground-floor storefront unit whose sliding glass doors are also lined with blood-red signs banning solicitation. It then cuts abruptly to the inside of the property, where the realtor is squatting on the floor making a phone call. The bleak interior of the location is twice emphasized. First, the sudden change from exterior to interior highlights the stark contrast between a seemingly busy neighborhood and the gutted interior of the unit. Second, the realtor's crouching figure in the mid-ground is cast against the glass doors with the now inverse for-sale signs that admit partial sunlight from the outside. This is a spatial relay that calls attention to the emptiness of the unaccounted-for foreground of the shot. An ensuing shot shows that empty space as truly empty, a mere continuation of space with visible signs of walls torn down and rooms demolished. This is an *emptied-out* space, a space of disembowelment.

Disembowcled, but not for long: these spaces are soon to be peopled by new occupants, at least according to the realtor's affirmative words about how they are fit for family living. More often than not, however, the various urban spaces *Vive L'Amour* shows remain in an odd state between unused and unusable. Indeed, the various commercial and residential spaces the realtor tries to sell are examples of this dis-utility. What is represented, in other words, is neither what things were nor what they will be; it is change materialized by the cinematic capture of the in-between moment of transition. The representation of the Ta-an Forest Park [*Da'an senlin gongyuan*] comes to the forefront as an emblematic image of a Taipei caught between stages—between demolition and rebuilding; between disembowelment and refilling; and, finally, between an old location in ruins and a new location that has yet to come into being.

This state of construction by destruction forms the basis for Yomi Braester's hypothesis about Taiwan's New Cinema, what he has termed the "poetics of demolition." For Braester, "like any history-rich city, Taipei offers a palimpsest of a layered growth."[19] Among the hundreds of years of Taipei's history, he focuses on Taipei's reconstruction period since the late 1970s which "entailed a massive demolition of old neighborhoods, the evacuation of entire communities, and the construction of new landmarks": a government-led urban replanning that results, Braester laments, in the "erasure of older Taipei spaces" and, ultimately, the "erasure of memories."[20] However, by "[embracing] the changing cityscapes and [establishing] a dialogue with the landmarks of destruction," *Vive L'Amour* is one prime filmic example that "exercises what may be called a poetics of demolition...a paradoxical practice of writing through erasure, building through tearing down, remembrance through amnesia, and identity formation through the unmaking of social ties."[21] As a "strategy of resistance," in short, this poetics of demolition enables films to "[negotiate] between spatial belonging and urban alienation" and to "take part in the public debates on urban planning and channel civic resistance to more complex politics of memory."[22] This "poetics of demolition" is, finally, a promise of political, ideological, and identificatory gains through the cinema, a belief in direct correspondences between cinematic representation and the kind of activism it ostensibly advocates, or, at least, a recuperative revision that redeems the ruins only by displaying them.

Such a reflectionist approach is flawed by its supposition of a neat corresponding relationship between social reality and its representation. Braester's close attention to the history of the specific place for the Forest Park is, nevertheless, helpful for a productive reading of the final sequence of *Vive L'Amour*. The space for the Forest Park had long been designated as the "Reserved Land for Park #7." For years after the Nationalist government relocated to Taiwan in 1949, the area was mainly a *juancun* (military dependents' village) occupied by military personnel and their families, a particularly poor neighborhood whose inhabitants lived in overcrowded shacks. As Taipei became more prosperous and urban beautification more valued, this squalid area increasingly became an eyesore, a past that the modernizing city was all too eager to jettison. After some 40 years, the government declared in the early 1990s that most of the buildings were illegal and the area was to be razed to clear the land for a stadium or a park. For people who had lived there for decades, homes were turned overnight into a space in which they themselves suddenly became occupants of a borrowed space: from residents to squatters, all it took was a policy change and the spatial memory, and the sense of belonging with it, was trashed and then erased.

After much controversy and great difficulty with evacuation, this piece of land was cleared, both literally and figuratively, in 1992. Construction of the Forest Park quickly ensued. What *Vive L'Amour* captures is the park at this particular "point of transition":[23] a perfect stage for the spatial drama that has been playing out in this film precisely because its ephemerality is situated right between appearance (or the projected park under construction) and disappearance (of the slum demolished). The irony is impossible to miss. Whereas the appearing of the park is the disappearing of a local community, the disappearance of that piece of urban history makes way for the very appearance of an emerging public green space.[24] The role of the park will need to be placed with all other buildings and structures that collectively make up the urban space of Taipei. That is the same dynamic of all the living spaces—again, both for the living and the dead—among which the characters navigate their way. And this is the context within which a productive analysis of the final sequence of *Vive L'Amour* must be placed.

The last sequence takes place after a night of entangled erotic encounters and alienation. As Xiao-Kang lies on Ah-Rong's bed masturbating, he is surprised by the sudden return of Ah-Rong with the realtor. Hiding under the bed, Xiao-Kang is both a part of and apart from the sexual act on the bed. Trapped and aroused, Xiao-Kang resumes his masturbatory act and the mechanical squeaks of the box springs seem the most fitting accompaniment to this strange ménage-a-trois. The morning after, the realtor leaves while Ah-Rong is still asleep. Her car doesn't start, so she walks into the Ta-an Forest Park in the gray light of an overcast morning.[25]

One of the first shots of *Vive L'Amour* shows Xiao-Kang on his moped riding along the edge of the Ta-an Park; what we see then are only the construction fences at its perimeter. The activity inside the park is shown by the piles of dirt dug up by the bulldozer parked quietly to one side. A low-angle shot accentuates the obtrusiveness of the few apartment buildings just outside the park in the background with balloons and banners signaling units for sale. The realtor then walks into frame from screen right and, as the camera pans left following her along the half-paved walkway, her figure is dwarfed by the imposing presence of the yellow dirt piled far higher than her height. What follows is a tracking shot of her wandering through the park; her deliberate pace, as if strolling in a lush forest, is utterly at odds with the visually stark rawness of the park still in construction—no lawn, only newly planted trees with few leaves, only piles of dirt and unpainted benches lining her path.

The visual message is as bleak as it is stark. Just like the disemboweled buildings, the destruction of this space is, literally, to make room for new uses of the space and to create new meanings for the space now in ruins, at least for the time being. After many scenes highlighting that fact, this sequence opens up to the larger confinement of the in-between-ness, mapping Taipei in a simple yet broad stroke. As the camera follows the realtor in the park, we are afforded an increasingly wider and deeper view of what is both inside and surrounding the park, by now an emblem of the state of spatial transition in Taipei. The realtor walks down a seemingly endless half-paved path, alone yet determined in her stride, until a sudden cut to an extreme long shot, showing that there are in fact many other city dwellers in the half-naked park. That she is actually not alone is almost shocking if one was absorbed in the solitude of the lone woman's stroll after another one-night stand. Visually, the scope of what the sequence involves—especially coming at the very end of the film—seems to get larger and emptier as any holds on personal connections or meanings are rendered less and less tangible. This sense of personal alienation at its most impersonal is played out against the background of buildings like a scroll painting unfolding.

*   *   *

The camera finally abandons the woman altogether—for a little while, at least—and begins a leftward circular pan, a panoramic scoping that slowly and yet insistently takes in all of the cityscape that the mechanical eye can see. With no longer a human actor serving as an anchor, this is an encounter between the cinematic apparatus and the city.

But the camera does come back to the woman. As it picks up her figure again, she is shown in a long shot walking among a sea of empty benches in a half-completed outdoor theater with one lone old man sitting in the foreground reading a newspaper, utterly indifferent to her appearance, before the film cuts to a medium shot of the woman. The camera has come back to her only to watch her cry in a sustained close-up that lasts six long minutes. When her sobbing finally subsides, she lights a cigarette as a brief moment of sunlight travels across her face. But then an uncontrollable sob wells up again and there the film ends.

It is perhaps justified to ask, along with Chris Berry, "Where is the love?"[26] when the film abruptly ends with no hope in sight. Hsiao-Hung Chang and Chih-Hung Wang ask a different question about the park: "Is the Ta-An Park an emblem of the fin-de-siecle wasteland or the brave new world of a new century?" By looking at the bizarre and almost inexplicable crying scene of the woman—the "heterosexual" woman, Chang and Wang are eager to point out—they propose a reading of the film by focusing on the disintegration of traditional family. Based on the failure of heterosexual relationships in this film, Chang and Wang argue a rather unusual dialectics that they claim the film puts forth.

> The radicalness of *Vive L'Amour* lies in its refusal to indulge in nostalgia when representing the breakdown of the traditional heterosexual family. It catches a glimpse of the emergence of new modes of desire amid the agitation and anxiety. On the one hand, it vacillates in the habit to look for a sense of belonging in emotions. On the other, it rhapsodizes over new modes of erotic interaction.[27]

If I paraphrase: even though the film does linger around the imminent loss of any traditional emotional anchor—mainly, the heterosexual family—it in fact valorizes some emergent possibilities of human relationships, best exemplified, of course, by homosexual, or, as they call it, "other" or "heterotopic" eroticism represented by the highly dramatized kiss between the two young men. If traditional, heteronormative love has indeed failed, the homosexual or alternative love is still without consummation.

*   *   *

Flowing Is the Unspeakable, Unspoken Desires

The desire for a heterotopic or alternative space falters in Tsai's cinema because both traditional and nontraditional modes of relationships crumble at the point of contact. Desire is granted spatial mobility only when left unspoken and unrecognized. Tsai's next film problematizes the flow of desire that hinges on spatial *proximity without reciprocity*. Perhaps his most infamous film, Tsai's 1995 *The River*, tells the story of a heartbreakingly alienated family whose recognition of emotional ties is achieved only through an ultimate act of misrecognition. The breakdown of spatial meaning in the visual form of the permeation and puncturing of the cinematic frame receives much further attention in what is arguably the most melodramatic film in Tsai's body of work. By melodramatic, I mean how the issues regarding home/family and the problems of mis/recognition lie at the core of the film's dramatization. If the previous two films work to loosen any traditional values familial space holds, this film goes further to uproot the significance of that space and disperse it into the general urban space at large. A discussion of this film will then prepare us to consider, with two other later films, how this dislocated Taipei may be resituated within a global context and how the notion of the global is formed and informed by the process of dislocation of the local.

The River is considered the final film of Tsai's Taipei Trilogy. It may be appropriate here to pause and consider the notion of "trilogy," as this book has earlier dealt with several such trios. A critical impulse to auteurize a filmmaker and his or her work by suggesting a trilogy is nothing new. Even within the context of this book, I have already discussed Hou Hsiao-Hsien's and Wang Tong's Taiwan trilogies. This hypothesis is based on an assumption that the three films would form a coherent framework within which links and connections could provide a consistent and sufficient understanding of them, together and individually. What is worth noting in this case is the emphasis on Taipei that my discussion so far has also explored. To stay within this critical hypothesis can be productive, if only provisionally. What this analytic method lacks or fails will then open up possibilities for an analysis that extends to include Tsai's films *after* the trilogy.

In the case of Tsai's Taipei Trilogy, one compelling reason for this grouping is that Xiao-Kang's character in all three films is played by the same actor as are his parents in *Rebels* and *The River*.[28] This diegetic continuity of the family—which is later elaborated on in *What Time Is It There?* (2001) after *The Hole* (1998)—*however dysfunctional*, is matched by the film's visualization of urban spaces, of anonymity and alienation. I have analyzed earlier the use of hotel rooms and corridors to signify the state of "homelessness" in *Rebels* that is echoed by the representation of "home for sale" in *Vive L'Amour*. Both films highlight the difficulty, if not total impossibility, of communication and intimacy through a spatial dialectics of connectedness and separation. *The River*'s elaboration on those themes is at its most striking in its representation of hotel rooms and gay bathhouses.

The River tells the story of Xiao-Kang who is suffering from a strange ailment in his neck. It is clear from the very beginning that the relationships among his family have seeped much more deeply into alienation than in *Rebels*. The parents are no longer sleeping in the same bedroom and Xiao-Kang's response to their questions about anything is almost always "None of your business." As the back cover of the film's U.S. DVD release dryly observes, "The son…drifts through life without a job; the mother is an elevator operator having an affair with a man who pirates pornographic movies; and the father pursues illicit pleasure in the city's gay saunas and is on a mission to stop the leaking water from the apartment upstairs." After randomly agreeing to play a corpse floating in Taipei's Tanshui River as a movie extra, Xiao-Kang begins to develop an unexplained pain in his neck, which soon grows to be so agonizing that he is unable to straighten his neck. After numerous efforts—from massaging with ointment and his mother's vibrator, to seeing Western, Chinese, and even a shaman-like doctor, the pain only gets worse. Almost as a last resort, the father takes Xiao-Kang on a trip to Taichung City to visit a witch doctor.[29]

Having to spend an unexpected extra night away from Taipei in a hotel, first the father, and then Xiao-Kang, pay a visit to a local gay sauna. In a bare and darkened room used for anonymous sexual encounters, one male body sits in the embrace of another while the latter pleasures the former with his hand. Only afterward, when the light is flicked on, do the father and son realize what they have done together. The father strikes a hard slap across Xiao-Kang's face, and Xiao-Kang storms out of the room. Back in the hotel room the next morning, Xiao-Kang's neck seems to have gotten better as he walks out of the hotel room onto a sunlit balcony.

There are at least three dominant spaces in this film and a careful consideration of them yields a productive understanding of the climactic scene of incest. On the one hand, there is the familial space of broken ties—the family's apartment—and, on the other hand, there are those anonymous spaces of floating desire and pleasure—hotels and saunas. Between these two, there is the city itself—streets, bridges, hallways—that connect the other two spaces. First of all, the traditional home space has lost its binding power, even in a physical sense. Aside from the fact that all three members now have their own bedrooms and the living room area is hardly a space where they interact, the focus is on the leak in the father's bedroom. Unlike the flooding of the apartment in *Rebels*, this leak has an overwhelming effect, but in a strangely isolated manner; it seems only to affect the father, while Xiao-Kang and the mother are oblivious to the increasing devastation of the leaking and flooding in the father's room. For example, in a scene where the mother is cutting up a durian fruit and sharing the creamy but famously pungent meat with Xiao-Kang, the father is busy bringing out buckets full of water leaking from above. While the mother and son are positioned facing toward the camera, the father's entrance from the background only triggers a slight glance from his estranged wife; a half-turned backward glance, to be exact, which further emphasizes the lack of interest of the absentminded looker.

The way the family members' gazes hardly ever meet is most horrifying in the scene when the parents go to the hospital after Xiao-Kang is hospitalized (less for his physical discomfort, the film seems to suggest, than for his psychological instability). The father and the mother meet in the hospital. The father enters an elevator, a long shot showcasing the various frames within the building with the interior of the elevator lit like a cage on display. Right before the door closes, the mother cuts through all the frames and enters the elevator. As the door slowly shuts, the two stand next to each other, stiff, without exchanging a single look. Exiting the elevator, the parents turn a sharp corner, and, in a long take, they walk down an excruciatingly long corridor—one not unlike those in the hotels or bathhouses—turn and exit through an unseen door before the film shows that a figure sitting in the foreground on a bench has all along been Xiao-Kang. This is a moment of shocking misrecognition, or, simply, *non*-recognition among family members who have long since stopped looking at each other or seeing one another.

The nonrecognition, especially in a setting that is architecturally and compositionally similar to that of the gay sauna, foreshadows the anonymity and its resulting drama in the later scene. This uninterrupted shot continues until the parents reenter the frame, run toward Xiao-Kang, and the boy in pain begins to wail and bang his head against the wall as the mother tries to comfort him to no avail and the father stands awkwardly by. This part of the scene recalls the opening sequence of *Rebels of the Neon Gods*. After Xiao-Kang cuts his hand by breaking the window glass, the mother rushes into the bathroom to help him clean the wound (off frame as they are both in the bathroom) while the father stands outside, concerned yet denied any direct participation. This seemingly connected yet separated visual relationship among the family members echoes the spatial arrangement of their home. This sense of homelessness at home is thus mostly vividly dramatized by their proximity without reciprocity.

When reciprocity does occur in various forms of physical contact, it is often indicative more of heightened alienation than of intimacy. The interaction between Xiao-Kang and Ah-Tse in *Rebels* results in either violence or rejection. In *Vive L'Amour*, the kiss Kang places on Ah-Rong's lips in the empty apartment only makes the solitude all the more harrowing. In *The River*, on the other hand, the pursuit of anonymous gratification is like a river of unspoken desire, a human Tanshui River as it were, along the darkened corridors of gay bathhouses. Before the climactic incest sequence, this visual motif is quite elaborately established in earlier scenes in saunas and hotels. Each corridor is lined with numerous doors, each of which opens onto an unknown room of unspoken desire.

After Xiao-Kang takes a dip in the Tanshui River as a movie extra, to return to an earlier moment in the film, he is taken to a hotel to clean up by a production assistant, his childhood friend, Xiao-Qi, who has invited him to the shoot. As she devises her seduction plot, Xiao-Qi is shown pausing in the corridor before opening the door while Xiao-Kang is inside taking a shower. When she finally opens and enters through the door, she systematically turns the room into a darker and even more anonymous space by making Xiao-Kang turn off the lights and pull shut all the curtains. Their entwined bodies engaging in rhythmic lovemaking movements are reflected in a mirror and create a doubly fragmented image of casual sex. The film suddenly cuts from this moving—albeit mechanical—image to an equally fragmented yet completely motionless image in a dark room where a male body is partially covered by an orange-colored bath towel across his midriff. Another man enters from off-frame and begins touching the first man only to be rejected in his attempt. The dejected man leaves and, after another minute or so of stillness, the first man in the room sits, revealing himself to be Xiao-Kang's father.

The parallelism drawn here is a troubling one. The contrast between the active (the movement in the scene between Xiao-Kang and Xiao-Qi) and the passive (the close-to-stillness treatment of the father's rejection of the faceless man) only heightens the unease that Xiao-Kang's sexual activity is cinematically associated with the father's pursuit of illicit homosexual pleasure. The next major scene in a gay sauna further strengthens the imminent threat of the absolute taboo of father-son incest by even closer articulation of the spatial proximity of the father and son's unspoken desire. The scene I have in mind takes place right after the father has had sex with a young man, the same actor who played Ah-Tse in *Rebels of the Neon God* and Ah-Rong in *Vive L'Amour*. Their sexual interaction—filmed in the same medium close-up as the next scene to be discussed—ends on a sour note as the young man refuses to perform oral sex on the older man, a fact made visually quite unpleasant to watch largely because of the camera's physical closeness to the characters and their action; it is almost as if the camera were keen on capturing less the intimacy between the two men than the *failure* of achieving just that. Moreover, it is the very association of father-son incest that looms dangerously close.

A telling moment about this anxiety—a "cultural anxiety" according to Zhang Ai-zhu, to whom I will turn shortly—comes right after the brief moment when the young man comes face-to-face with Xiao-Kang as they cross paths at the entryway of the gay sauna. The scene begins after the father and the young man have had their illicit rendezvous in a dark room of a sauna. Their ill-matched sexual act is intercut with Xiao-Kang painstakingly dressing for the evening due to the ailment in his neck. Xiao-Kang finally makes it to the sauna precisely at the moment when the young man is on his way out. The short exchange of looks is as fleeting as it is awkward. The young man quickly exits the building, as Xiao-Kang reluctantly stands in front of the unattended reception desk. In the background is a bead curtain still fluttering after the young man has emerged from behind it. The slight movement of the curtain is what eventually remains on screen after Xiao-Kang suddenly walks out of frame and leaves.

Walking along on a deserted pedestrian bridge lit by streetlights and flickering neon, Xiao-Kang is shown in a long shot making his way toward the camera. Soon the young man appears behind him. Overtaking him as they reach a turn on the bridge, the young man marches on as Xiao-Kang follows behind. The camera pans slightly to the right to catch their backs as they disappear into the night. The bridge is a corridor of Taipei City and, particularly at night, its course the channel of dark desire. What is particularly interesting here, however, is how the camera still remains relatively stable; the most involvement it exhibits is a slight pan, but it never moves from a fixed vantage point of observation. In other words, the chance/missed connection between Xiao-Kang and the young man is contrasted to the previous scene of the anonymous/disconnected encounter with the father.

In preparation for the climactic incest incident near the end of the film, the sequence begins with a very similar visual composition. Here inside the gay sauna, Xiao-Kang is shown walking toward the camera along a darkened corridor lined with closed doors to private rooms.

Just as in the pedestrian bridge scene described above, the camera remains still as he approaches. The camera also pans slightly as Xiao-Kang turns a corner. As he walks down the second corridor with his back to the camera, however, the camera begins to follow him. The movement of the camera is smooth, as it stays just close enough to watch him in the passageway of unspoken desire. Unspoken is a literal description of the activities represented here. This long continuous take shows a number of half-naked men walking the corridor, opening and closing each door. No words are exchanged, only anonymous bodies in movement. Behind each door, it seems, there's an equal chance of pleasure or disappointment as the seekers eagerly march on, Xiao-Kang and the camera along with them.

This is a space of desire that is constantly put to the test in agonizing anticipation and sore disappointment. But that is not the only reason for the lingering portrayal of the gay sauna space full of tentativeness and hesitation. In an interview with Daniele Rivere, director Tsai Ming-Liang talks about his own internal struggle when filming this scene. A milder scenario was to have Xiao-Kang and his father just "run into each other." Once on location in the middle of preparation, however, Tsai couldn't help but ask himself why he recoiled. He confesses,

> I realized at once that what I actually wanted to do was to go much further...and have father and son make love in the dark. Why hadn't I dared to have that thought until then? Lest I'd have been afraid of doing it. I quickly decided to do the scene that way. I discussed it with the actors and we did the shoot.[30]

For Hsiao-Hung Chang, this hesitation, along with the ambiguous critical discourse about the scene, is a clear indication of the "cultural unrepresentability" of father-son incest.[31]

Zhang Ai-zhu agrees with Chang and attributes this cultural "anxiety" to the lack of corresponding images from the "reservoir of cultural icons" to help give meaning to the horrifying visualization. She then proceeds to interpret this scene by appropriating and perverting the "representational frame" of the Pietà in order to "re/present" the unrepresentable scene of the father-son incest. That is, even though the composition of the sex scene between the father and son is similar to that of the Pietà, in *The River* the father takes the place of the mother while the desexualization of the Pietà image is recharged with homosexuality. The literal application of psychoanalytic theory notwithstanding, she makes a very interesting point about space. For her, what makes it possible for the desexualized hetero-normative icon of the Pietà to be appropriated into visualized homosexual incest is the space in which it takes place: the gay sauna as a "temporary" and "transitional" space.[32] Rather than focusing only on the very shot of the incest, I argue that it is important to demonstrate how *The River* represents the temporary and transitional qualities of this space of unspoken desire.

To return to Xiao-Kang cruising the corridor in the sauna, his walk down the hallway, followed by the camera, is punctuated by the continuous opening and closing of the seemingly endless doors. After he makes a turn and walks down a third corridor, a sudden cut shows Xiao-Kang entering a darkened room and sitting down on the floor mattress. In the next two minutes or so, three men in a row open the door, look inside and close the door again: three looks, three rejections. After that, Xiao-Kang locks the door of the room. Before a possible reading of this gesture as either lack of interest or an act of self-defense against further rejection or humiliation, yet another sudden cut shows the corridor where Xiao-Kang turns one doorknob after another only to find all the doors are locked, an indication that all the people cruising in the previous shot have settled with a partner for the time being. All doors but one, we find out with Xiao-Kang as he walks up to the very last door right in front of the camera, which remains unlocked.

Up to this point, the camera has been static, quietly observing our desperate character. However, as he opens the door and enters the room, the camera moves. Starting like the two previous pan-and-follow movements I discussed in the above passages, the camera here moves to face the door head-on for the first time. As if finally coming face-to-face with this half-closed space of unspoken desire, the camera has to stop short while Xiao-Kang disappears into the immense darkness that swallows his figure right away. The next shot is the homosexual Pietà. After Xiao-Kang sits down on the floor mattress, the father approaches him with both arms from behind. Xiao-Kang then rests his still agonized neck on the father's chest as the latter pleasures him with his hands. After he orgasms, Xiao-Kang half turns toward the father, and the two bodies, glistening with sweat by now, entwine in a tight embrace.

All my close analysis of various scenes of this film has prepared us for this moment of contact when the film's long journey for intimacy finally reaches its destination; the thematic and visual organization that have long worked toward this moment of intimacy have come to fruition here. It is then not surprising that the sequence immediately cuts to the mother, who sits at home alone eating leftovers. Flooding water flows into the dining area and she bolts to the father's room to find out why. There stands before her another door to hidden secrets, only this one is under her own roof, at her own home. She opens the door deliberately and sees the leak from the ceiling for the first time, now so bad that it causes a downpour of water like the rainstorm outside. The low-angle shot with her looking up from the lower left corner of the frame ends with her slamming the door shut as the scene cuts to the sauna room where the father has just flicked the light on in a similar low-angle shot. He stares toward the lower left-hand corner of the frame for a moment before stepping over into the frame and slapping his son in the face. Xiao-Kang then gets up from the floor and runs out of the room and out of the frame. The family members are thus cinematically connected by their irrevocable separation: the disintegration of home into this ultimate homelessness, at home as well as away from it.

*   *   *

Where to Go from Here?

The disintegrated domestic space and disconnected human relationships best describe the fragmented urban space of Taipei. Li Qing-Zhi, for example, has called Taipei City an "unsolvable puzzle,"[33] a highly suggestive imagery of fragments that do not come together as a complete picture. The endless constructions captured in Tsai Ming-Liang's films are visual reminders of both the breaking up of urban space—by roads, bridges, high-rises—and the breaking down of spatial history—by demolition, rebuilding, commercialization. Compared to the historically rich Taiwan in the earlier films of New Taiwan Cinema by Wang Tong and others, Tsai's Taipei in the 1990s seems to have lost its historical specificity as the sense of being transitional and temporary saturates the screen. In *The Hole*, for example, Taipei on the eve of the millennium is portrayed as a collection of nameless and faceless structures where people live under the threat of disease with no exit. In the bleakness of the present and the hopelessness of the future, the only consolation comes from flights of fanciful song and dance sequences, bringing temporary relief in their artificial colors and lightness.[34] Fragmented, isolated as well, this Taipei is almost an island by itself.

It is not until *What Time Is It There?* that we clearly see Taipei within a larger, global context. This film reunites Xiao-Kang's family, but the father dies after the beginning sequence, leaving only Xiao-Kang and his mother, who quickly develop different obsessions. The mother, on the one hand, is obsessed with blocking any outdoor light from entering the apartment so as to make the space a friendly place for the father's spirit to return to. The father's presence is now represented by his absence; his death has finally made his presence visible both with the enlarged photos of him in the apartment and, even more significantly, through his wife's thoughts of him materialized in actions. On the other hand, now a street peddler selling watches on a pedestrian bridge in front of Taipei Train Station, Xiao-Kang becomes obsessed with the different times between Taipei and Paris after he sells his own watch with dual time zones to a young woman before she leaves for Paris. The narrative line in Paris and that in Taipei are connected by the time differences between them. Told that Paris time is seven hours behind Taipei time, Xiao-Kang starts to change the time of any timepiece he can get his hands on to Paris time, including an enormous clock atop a high-rise office building. This film, in short, tells a touching story about two cities and four persons, three alive and one dead.

The film's elaborate treatment of these different times and spaces eventually congregates into a *simultaneous existence* of all of those temporalities and spatialities in all places, at all times. At one point, for example, Xiao-Kang is watching Francois Truffaut's *400 Blows* late at night at home in his room in Taipei. In the meantime, the young woman in Paris has a real-life encounter with the film's child actor, Jean-Pierre Leaud, now a seasoned, mature man, in a cemetery in Paris. The two narrative lines converge on a single person, whose past and present, real and imaginary, defy temporal or spatial categorization. Here Paris and Taipei, past and present, diegesis and extra-diegesis, meet, only on a stage large enough to let all these singular entities play out their specificities at the same time. If the global poses a threat to the loss of all these localities and individuals, *What Time Is It There?* opens up new possibilities to see it not as a set frame, but rather as a relation, a mode of understanding the world in times of change and transition. Where is nation? After a century of contested history, it remains to be seen, but the cinema will continue to help us to see it, however elusive it may be.

Afterword

Cinema after Nation

Chapter 6 concludes with a striking image in *What Time Is It There?* The character Xiao Kang is morbidly obsessed with the time difference between Taipei and Paris, roaming all over the city and changing the time on any timepieces he can get his hands on. In a daring move, he climbs atop a high-rise office building and changes the time of the clock tower from local to Paris time. An extreme high-angle and extreme long shot captures Xiao Kang's lone figure against the cityscape of Taipei, leaning over the railing and moving the clock's hands with a TV antenna. In the foreground there is an oversize advertisement banner, in the background a distinctive sign for Far-Eastern Department Stores, and on the lower right-hand corner a conspicuously empty lot freshly razed for future construction. Xiao Kang stands on the roof of a stock brokerage firm with its sign right above the clock with which he is tampering. The loud hum from the streets, the quintessential music of the city, rises from below as the moving traffic is reflected on the darkened windows of the office building.

This composite urban picture in *What Time Is It There?* is an image of coalescence, if not willing complicity, of a postcolonial city. Here in the twenty-first-century Taipei, a listless individual manipulates the time of a clock atop a stock exchange office building, which represents one of the most sophisticated forms of the abstracted but incessant flow of capital in a time of globalization. A further irony is that Xiao Kang is in fact *slowing down* the clock, turning it back seven hours, to synchronize a foreign time with that of the local space.

What I am reading into this treatment of time and space within the context of the city is a stark contrast between a time that occupies the central locus of contention (national/colonial, traditional/Western) and a time that, to put it bluntly, has lost its momentum. The spatial

significance inscribed within the frame, too, has changed from indexing a place that struggles against colonial erasure of personal memory
and national history, to one in which the core spatial problem is not
so much the contentious relationships among different meanings as
the imminent loss of any possibility of discernible meaning at all. As
a part of the larger general study of contemporary visual culture from
colonial time to the postcolonial and global era, this book offers a
partial view of these transformations in the case of Taiwan cinema, in
both its colonial and postcolonial times, before and after the framework of the national.

I asked, too, where would we go from "there"? This question
clearly cannot yield definitive answers. Rather, I hope to argue for
an open historiography, one in which various frameworks, such as
genres, periods, and locations, are part and parcel of formal and
cultural considerations of film texts. This historiography will be a
crucial tool in coming to new understandings not only of the past
but also of the present and future of Chinese-language film histories. That my effort in this book has been to make some sense out of
the relationship between modernity and the cinema is one example
of this historiographical practice. Through close analyses of narrative and narration as well as consideration of their formal and visual
materialization in genre and style, I have attempted to demonstrate
that, to understand the cinematic representation of history, one must
attend to the multiplicities of both temporal and spatial elements. In
the more recent context as well, the global does not signal another,
all-out different landscape as an outcome of this trend, movement,
or process of hegemonic maneuvering that can be all too pervasively
categorized as globalization.

Indeed, where do we go from here? Whether with the forward-
looking or the backward glance, cinematic representation yields
meaning in its formal materialization of space and time. Cinematic
form is a form of theorization. Filmic text itself, furthermore,
must be taken seriously as a materialization of historiography
and even meta-historiography. In order to come to closure in this
book, I feel compelled to visit a few more cinematic moments to
find possible directions in the search for future studies of Taiwan
and other Chinese-language cinemas. If, as shown in the case of
Wang Tong and other earlier New Cinema filmmakers in Taiwan,
cinematic retrospection has provided a cinematic means for rethinking and remapping Taiwan's colonial pasts, Tsai Ming-Liang is
one striking example showing that new challenges have arisen as

temporal and spatial meanings are undertaking significant changes and transitions.

Nor, I hasten to emphasize, is Tsai an isolated case. Like *What Time Is It There?* a number of important Chinese-language films emerging around the turn of the twenty-first century also deal with some similar historical questions. For example, Edward Yang's *Yi Yi* (aka *A One, and a Two*, 2000) brilliantly maps personal memory onto collective history, showing the main characters in Taiwan seeking reconciliation without resolution by taking a trip to Japan. Hou Hsiao-Hsien's exquisite visual masterpiece *Flowers of Shanghai* (1999), on the other hand, abandons all immediate temporal and spatial referents to contemporary Taiwan and immerses itself to the extreme in the meticulously reconstructed past at the turn of the nineteenth century. The only gesture toward the Now is the consistent and repetitive panning camera movement throughout the entire film which patiently and unrelentingly scrutinizes the very constructedness of the space of cinematic representation at the end of the twentieth century.

Taiwan's cinema does seem to have reached new heights in the early years of the twenty-first century, a phenomenon best exemplified by the unprecedented box office success of Wei De-Sheng's *Cape No. 7*, both domestically and overseas in 2008, and that of another blockbuster, *Monga*, directed by veteran New Cinema actor Niu Cheng-Ze in 2010. The noted difference between *Cape No. 7* and its contemporaries, on the one hand, and the New Taiwan Cinema of the 1980s, on the other, offers much to ponder about what is considered by some a potential "Post-New" Taiwan Cinema, the desire for which has been evinced by a conference devoted to it held in Taiwan's Academia Sinica in 2009. For some, the first new cinema focuses its efforts on the aesthetic exploration of the realistic portrayal of everyday life, whereas the emerging, some dub as the "second" new cinema today, revitalizes Taiwan's film industry by putting forth films that are largely genre driven. The notion of "newness"—implying a severance from the past and promising hope—is extremely tempting and, for that reason, in great need of historicizing. As I have shown throughout the book, from colonial propaganda to postcolonial educational films, from Taiwanese-dialect films to Healthy Realist Mandarin cinema, between the pressure of Hong Kong films and Hollywood imports, and between government cultural policies and industry demands, the first New Cinema of the early 1980s responded to the stagnant genre filmmaking with audacious stylistic exploration. The re-cinematization of Taiwan in the early 1980s took the form of a vigorously reinvented realism. Its subsequent successes and failings are a familiar story. In this context, however, the more recent wave of the "second" new or "post-new" cinema in the twenty-first century begs careful scrutiny.

Indeed, Taiwan cinema in the new millennium begins in some ways that have been long anticipated in my laying out of Taiwan's film history in contention with its national history, since the colonial times if not earlier. Various cinematic vignettes, in parts and with many interruptions, fragment by fragment, have helped us slowly see Taiwan *on its own terms*, an impossible task which had launched my entire project in the first place. What, I asked at the beginning of this book, would Taiwan look like if we did not have cinema to help us see it? What have we witnessed and what will emerge on the horizon? In 2006, a quiet and beautiful film, *Island Etude*, directed by En Chen, cinematographer of Hou Hsiao-Hsien's *A City of Sadness*, follows another deaf-mute character on a circuminsular cycling adventure. This seven-day-six-night trip takes the character to places on the island that are familiar and yet unremarkable. Unlike Brothers Wang and Liu's tour a half-century ago, the cyclist visits neither monuments nor historical sites; he gets close to Taipei City only to bypass it. It is a journey in which one is compelled to immerse oneself—at least for the duration of the film, with its diegetic fantasy and extradiegetic desire—in a totality of a Taiwan that is finally, if only temporarily and cinematically, free of contention.

Afterword to the Paperback Edition: What Was Nation and Why Isn't It Going Away?

In 2011, *Seedig Bale* was released in two parts. Directed by Wei De-Sheng and produced by John Woo, this epic drama chronicles the Wushe Incident (*Wushe shijian*) in 1930, a bloody uprising against the Japanese rule by an indigenous tribe in Central Taiwan. Touted as the most expensive production in Taiwan cinema history and carrying the hope of bringing Taiwan to the center stage of global cinema, *Seedig Bale* went on to feature in many international film festivals, from Venice to Busan International Festivals, and the Academy Awards in the United States. The fervent anticipation for global recognition partially mirrored the breakout success of New Taiwan Cinema in the 1980s, but this time it was fueled by domestic audience's enthusiasm. Besides a few nominations in some "minor" film festivals in Asia, however, the film returned home without any acknowledgment many in Taiwan had so passionately desired; vindication once again denied to Taiwan's national cinema in playing a stellar role in the global cinema.

Out of the four and a half hours running time of the two-part original, the international version of *Seedig Bale* was edited down to a single film of two and half hours. Defending against criticism of the shorter version, Director Wei stated that the lengthy original was in response to "ethnic pressure for historical details" while the reedit allowed him to "focus on the story" and thus make the film more commercially viable outside Taiwan.[1] It is not without regret that the local or indigenous history of Taiwan is rendered insignificant and dispensable in the global context. A further irony probably hits home ever harder in that the climax of the "story" thus emphasized—with less history, more drama—is in fact fictional; the final attack on the Japanese to take back the village never took place. That it is harsh, even unrealistic, to fault a filmmaker for making his work readily accessible in different contexts, on the one hand, and to demand historical accuracy in cinema or other cultural production as the only legitimate yardstick, on the other hand, is beside the point.

In the pursuit for international recognition—especially after the enthusiastic reception domestically—the most keenly felt anxiety arises from the desire to render a distinctive, globally legible image of a Taiwanese nation. The question remains what I have asked at the initial publication of this book: What is Taiwan's national cinema? And that question needs paraphrasing: What would Taiwan look like without its cinema?

But where do I begin? Before *Seedig Bale* and other blockbusters focusing on Taiwan's local history and vernacular culture flourished in the recent decade, before *Cape No. 7* became the biggest surprise success story in many years, before it was a feasible project and its phenomenal success conceivable? And what if we go further back in time, before *Crouching Tiger, Hidden Dragon*, before Edward Yang's *Yi Yi*, before Tsai Ming-Liang's Taipei trilogy, before Hou Hsiao-Hsien, before New Taiwanese Cinema in the 1980s, before Healthy Realism and Taiwanese-dialect films in the 1960s and 1970s, before Qiong Yao and Bruce Lee, before the one-armed swordsman's martial arts prowess and the butterfly lovers' heart wrenching Yellow Plum Melody, before 1949, before 1945, and why not go as far as we can to 1895 when cinema was reportedly invented? What might Taiwan look like if we did not have films to help us see it? What if, this may not be an unfounded anxiety for any serious students of Taiwan cinema, the cultural references I just enumerated were not in the general registers? What if, to put it differently, *Crouching Tiger* is but a kung fu flick that people in the know might consider overrated, Edward Yang was a master of cinematic arts whose premature death renders his film even more sadly obscure, Hou Hsiao-Hsien is a director who makes slow films, and Tsai Ming-Liang is someone who makes even slower films?

Almost two years after the book's first publication, the historiographic work I sought to initiate seems to me even more urgent now. To be sure, some 20-plus years after *In Our Times*, we are enormously enamored with and yet profoundly puzzled and excited by the recent accomplishments and promises of films such as *Cape No. 7* and *Seedig Bale*. In fact, many more films combine cinematic elements—from genres to styles, and from domestic market to transnational distribution, and, most notably, from Taiwan, across the Straits, to the Mainland—and enjoy tremendous success. Take, for example, *You Are the Apple of My Eye* (2011). The film swept box offices in Taiwan, extended its popularity to Hong Kong and Southeast Asia, and successfully opened in China after some minor reedit. This film, adapted from a popular online serialized fiction and unabashedly in the genre of television Idol/Schoolyard Youth Drama (*ouxian/xiaoyuan qingchun ju*), further complicates the fast merging and converging audiovisual realm constituted by recycled genres while capitalizing on the fast transformation and speedy reach of new media. If there is possibly a "new new cinema" or a "post-new" cinema in Taiwan, one way to come to terms with the fact that this phenomenon is precisely to resist the temptation of a definitive "new" as some sort of designation of break, lest the celebration of the new blocks the historical paths to an understanding, many understandings, of the present. The lure of the "new," doubly so when the first new has long failed us, tempts us even further from history with the second—who needs history when we can start anew, breaking free from the past? But when does the new begin? Not unlike Walter Benjamin's angel of time, progress befuddles us, sweeps us off our feet, but the gaze of history always casts a glance, never parting, at the past that, looking back, is also our future.

Appendix 1: List of Chinese Characters

2/28 Incident	二二八事件
Bai Ke	白克
benshengren	本省人
bianshi (benshi/benzi)	辯士
bingbian	兵變
Bu Wancang	卜萬蒼
Cathay Film Company	國泰影業公司
Central Motion Picture Corporation	中央電影公司
Central Pictures Corporation	中影股份有限公司
Chang Cheh	張徹
Chang Tso-Chi	張作驥
Chen Feibao	陳飛寶
Chen Huai-En/En Chen	陳懷恩
Chen Yi	陳儀
chengzhang	成長
Chiang Wei-Shui	蔣謂水
Chiao Hsiung-Ping	焦雄屏
dahan minzu	大漢民族
Da'an senlin gongyuan	大安森林公園
doka	同化
Du Yun-Zhi	杜雲之
Edward Yang	楊德昌
Fang-Nai Pavilion Theater	芳乃亭
Feng Fei-Fei	鳳飛飛
gaoshanqing	高山青
Ge-Zai Opera	歌仔戲
Gong Hong	龔弘
guxiang	故鄉
guangfu	光復
guomin	國民

guopian	國片
He Fei-Guang	何非光
Hou Hsiao-Hsien	侯孝賢
Hu Die	胡蝶
Huang Shi-De	黃時得
Ichikawa Sai	市川彩
jiankang xieshi zhuyi	健康寫實主義
Jinmen	金門
jinru shandi qingyong guoyu	進入山地請用國語
juancun	眷村
keban yingxiang	刻板印象
Kenny Bee	鍾鎮濤
Ke Yi-Zheng	柯一正
kominka	皇民化
Koxinga	國姓爺
Lee Chia	李嘉
Lee Daw-Ming	李道明
Lee Hsing	李行
Li You-Xin	李幼新
Li Xianlan	李香蘭
Liang Zhe-Fu	梁哲夫
Liao Huang	廖煌
Lin Hsien-Tang	林獻堂
Liu Ming-Chuan	劉銘傳
Liu Na'ou	劉吶鷗
Liu Sen-Yao	劉森堯
Liu Xi-Yang	劉喜陽
Lu Su-Shang	呂訴上
Ma-zu	馬祖
Mao Xin-Shao/Mao Wang-Ye	毛信孝／毛王爺
Matuura Shozo	松浦章三
Mei-Tai Troupe	美臺團
Misawa Mamie	三澤真美惠
Niu Chen-Ze	鈕承澤
nuhua	奴化
nuli	奴隸
Oshima Inoshi	大島豬市
ouxian/xiaoyuan qingchun ju	偶像／青春校園劇
piaoyou qunzu	漂游族群
Qiong Yao	瓊瑤
qiuzhi yu	求知慾

quanguo gejie	全國各界
renmin jiyi	人民記憶
Ruan Lingyu	阮玲玉
sanhai	三害
shandi	山地
Shao	邵族
Shigehiko Hasumi	蓮實重彥
Shihmen Reservoir	石門水庫
shumin	庶民
Sino-Japanese Amity	日華親善
Society for Chinese Cinema Studies	中國電影史料研究會
Sun Moon Lake	日月潭
Taiwan Agricultural Education Studios	臺灣農教片場
Taiwan Cultural Association	臺灣文化協會
Taiwan jinyan	臺灣經驗
Taiwan Motion Pictures Studios	臺灣電影攝製場
Taiwan Nichinichi Shimpo	臺灣日日新報
Taiwan People's Daily	臺灣民報
Taiwan Self-Governance Alliance	臺灣自治聯盟
Taiwanese People's Party	臺灣民眾黨
Takamatsu Toyojiro	高松豐次郎
Tanaka King	田中欽
Tao De-Chen	陶德辰
Tian-Ma Teahouse	天馬茶房
town and village self-governance	城鄉地方自治
Three Principles of the People	三民主義
Tsai Ming-Liang	蔡明亮
Tsai Pei-Huo	蔡培火
waishengren	外省人
Wan Jen	萬仁
Wan-Xiang Film Company	萬象影片公司
Wang Tong/Wang Tung	王童
Wang Yun-Feng	王雲峰
wenhua cun	文化村
Wei De-Sheng	魏德聖
Wu Feng	吳鳳
Wu Nien-Jen	吳念真
wunu	舞女
Wushe Incident	霧社事件
Xiamen/Amoy	廈門
Xiao Ye	小野

xieyuan xiangyi	血緣相依
Yamaguchi Yoshiko	山口淑子
Yang Zhao-Jia	楊肇嘉
Yellow Plum Melody	黃梅調
yiqie wei mingtian	一切為明天
yixiang	異鄉
Tseng Wen Reservoir	曾文水庫
Zeng Zhuang-Xiang	曾壯祥
Zhan Tian-Ma	詹天馬
zhandou wenyi	戰鬥文藝
Zhang Han-Shu	張漢樹
Zhang Yi	張毅
Zhang Yimou	張藝謀
Zhang Yong-Xiang	張永祥
Zheng Cheng-Gong	鄭成功
zhengtixing	整體性
zhengzong	正宗
zhihua	殖化
Zhou Xuan	周璇

Appendix 2: List of Film Titles in Chinese

I cite commonly used English film titles and indicate alternatives when available. For those films first appearing in English publication, especially in the Taiwanese-dialect cinema section, the translations are mine.

Awakening from a Nightmare	惡夢初醒
Banana Paradise	香蕉天堂
Beautiful Duckling	養鴨人家
Blood Stains	血痕
A Borrowed Life	多桑
Both Sides Are Happy	兩相好
Boys from Fengkuei	風櫃來的人
The Bride from Hell	地獄新娘
Brother Wang and Brother Liu 007	王哥柳哥007
Brother Wang and Brother Liu Have a Happy New Year	王哥柳哥過好年
Brother Wang and Brother Liu Have Hundredsof Children and Thousands of Grandchildren	王哥柳哥百子千孫
Brother Wang and Brother Liu Tour Taiwan	王哥柳哥遊台灣
Brother Wang and Brother Liu Tour the Underworld	王哥柳哥遊地府
The Burning of the Red Lotus Temple	火燒紅蓮寺
Cape No. 7	海角七號
A City of Sadness	悲情城市
Darkness and Light	黑暗之光
Daughters of the Nile	尼羅河女兒
Descendants of the Yellow Emperor	黃帝子孫
The Ditsy Bride and Her Goofy Groom	三八新娘憨女婿
Dr. Sun Yat-Sen	國父傳

Dust in the Wind	戀戀風塵
The Early Train from Taipei	台北發的早班車
The Eyes of the Buddha	大佛的瞳孔
Flowers of Shanghai	海上花
The Goddess	神女
Good Morning, Taipei	早安台北
Green, Green Grass of Home	在那河畔青草青
He Never Gives Up	汪洋中的一條船
Head of the Street, End of the Lane	街頭巷尾
Heart with a Million Knots	心有千千結
Hill of No Return	無言的山丘
His Son's Big Doll/The Sandwich Man	兒子的大玩偶
The Hole	洞
How I Lived My Life	我這樣過了一生
Hua-Lien Harbor	花蓮港
In Our Time	光陰的故事
Little Dragonhead	小龍頭
Expectations	指望
Jumping Frog	跳蛙
Say Your Name	報上名來
Island Etude	練習曲
Kang-Ding Tours Taipei	康丁遊台北
The Last Train from Kaohsiung	高雄發的尾班車
The Legend of Ali Mountain	阿里山風雲
The Love Eterne/Butterfly Lovers	梁山伯與祝英台
Love Waves	情潮
Lovable You/Cute Girl	就是溜溜的她
My New Friends	我新認識的朋友
Monga	艋舺
One-Armed Swordsman	獨臂刀
Osmanthus Lane	桂花巷
Oyster Girls	蚵女
The Peach Girl	桃花泣血記
Play While You Play/Cheerful Winds	風兒踢踏踩
Raise the Red Lantern	大紅燈籠高高掛
Rebels of the Neon God	青少年哪吒
Red Persimmons	紅柿子
Reunion	我們都是這樣長大的
The River	河流
The Road	路
The Seashore of Goodbye	惜別的海岸

Seedig Bale	塞德克·巴萊
Sisters	姐妹花
Six Talents' Romance of the West Chamber	六才子西廂記
Song of the Fisherman	漁光曲
Star, Moon, Sun	星星, 月亮, 太陽
Story of a Small Town	小城故事
Strawman	稻草人
Street Angels	馬路天使
A Summer at Grandpa's	冬冬的假期
Super Citizens	超級市民
Taipei Story	青梅竹馬
Terrorizers	恐怖份子
That Day, on the Beach	海灘上的一天
A Time to Live, a Time to Die	童年往事
Toys	小玩意
What Time Is It There?	你那邊幾點？
Whose Fault Is It?	誰之過？
Yi Yi/A One, and a Two	——
You Are the Apple of My Eye	那些年, 我們一起追的女孩
Xue Ping-Guei and Wang Bao-Chuan	薛平貴與王寶釧

Notes

Introduction: Taiwan Cinema and the Historiography of Absence

1. Kristin Thompson and David Bordwell, *Film History: An Introduction*, New York: McGraw-Hill, Inc., p. 779. Interestingly, later editions of this book in 2003 and 2009 incorporated new information but only on what has transpired after 1982, keeping the exact same paragraph that introduces Taiwan into the authors' vast mapping of world cinema history. See Thompson and Bordwell, 2003, p. 659, and 2009, p. 652.
2. Robert Sklar, *A World History of Film*, New York: Harry N. Abrams, Inc., 2001, p. 470.
3. Andrew Higson, "The Concept of National Cinema," *Screen*, vol. 30, no. 4, 1989, pp. 36–37.
4. Higson, "The Limiting Imagination of National Cinema," in *Cinema and Nation*, edited by Mette Hjort and Scott Kenzie, London and New York: Routledge, 2000.
5. Stephen Crofts, "Reconceptualizing National Cinemas," in *Film and Nationalism*, edited and with an intro by Alan Williams, New Brunswick, New Jersey, and London: Rutgers University Press, 2002.
6. Higson, "The Limiting Imagination of National Cinema," pp. 67–69.
7. See Dudley Andrew, "Islands in the Sea of Cinema," in *National Cinemas and World Cinema*, edited by Kevin Rockett and John Hill, Dublin, Ireland: Four Courts Press, 2006, p. 15.
8. Chen Kuan-Hsing, "Taiwan New Cinema, or a Global Nativism?" in *Theorizing National Cinema*, edited by Valentina Vitali and Paul Willemen, London: BFI Publishing, 2006, pp. 138–147.
9. Shih Shu-Mei, "Globalisation and the (In)Significance of Taiwan," *Postcolonial Studies*, vol. 6, no. 2, 2003, pp. 143–53.
10. Chris Berry "If China Can Say No, Can China Make Movies? Or, Do Movies Make China? Rethinking National Cinema and National Agency," in *Modern Chinese Literary and Cultural Studies in the Age of Theory*, edited by Rey Chow, Durham and London: Duke University Press, 2000, p. 177.

1   Colonial Archives, Postcolonial Archaeology: Pre-1945 Taiwan and the Hybrid Texts of Cinema before Nation

1. Lu Su-Shang, *Taiwan dianying xiju shi* (The History of Taiwan's Film and Drama), Taipei: Yin-Hua Publishing, 1961.
2. The figure of the "slave" (*nuli*) as antithetical to "national people" (*guomin*) had occupied a significant part of Chinese nationalist thinking since as early as the late Qing dynasty. Rebecca Karl demonstrates convincingly that the binary between the "slave" as passive and *guomin*, the "true" national subject, as active, is particularly effective in the nationalist discourse to situate China's struggle within the larger global context. That dichotomy serves to link up China's struggle against imperialist invasion with other regions of the world through a shared condition of "statelessness." See Karl, *Staging the World: Chinese Nationalism at the Turn of the Twentieth Century*, Durham: Duke University Press, 2002, p. 54 and p. 79.
3. Du Yun-Zhi, *Zhongguo dianying shi* (The Film History of China), vol. 3, Taipei: Taiwan Commercial Press, 1972, pp. 1–3; and, Du, *Zhonghua minguo dianying shi* (The Film History of the Republic of China), Taipei: The Council for Cultural Affairs, Administrative Yuan, 1988, pp. 439–440. Another noteworthy change is that in the original the author's preface (mostly personal reminiscences) and abstract (brief explanation of periodization emphasizing its focus after 1949 on "free China" only, i.e. Taiwan and Hong Kong) are replaced by a preface written by the Council's director at the time of the publication. The new preface takes care to avoid political partisanship by lauding film as art and its importance as historical document.
4. Another demonstration of this significant shift in film historiography can be found in critical works done on New Taiwan Cinema in the 80s and early 90s, an analysis of which will be provided in chapter 5.
5. See Lee Daw-Ming, "Taiwan dianying diyizhang: 1900–1915" (The First Chapter of Taiwan's Film History: 1900–1915), *Film Appreciation*, no. 73, p. 28, and "Dianying shi ruhe laidao Taiwan de?" (How Did Film Arrive in Taiwan?), *Film Appreciation*, no. 65. p. 107.
6. Lee, "Riben tongzhi shiqi dianying yu zhengzhi de guanxi" (The Relationship between Film and Politics during the Japanese Colonization), *History Monthly*, Nov. 1995, p. 123.
7. See Li Tian-Duo, *Taiwanese Cinema, Society, and History*, Taipei: The Society for Chinese Cinema Studies, 1997, pp. 36–37.
8. See Huang Ren and Wang Wei, eds., *One Hundred Years of Taiwan Cinema*, Taipei: Chinese Film Critic Association, 2004, pp. 11–13; and Edmund K. Y. Wong, ed., *The Chronicle of Taiwan Cinema 1898–2000*, Taipei: The Council for Cultural Affairs, Administrative Yuan, 2005, p. 107.
9. Ye Long-Yan, *The History of Taiwanese Movies during the Japanese Colonization*, Taipei: Yushanshe, 1998, pp. 51–53. Chapter 2 will analyze in greater detail Ye's impressive oeuvre of Taiwan's film history, particularly those on Taiwanese-dialect cinema of the 1950s and 1960s.

10. Ye, *The History of Taiwanese Movies during the Japanese Colonization*, pp. 64–71.

11. In *One Hundred Years of Taiwan Cinema*, the authors single out the 1906 exhibition of newsreels on the Russo-Japan war and claim that, by showing the courage and patriotism of the Japanese soldiers, those films "changed the impression the Taiwanese had had of Japan and they began to worship the Japanese Emperor, to worship Japanese soldiers." Though such a sea change of attitude toward Japan was unlikely, it is clear that film as propaganda was a top priority for the colonial government. See Huang, pp. 16–17.

12. Both Lee Daw-Ming and Ye Long-Yan provide detailed, at times identical, accounts of this documentary, stressing its importance for the wish of Japanese colonizers to introduce Taiwan to Japan, a desire to cast this island as a fast-modernizing, model colony. See Lee, "The Relationship between Cinema and Politics during Japanese Occupation," *History*, Nov. 1995, pp. 123–125, and Ye, *The History of Taiwanese Movies*, pp. 71–78.

13. Ye, *The History of Taiwanese Movies*, pp. 164–165. See also Yingjin Zhang, *Chinese National Cinema*, New York and London: Routledge, 2004, p. 116.

14. See Huang, pp. 18–33.

15. Deslandes, Jeanne, "Dancing Shadows of Film Exhibition: Taiwan and the Japanese Influence," *Screening the Past*, November 2000. This journal is published online by La Trobe University, Australia. See http://www.latrobe.edu.au/screeningthepast/.

16. See Donald Ritchie, *A Hundred Years of Japanese Cinema: A Concise History*, Tokyo, New York and London: Kodansha International, 2001, pp. 18–22; and Isolde Standish, "Mediators of Modernity: 'Photo-interpreters' in Japanese Silent Cinema," *Oral Tradition*, vol. 20, no. 1, March 2005, pp. 93–110.

17. Abe Mark Nornes, "For an Abusive Subtitling," in *The Translation Studies Reader*, Lawrence Venuti, ed., New York and London: Routledge, 2000, p. 451.

18. Ye, *The History of Taiwanese Movies*, particularly pp. 184–194 and pp. 326–330. Besides Ye's book, other major historical works on Taiwan cinema also include specific sections on the *benzi*. See, for example, Huang Ren, *A Hundred Years of Taiwanese Cinema*, pp. 38–40, and Chen Feibao, *Taiwan dianying shihua* (A History of Taiwan Cinema), Beijing: Zhongguo dianying chubanshe, 1988, pp. 4–8.

19. Wang is noteworthy also because he composed the film scores for the famed Shanghai Lian-Hua Studio's 1931 film *The Peach Girl*. See Ye Long-Yan, *The History of Taiwanese Movies*, p. 185. The traffic between Taiwan and Shanghai before 1945 is well documented, a point to which I return later.

20. The 2/28 Incident refers to a series of events beginning on February 28, 1947, when conflicts between Taiwanese locals and the recently arrived Nationalist regime resulted in bloody military suppression and the declaration of martial law. See chapter 2 for a more detailed account.

21. Huang, *A Hundred Years*, p. 39.
22. Ye, *The History of Taiwanese Movies*, pp. 190–191. According to his account, some *benzi* from the Mei-Tai Troupe would even make sensational speeches after the screening, a practice only barely tolerated by the colonial government.
23. Chen, *A History of Taiwan Cinema*, pp. 5–6.
24. Ye, *The History of Taiwanese Movies*, pp. 59–86.
25. Ibid., p. 130.
26. Misawa Mamie, *Silver Screen in the Colony: Research on Taiwan Governor Office's Film Policies, 1895–1942*, Taipei: Avanguard, 2002, pp. 56–66.
27. Ye, *The History of Taiwanese Movies*, pp. 131–135.
28. Ibid., pp. 140–162.
29. Questions of Liu's involvement with the Japanese regime during Shanghai occupation would require further research.
30. See Yingjin Zhang, *Chinese National Cinema*, p. 117; Ye, *The History of Taiwanese Movies*, pp. 131–132; and Chen Feibao, *A History of Taiwan Cinema*, p. 18.
31. For a complete list, see Huang Ren, *One Hundred Years of Taiwan Cinema*, pp. 46–49.
32. For detailed history of this organization, see Lin Bo-Wei, *Taiwan wehua xiehui cangsang* (The History of Taiwan Cultural Association), Taichung, Taiwan: Taiyuan, 1993; Zhang Xian-Yan, "Taiwan wenhua xiehui de chengli yu fenlie" (The Establishment and Disbandment of the Taiwan Cultural Association) in *Taiwanshi lunwen xunji* (Selected Essays on Taiwan History), Taipei: Yushangshe, 1996, pp. 131–159; and, most importantly, Tsai Pei-Huo et al., *Taiwan mingzu yundongshi* (History of Taiwan's National Movement), Taipei: Zili wanbaoshe, 1971, particularly chapter 6 on the Taiwan Cultural Association, pp. 281–354.
33. In his *Chinese National Cinema*, Yingjin Zhang quotes from Chen Feibao's *A History of Taiwan Cinema*, stating that the Association's clear intentions were to "elevate Taiwan culture, awaken the Han national consciousness and resist national oppression by the Japanese" (Chen, p. 8; and Zhang, p. 115), which is in turn quoted from in *History of Taiwan's National Movement*, Tsai Pei-Huo et al., p. 287.
34. Harry J. Lamley, "Taiwan under Japanese Rule, 1895–1945: The Vicissitudes of Colonialism," in *Taiwan: A New History*, Murray A. Rubinstein, ed., Armonk, New York, and London: M. E. Sharpe, 1999, p. 232.
35. Tsai Pei-Huo et al., *History of Taiwan's National Movement*, pp. 306–308.
36. Ye, *The History of Taiwanese Movies*, pp. 135–137.
37. *Taiwan People's Daily*, April 25, 1926, quoted in Ye Long-Yan, *Hsinchushi dianyingshi* (The Film History of Hsinchu City), Hsinchu, Taiwan: Hsinchu Municipal Cultural Center, 1996, pp. 64–65.
38. Zhang, p. 116; and Ye, pp. 136–138.
39. Huang, *One Hundred Years of Taiwan Cinema*, p. 41. Later on imports from China and Chaplin's films were also included.
40. Lin Hsien-Tang, one of the key founding members of the Association, made an around-the-world tour in 1927–28 and published his travelogue as an

extremely popular weekly column in *Taiwan People's Daily* for four years, starting in 1931. The film selection for the Mei-Tai Troupe was clearly in line with this broad tendency.

41. Chen, *A History of Taiwan Cinema*, p. 9.
42. Tsai et al., *The History of Taiwan's National Movement*, pp. 317–319, and Ye, *The History of Taiwanese Movies during the Japanese Colonization*, pp. 137–138.
43. Leo T. S. Ching provides the definitive study to date on the questions of national identity in colonial Taiwan. See Ching, *Becoming "Japanese": Colonial Taiwan and the Politics of Identity Formation*, Berkeley and Los Angeles: University of California Press, 2001. See especially chapter 3, "Between Assimilation and Imperialization: From Colonial Projects to Imperial Subjects," pp. 89–132.
44. Ye, *The History of Taiwanese Movies during the Japanese Occupation*, pp. 279–284. A significant case is the prominent wartime actress, Yamaguchi Yoshiko, a Japanese national born in Manchuria, adopted by a pro-Japan Chinese banker and subsequently renamed Li Xianlan. Her dual identities enabled her to be the representative figure for the quintessential slogan for Japan's colonial project in Taiwan, the Sino-Japanese Amity. She visited and made films in Taiwan and was a high-profile figure in wartime cinema not only in Taiwan and Japan but also in Shanghai. For more on Yamaguchi, see Yiman Wang, "Screening Asia: Passing, Performative Translation, and Reconfiguration," *positions: east asia cultures critique*, vol. 15, no. 2, Fall 2007, pp. 319–343.
45. *China Times*, Xiangtu Section, November 11, 1983.
46. A recent example took place in 2000. As an effort to promote a new film about blindness, filmmaker Wu Nien-Jen was enlisted to play the *benzi* at the premier of Chang Tso-Chi's *Darkness and Light* to explain the film for the benefit of over a hundred vision-impaired viewers invited to the screening. See *United News*, Sec. 25, February 19, 2000.

2   Cinema among *Genres*: An Unorthodox History of Taiwan's Dialect Cinema, 1955–1970

1. Throughout the book, I use "Taiwan's dialect cinema" and "Taiwanese-dialect cinema" interchangeably. However, it is important to note that dialect cinema includes more than films made in the conventionally considered Taiwanese dialect, the so-called Hokkien or Minnanese; even that designation has been challenged in recent years and modified as Hoklo or Ho-Lo to reflect even more specific regional differences. I use "Taiwan's Dialect Cinema" in the title of the chapter to signal this complexity. See below, for example, for an account on the controversy between the Hokkien and Amoy-dialect films.
2. See Ye Long-Yan, *Guangfu chuqi Taiwan dianying shi* (Taiwan Film History in the Early Years after Restoration), Taipei: National Film Archive, 1994, p. 22.

3. The following narrative draws from multiple sources. Points that warrant specific citations will be duly noted. What informs my summary here are as follows: Ye, *Taiwan Film History in the Early Years after Restoration*, pp. 22–53; Lu Feii, *Taiwan Cinema: Politics, Economy, Aesthetics, 1949–1994*, Taipei: Yuanliu, 1998, pp. 33–43; Yingjin Zhang, *Chinese National Cinema*, New York and London: Routledge, 2004, pp. 114–124; Huang Ren and Wang Wei, eds., *One Hundred Years of Taiwan Cinema*, Taipei: Chinese Film Critic Association, 2004, pp. 83–112; and Chen Feibao, *Taiwan dianying shihua* (A History of Taiwan Cinema), Beijing: Zhongguo dianying chubanshe, 1988, pp. 31–50.

4. Huang Shi-De, a prominent writer in the colonial period, remembered those early days of political vacuum as a stunning display of self-governance by the Taiwanese. Reading through all the newspapers during those seventy days, Huang discovered not one single crime committed. Huang's accounts basically attribute the surprising stability in Taiwan between two regimes to how "the Taiwanese were proud to be again part of the Great Han Nation (*dahan minzu*) and voluntarily kept the best behavior befitting that honor." Such statements exemplify the sentiment of national restoration. See Wu Wen-Xing, ed., *Renshi Taiwan: huiwei 1895–2000* (Know Taiwan: Reminiscences between 1895–2000), Taipei: Yuanliu, 2005, p. 112.

5. Huang Ren, *One Hundred Years of Taiwan Cinema*, p. 95; and Ye Long-Yan, *Taiwan Film History in the Early Years after Restoration*, pp. 42, 45–46.

6. See Lu Feii, *Taiwan Cinema: Politics, Economics, Aesthetics*, pp. 33–34.

7. Ibid., p. 54.

8. Ibid., pp. 37–38.

9. Homi Bhabha, "DissemiNation: Time, Narrative, and the Margins of the Modern Nation," in *Nation and Narrative*, edited by Bhabha, London and New York: Routledge, 1990, pp. 291–322, cited in Lu, *Taiwan Cinema*, p. 37.

10. My account here is a summary adapted from Wu Wen-Xing's *Know Taiwan*, p. 116. For more detailed accounts see, for example, Steven Phillips, "Between Assimilation and Independence: Taiwanese Political Aspirations Under National Chinese Rule, 1945–1948," in *Taiwan: A New History*, edited by Murray A. Rubinstein, Armonk, New York, and London: M. E. Sharpe, 1999, pp. 292–96; and Denny Roy, *Taiwan: A Political History*, Ithaca and London: Cornell University Press, 2003, pp. 67–74.

11. Zhang Sheng, "*Descendants of the Yellow Emperor*," *United News*, "Arts and Literature" Section, March 1, 1957.

12. Huang, *One Hundred Years of Taiwan Cinema*, p. 177. According to Chen Feibao, this film was a surprise box office success whose twenty-four-day run in Taipei alone was an unusual phenomenon. Yingjin Zhang concurs and considers Taiwanese-dialect films as a "recognized cultural force." See Chen, *A History of Taiwan Cinema*, p. 75, and Zhang, *Chinese National Cinema*, p. 128. Some accounts, Zhang's included, mention another opera film, *Six Talents' Romance of the West Chamber* as the true earliest Taiwanese dialect film. A crude production shot on 16mm, this film premiered as early as 1955 but without any commercial success. See Zhang, p. 128; for a more detailed history of this film, see Ye Long-Yan, *Zhengzong*

taiyu dianying xingshuailu (The Orthodox Chronicles of the Vicissitudes of Taiwanese-Dialect Films), Taipei: Boyang, 1999, pp. 65–68.

13. Mary Farquhar and Chris Berry, "Shadow Opera: Towards a New Archaeology of the Chinese Cinema," *Post Script*, vol. 20, nos. 2 & 3, p. 26.

14. See Ye, *The Orthodox Chronicles*, pp. 59–60; and Huang, *One Hundred Years of Taiwan Cinema*, pp. 175–176. It appears that Chris Berry and Mary Farquhar have only seen this version when they cite the film as an example of Mandarin film; see their discussion of this film in *China on Screen: Cinema and Nation*, New York: Columbia University Press, 2006, p. 193.

15. Huang, *One Hundred Years of Taiwan Cinema*, p. 176.

16. Ye Long-Yan takes great care explaining the complex situation concerning Taiwanese and Xiamenese films in the crucial years of 1955–56. Implied in his narrative is the same desire for an "authentic" history that restores Taiwan to its rightful historical place that I discussed in chapter 1. The title of his book reflects that desire. See Ye, *The Orthodox Chronicles*, pp. 54–72.

17. *Koxinga* literally means a lord or master with an imperial and *national* (*guo*) surname, an appellation solidifying Zheng's affinity with the Ming Dynasty; that is, the Chinese Nation connection.

18. For instance, the National Institute of Compilation and Translation, a branch of the Ministry of Education in charge of the approval of textbooks used in K-12 education in Taiwan, devotes an official website to this historical figure and the controversies surrounding him, specifically on the discrepancies between "legends and textbooks." See http://www.nict.gov.tw/tc/learning/b_3.php

19. Synchronous placement of both the colonizer and the colonized is an unattainable desire. However, the cinematic apparatus can project an imaginary field of space and time that accommodates that impossible matrix of historical coordinates. The cinema is capable of constructing a diegesis that allows for a making of colonial modernity when the colonial and the modern would otherwise be mutually exclusive. I discuss this perverse colonial temporality thus spatialized in cinematic representation as the "will-have-been" in a different context in "Framing Time: *New Women* and the Cinematic Representation of Colonial Modernity in 1930s Shanghai," *positions: east asia cultures critique*, vol. 15, no. 3, Winter, 2007, pp. 553–580.

20. Later in the same decade, the largest dam in Taiwan would be under construction. First conceived during Japanese occupation, Tseng Wen Reservoir had been in planning since the late 1950s. While the actual building did not begin until 1966 and was completed in 1973, water conservancy had been central to Taiwan's infrastructural planning in the early decades of Nationalist rule.

21. Berry and Farquhar, *China on Screen: Cinema and Nation*, p. 191.

22. An important example of this genre is *Kang-Ding Tours Taipei* (1969), a film portraying migrant workers and their hardships in Taipei. The message that the fast economic growth and rapid social transformation have accelerated the widening gap between the rural and urban areas still does not prevent a comic resolution.

23. According to Ye Long-Yan, prevalent genres during this period do not include thriller or suspense. However, if one reads his categorization carefully, two major genres rely heavily on this particular mode: "social event" and "folk story" films. Many of the films in those two categories recount either real-life or legendary events involving treachery, violence, and even murders: the former often ends with justice served by legal means and the latter by moral resolution. The cinematic mode of narrativization in those films highlights suspense and even horror. A good example is director Xin Qi's *The Bride from Hell* (1965), which tells the story of an abused woman who seeks revenge by posing as a ghost and the wrongs done to whom are righted in the end when her victimizer is arrested by the police. For Yeh's twelve principle genres, see *The Orthodox Chronicles*, pp. 201–205.

24. According to Chen Long-Ting, this figure was Mao Xin-Shiao, nicknamed Mao Wang-Yeh, an unofficially titled royal person. When Chiang Kai-Shek visited Sun Moon Lake, Mao led a group of fellow Shao people to greet him at the dock and entertained him with traditional song and dance. Mao later organized a performance troupe and established the Shao Cultural Village featured here in *Brother Wang and Brother Liu*. See Chen's "Image and Identification of Taiwan in Taiwanese Dialect Cinema" in *Essays on Taiwanese Dialect Cinema*, Taipei: National Cheng-Chi University, 2007.

25. Berry and Farquhar, *China on Screen*, p. 191.

26. There is one significant exception when the young couple escape from their homes to live together despite their respective parents' strong objection. After a big argument, resulting in tattered clothes and broken furniture, both sides summon their parents to come pay for the damage. An extraordinary scene ensues when the young couple reenact their fight in front of several bystanders, the couple's parents included, for their arbitration. The mess in the room becomes a visual marker of the crisis, but the symmetrical, frontal composition keeps the situation composed until all is resolved and a happy ending ensured.

27. This notion of a "southern" perspective would take on even greater significance when Taiwan's pro-independence movement began to challenge the Nationalist hegemony starting in the 1980s. As an antithesis to the North, with Taipei as the symbol for not only the Nationalist regime but also Japan's colonial rule, the South comes to stand for an imaginary origin of a local, Taiwanese consciousness. The highly contested presidential elections in Taiwan since 2000 show this geographical division's long-lasting legacy.

28. Chen, "Image and Identification of Taiwan in Dialect Cinema," p. 18.

29. For but one example, *Wild Rose*, a 1930s Shanghai leftist classic, has a very similar plot, which also prefigures Hou Hsiao-Hsien's early films I discuss in the Interlude.

30. Andrew F. Jones, *Yellow Music: Media Culture and Colonial Modernity in the Chinese Jazz Age*, Durham: Duke University Press, 2001, p. 112. Emilie Yue-yu Ye, on the other hand, provides an interesting sketch of the interactions between music and film in Shanghai 1930s and 1940s as well as a detailed account in Taiwan after 1975 in her *Gesheng meiying: gechu*

xushi yu zhongwen dianying (Phantom of the Music: Song Narration and Chinese-Language Cinema), Taipei: Yuanliu, 2000. Her study, however, does not cover Taiwanese-dialect cinema.

31. See Guo Dai-Xuan, "Taiyu dianying ui liuxing gecu xushi yanjiu" (Studies of Song Narration in Taiwanese Dialect Cinema and Popular Music), in *Essays on Taiwanese Dialect Cinema*, Taipei: National Cheng-Chi University, 2007, pp. 130–131. Guo also notes that the lyrics were written with seven words per line, emulating the traditional operatic style of composition.

32. See Liao Gene-Fon, *Xiaoshi de yingxiang: taiyupian de dianying zaixian yu wenhua rentong* (Fading Sight and Sound: Cinematic Representation and Cultural Identity in Taiwanese Dialect Cinema), Taipei: Yuanliu, 2001, pp. 75–86.

33. Guo, "Song Narration," p. 133.

34. Andrew Higson, "The Limiting Imagination of National Cinema," in *Cinema and Nation*, edited by Mette Hjort and Scott Kenzie, London and New York: Routledge, 2000, p. 69.

35. Zhang, *Chinese National Cinema*, p. 131.

36. Ye, *The Orthodox Chronicles*, pp. 131–133. It should be noted that, according to Ye, the phenomenon of overproduction was not due to foreign market speculation but, rather, it occurred within Taiwan's own market itself. In Ye's account, the phenomenon of copycat productions occurred as early as 1956. The example of *Brother Wang and Brother Liu*, discussed earlier, is a case in point. The same problems occurred with melodrama with its popular songs and with genres such as crime drama, even films featuring beggars as central characters. For a detailed account, see Ye, pp. 129–131.

3 Tracing a Journeyman's Electric Shadow: Healthy Realism, Cultural Policies, and Lee Hsing, 1964–1980

1. Chiao Hsiung-Ping, *Shidai xianying: zhongxi dianying lunxu* (Images of Time: Discourses on Chinese and Western Films), Taipei: Yuanliu, 1998, p. 149.

2. Yellow Plum Melody refers to a regional operatic style with very singable tunes and stylized performances. Though similar to Beijing Opera in its reworking of familiar historical events and folklore, this popular genre in its filmic form is best known for its elaborate sets and costumes as well as the star power of its "male" leads, who were always played by female actors.

3. In 2005, the Nationalist Party withdrew its ownership and, after major restructuring, the company was regrouped as a private enterprise and renamed the Central Pictures Corporation (CPC). For details of this change, see the official CPC website at http://www.movie.com.tw/.

4. To those two genres that Chiao mentions I would add the martial arts film, a vibrant genre that has been prominent since the 1920s in China and continues to be popular in Hong Kong and Taiwan as well as extends its reception in the global market most notably since *Crouching Tiger, Hidden Dragon* (1999).

5. Theodor W. Adorno, *The Culture Industry: Selected Essays on Mass Culture*, edited and with an introduction by J. M. Bernstein, London and New York: Routledge, 1991, pp. 98–99.
6. Martin Jay, *Adorno*, Cambridge, Massachusetts: Harvard University Press, 1984, p. 122.
7. Adorno, *The Culture Industry*, pp. 100–101.
8. Lu Feii, *Taiwan Cinema: Politics, Economy, Aesthetics, 1949–1994*, Taipei: Yuanliu, 1998, pp. 266–267.
9. Cheng Ming-Lee, ed., *Politics and Contemporary Taiwanese Literature*, Taipei: Shibao, 1994, pp. 13–23.
10. Zhang Dao-Fan, "The Cultural Policy We Need," quoted in Cheng Ming-Lee, ed., *Politics and Contemporary Taiwanese Literature*, Taipei: Shibao, 1994, p. 13-23.
11. Ibid., p. 17.
12. Chiang Kai-Shek, in *San Min Chu I: The Three Principles of the People* by Sun Yat-Sen, "Two Supplementary Chapters" by Chiang. Taipei: Government Information Office, 1990, p. 266.
13. Ibid., p. 300.
14. Ibid., p. 302.
15. For detail see Cheng, *Politics and Contemporary Taiwanese Literature*, pp. 28–33; and Li Tian-Duo, *Taiwanese Cinema, Society, and History*, Taipei: The Society for Chinese Cinema Studies, 1997, pp. 80–85.
16. For the complete list of the awards, see the official website of the Golden Horse Awards at http://www.goldenhorse.org.tw/
17. Huang Ren and Wang Wei, eds., *One Hundred Years of Taiwan Cinema*, Taipei: Chinese Film Critic Association, 2004, p. 269.
18. Ibid., p. 266. It is interesting to note that, at this time, Hong Kong's Shaw Brothers still employed Japanese technicians in charge of color cinematography, which, undoubtedly, would be an added motivation for the CMPC to push for a complete domestic production.
19. Paul Heyse, "Letter to Georg Brandes, March 3, 1882," quoted in Sigrid von Moisy, *Paul Heyse: Münchner Dichterfürst im bürgerlichen Zeitalter. Ausstellung in der Bayerischen Staatsbibliothek 23. Januar bis 11. April 1981*, München: C. H. Beck, 1981, pp. 216–217. I thank Toril Moi for calling my attention to this quote. It is striking to see that such an overt idealist notion would appear with the same zeal and conviction in discourses by advocates of Taiwan's Healthy Realism some eighty years later.
20. Taiwan's National Film Archive later published a detailed transcript of this panel discussion along with several articles focusing on Healthy Realism in *Film Appreciation*. This special issue remains until today the most substantial discussion of this movement. Even though Healthy Realism is acknowledged as an important period of Taiwan's film history, mentions of it are often more descriptive than critical or analytical. For the special issue, see *Film Appreciation*, no. 72, 1994, pp. 13–58.
21. See the transcript of the panel on Healthy Realism, "Fragments of Time," *Film Appreciation*, no. 72, Nov./Dec. 1994, p. 19.

22. Liao Gene-Fon, "Towards a Definition of Healthy Realist Films: Memorandum on Taiwan's Film History," *Film Appreciation*, no. 72, 1994, p. 43.

23. See Guo-Juin Hong, "Strategies of Defiance: Towards a Thesis on Anti-Realist Documentary," *Film Appreciation*, no. 111, April-June, 2002, pp. 11–12.

24. André Bazin, "An Aesthetic of Reality: Neorealism," *What Is Cinema?* vol. II, Berkeley, Los Angeles and London: University of California Press, 1971, p. 26.

25. For more elaboration on reality and representation, see Fredric Jameson, *The Political Unconscious: Narrative as a Socially Symbolic Act*, Ithaca, New York: Cornell University Press, 1981, p. 35.

26. See Liu Xian-Cheng, "Liuling niandai Taiwan jiankang xieshi yingpian zhi shehui lishi fenxi" (A Socio-Historical Analysis of Taiwan's Healthy Realist Films in the 1960s), *Film Appreciation*, no. 72, pp. 48–58.

27. In the following, unless otherwise noted, all biographical information about Lee Hsing and his work is from a detailed chronology in *Xinzhe yingji: Lixing, dianying, wushi nian* (Tracing a Journeyman's Shadow: Fifty Years of Lee Hsing's Films), edited by Huang Ren, Taipei: Shibao, 1999, pp. 434–460.

28. Yingjin Zhang, *Chinese National Cinema*, New York and London: Routledge, 2004, p. 134.

29. Ibid., p. 135. Zhang calls the years between 1964 and 1969 a "golden age in Taiwan cinema" because of "the rise of Mandarin cinema" and "the number of consistent releases." For detailed statistics of the production number between 1949 and 1994, see Lu Feii's *Taiwan Cinema: Politics, Economy, Aesthetics*, pp. 429–475.

30. Berry and Farquhar, *China on Screen: Cinema and Nation*, New York: Columbia University Press, 2006, p. 98.

31. See Zhang Jing-Pei, "Miandui dangdai daoyan Lixing" (Face to Face with Director Lee Hsing), in Huang, ed., *Tracing a Journeyman's Shadow*, pp. 48–53.

32. I discuss this very different kind of temporal crisis of modernity vis-à-vis the nation in "Framing Time: *New Women* and the Cinematic Representation of Colonial Modernity in 1930s Shanghai," *positions: east asia culture critique*, vol. 15, no. 3, Winter 2007, pp. 553–580.

33. Judith Butler, *Precarious Life: The Powers of Mourning and Violence*, London and New York: Verso, 2004, pp. 51–52.

34. Berry and Farquhar, *China on Screen*, p. 76.

Interlude: Hou Hsiao-Hsien before Hou Hsiao-Hsien: Film Aesthetics in Transition, 1980–1982

1. James Udden, "Taiwanese Popular Cinema and the Strange Apprenticeship of Hou Hsiao-Hsien," *Modern Chinese Literature and Culture*, vol. 15, no. 1, Spring, 2003, pp. 135–136.

2. See Shigehiko Hasumi, "Dangxia de xiangchou" (Homesickness Now) in *Hou Hsiao-Hsien*, Taipei: National Film Archive, 2000, pp. 134–136. This volume is in part a translation of a collection of French essays on Hou with additional contributions from Asian film scholars and historians. Not surprisingly, the original French edition did not include discussion of those three early films.

3. Lin Wenchi has an excellent Chinese article which also traces Hou's distinct cinematic styles from those early films by engaging with the question of film narrative and realism. See Lin, "Hou xiaoxian zaoqi dianying zhong de xieshi fengge yu xushi" (The Realist Style and Narrative in Hou Hsiao-Hsien's Early Films), in *Ximeng rensheng: Hou xiaoxien dianying yanjiu* (The Puppet Master: Studies of Hou Hsiao-Hsien's Cinema), edited by Lin Wenchi, Sheng Shiao-Yin, and Li Zhen-Ya, Taipei: Maitian, 2000, pp. 93–111.

4. Udden, "Taiwanese Popular Cinema and the Strange Apprenticeship of Hou Hsiao-Hsien," p. 136.

5. Ibid., p. 141.

6. Jason McGrath provides an excellent study of the phenomenon of holiday films in recent China. See McGrath, *Postsocialist Modernity: Chinese Cinema, Literature, and Criticism in the Market Age*, esp. chapter 6, "New Year's Films," Stanford, California: Stanford University Press, 2008, pp. 165–202.

7. Recall here Andre Bazin's famous declaration that "realism in arts can only be achieved in one way—through artifice." See Bazin, "An Aesthetic of Reality: Neorealism," *What Is Cinema?* vol. II, Berkeley, Los Angeles, and London: University of California Press, 1971, p. 26.

8. Film critic Li You-Hsin maintains that one major reason for Hou's use of non-professional actors through most of the 1980s was tied to his unpleasant experience with stars like Feng. Though a box office draw, Feng insisted on keeping her signature looks by wearing a great numbers of hats of various styles both in *Lovable You* and later in *Play While You Play*. This extradiegetic element of stardom, with its many accessories to boot, contributes greatly to the incongruous visual field in Hou's first three films I discuss here. See Li, ed., *Gangtai liuda daoyan* (Six Major Directors of Hong Kong and Taiwan), Taipei: Zili wanbaoshe, 1986, pp. 123–125.

9. Udden, pp. 136–139.

10. Policy films refer to a group of government subsidized productions made between 1974 and 1980 which depict mostly Sino-Japanese war. They appeared after a series of international defeats, especially Japan's normalization of diplomatic relations with the Communist China. For a detailed account, see Li Tian-Duo, *Taiwanese Cinema, Society, and History*, Taipei: The Society for Chinese Cinema Studies, 1997, pp. 155–166.

11. I will not spend much time at this point but one major scene in *Green* is about school children being required to bring fecal samples for a health inspection. Going further than the previous examples, the later *Green*'s portrayal of scatological subject matters play with two things at once: the government's effort in improving children's health care, a point any Healthy Realist film would highlight but most likely with more deference, and a sense of nostalgia

for some degree of innocence that has nothing to do with state policy. The latter of these will take on great significance when I discuss the question of the personal experience of growing up in chapter 5.

12. Li You-Hsin, *Six Major Directors*, p. 123.
13. Ibid., p. 125. Li quotes Liu here without giving the original source.
14. See James Udden, "The Strange Apprenticeship of Hou Hsiao-Hsien," p. 137.

4 A Time to Live, a Time to Die: New Taiwan Cinema and Its Vicissitudes, 1982–1986

1. Kristin Thompson and David Bordwell, *Film History: An Introduction,* New York: McGraw-Hill, Inc., 1994, p. 779.
2. See Chiao Hsiung-Ping, ed., *Taiwan xindianying* (New Taiwan Cinema), Taipei: Shibao, 1990, pp. 15–17. The following attributes of New Cinema are a summary of Chiao's prologue to this edited volume, a collection of important writings on New Cinema as it unfolded in the 1980s.
3. June Yip, *Envisioning Taiwan: Fiction, Cinema, and the Nation in the Cultural Imaginary,* Durham and London: Duke University Press, 2004, pp. 53–60.
4. Yip, *Envisioning Taiwan,* p. 52.
5. It is important to note that the number of films produced during this period did not decrease. In fact, feature film production continued to grow, from 95 in 1978 to 144 in 1982. Two specific popular genres of crime thrillers and student films spawned dozens of imitations each year, resulting in a frenzy of low-quality production, which was no competition for Hong Kong and Hollywood films. See Yingjin Zhang, *Chinese National Cinema,* New York and London: Routledge, 2004, pp. 241–242. For more detailed description and statistics of film production, see Lu Feii, *Taiwan Cinema: Politics, Economy, Aesthetics, 1949–1994,* Taipei: Yuanliu, 1998, pp. 255–296 and pp. 433–475.
6. See various articles in Chiao's *New Taiwan Cinema,* and Wu Chi-Yan, *Didu kaifa de jiyi* (Memories of Underdevelopment), Taipei: Tangshan, 1993.
7. Thompson and Bordwell, *Film History: An Introduction,* p. 777.
8. Ibid., p. 779.
9. See John Lent, *The Asian Film Industry,* London: Christopher Helm, 1990, p. 62.
10. Ibid., p. 62. This is Lent quoting from *Free China Review,* a government publication catering specifically to overseas readership.
11. Yip, *Envisioning Taiwan,* pp. 55–56.
12. Jen Hong-Zhi, "Taiwan xindianying de lailu yu chulu" (The Past and Future of New Taiwan Cinema), in Chiao's *New Taiwan Cinema,* pp. 25–39.
13. Ibid., p. 26.
14. Edmund K. Y. Wong, "The Last Beam of Morning Light," *Dianying Biweekly,* nos. 129–130, February 1984.
15. These dates are quoted from Edmund K. Y. Wong, ed., *The Chronicle of Taiwan Cinema 1898–2000,* vol. 2, Taipei: The Council for Cultural Affairs, Administrative Yuan, 2005.

16. This is I. C. Jarvie quoted in Roy Armes' *Third World Film Making and the West*, Berkeley and Los Angeles: University of California Press, 1987, pp. 159–160.

17. James Clifford, *The Predicament of Culture: Twentieth-Century Ethnography, Literature, and Art*, Cambridge, Massachusetts: Harvard University Press, 1988, p. 272.

18. Ibid., p. 273.

19. See Jen, "The Past and Future of New Taiwanese Cinema," p. 27.

20. Among those "new" directors, Hou Hsiao-Hsien was, of course, an exception, since he had started his filmic career much earlier and had already made three prior feature films, as I discussed in the Interlude.

21. Other film critics and scholars have made similar points on the commonalities among New Cinema films. See for example Chiao's "Introduction," *New Taiwan Cinema*, Jen's "The Past and Future of Taiwanese Cinema," Wu's *Memories of Underdevelopment*, and Robert Ru-Shuo Chen, *Taiwan xingdianying de lishi wenhua jingyan* (The Historical and Cultural Experience of New Taiwan Cinema), Taipei: Wanxiang, 1993.

22. Vivian Huang, "Taiwan's Social Realism," *The Independent*, vol. 13, no. 1, Jan.–Feb., 1990.

23. Chiao Hsiung-Ping, "The Year of Breaking Through," *Dianying Biweekly*, no. 179, January, 1986.

24. Zhang, *Chinese National Cinema*, pp. 240–241.

25. Ibid.

26. Xiao Ye, "Xindianying zhong de Taiwan jingyan" (Taiwanese Experience in the New Cinema), in *Yige yundong de kaishi* (The Beginning of a Movement), Taipei: Shibao, 1986, pp. 230–233.

27. Chiao Hsiung-Ping, "Achievements against the Odds," *Lien-Ho Literature Monthly*, February, 1987. The statistic data in the following are based on Chiao's report.

28. The title refers to an advertising practice of a hired hand wearing sandwich boards, often in some flashy if also ridiculous costume, and parading the streets to promote certain products or services.

29. Emile Yuen-Yu Yeh and Darrell William Davis compare Hou and Yang as follows. "Though [Hou and Yang] are the same age (b. 1947), and are both mainland transplants and founders of the New Cinema, their films are radically different, along with their approaches to story structure and the profilmic." They go on to summarize that "Hou's approach is more intuitive while Yang is calculating, painstaking, a perfectionist." See Yeh and Davis, *Taiwan Film Directors: A Treasure Island*, New York: Columbia University Press, 2005, p. 91.

30. See Chen Feibao, *Taiwan dianying daoyan yishu* (The Art of Taiwan's Film Directors), Taipei: The Association of Taiwan Film Directors, 1999, p. 147. It is interesting to note that, when comparing Yang to Italian Neorealists, John Anderson believes Yang's works to have shown "a far wider field of vision and a more *humanistic* worldview...than have his Italian predecessors" [my emphasis]. See Anderson, *Edward Yang*, Urbana and Chicago: University of Illinois Press, 2005, p. 3.

31. Godfrey Cheshire, "Time Span: The Cinema of Hou Hsiao-Hsien," *Film Comment*, vol. 29, no. 6, Nov.–Dec. 1993, pp. 56–63.

32. Ibid.
33. Fredric Jameson, "Remapping Taipei," *New Chinese Cinemas*, New York: Cambridge University Press, 1994, pp. 122–123.
34. As I discussed in the Interlude, James Udden provides a very detailed formal analysis of this dramatic editing style in his "Taiwanese Popular Cinema and the Strange Apprenticeship of Hou Hsiao-Hsien." *Modern Chinese Literature and Culture*, vol. 15, no. 1, Spring, p. 20.
35. Chiao in her *"Dust in the Wind*—a Review" also uses this sequence as an example to illustrate Hou's editing style in terms of its understated yet suggestive treatment of conflicts.
36. Here Jen talks broadly about the new dramaturgy in New Cinema in general. See Jen, "the Past and Future of New Cinema," pp. 26–27.
37. An interesting variation of the screen direction can be seen in the train shot right after the motorcycle theft. Opposite to the beginning sequence, this time we see the track from the tail end of the train. As the track extends *backwards* into a darkened tunnel and ultimately links to the capital, a subliminal sense of disillusionment is suggested.
38. Cheshire, "Time Span: The Cinema of Hou Hsiao-Hsien," p. 60.
39. Chen, *The Historical and Cultural Experience of New Taiwanese Cinema*, p. 171.
40. John Anderson also compares Yang with Western filmmakers such as Claude Chabrol of France and the Italian Neorealists. See Anderson, *Edward Yang*, pp. 2–3.
41. Edmund K. Y. Wong, "Edward Yang's *Taipei Story*," *United News*, February 5, 1985.
42. Chiao Hsiung-Ping, "The Year of Turning Point," *Dianying Biweekly*, no. 179, January, 1986.
43. Similarly, Lu Tonglin summarizes Yang's thematic concerns regarding the city as "a society cut off from its past but at the same time without a viable future." I take this to mean that Taipei as a modern city, at least in Yang's cinema, occupies a temporal vacuum whose history is suspended in the present, spatialized by its architectural as well as cinematic confines. See Lu, *Confronting Modernity in the Cinemas of Taiwan and Mainland China*, New York and Cambridge, U.K.: Cambridge University Press, 2002, p. 119.
44. Fredric Jameson, "Remapping Taipei," p. 119. Another point of interest is that Jameson adapts the translation of this film's title as *The Terrorizer*. I personally think that the plural form is more appropriate, which is used by Thompson and Bordwell in *Film History: An Introduction*. As the following discussion will show, all the characters in this film are potential terrorizers. As in the case of Vittorio De Sica's *Ladri di biciclette*, a certain thematic interpretation seems to support the translation to be *Bicycle Thieves*, rather than *The Bicycle Thief*.
45. Ibid., pp. 119–120.
46. Ibid., p. 120. Here Jameson refers to Renata Salecl's discussion of neoethnicity in a Yugoslavian context.
47. Ibid., p. 123–124.
48. Jameson, p. 147.
49. Chen, *The Historical and Cultural Experience of New Taiwan Cinema*, p. 104.

50. This controversy is documented in *Xindianying zhi si* (The Death of New Cinema), edited by Mi Zhou and Liang Xin-Hua, Taipei: Tangshan, 1991, pp. 29–78.

51. Ibid. Mi Zhou, "The Illusion of *All for Tomorrow*: A Crisis in Historical Consciousness and Cultural Self-Awareness," pp. 39–46.

5   Island of No Return: Cinematic Narration as Retrospection in Wang Tong's Taiwan Trilogy and Beyond

1. Xiao Ye, "Xindianying zhong de Taiwan jingyan" (Taiwanese Experience in the New Cinema) in *Yige yundong de kaishi* (The Beginning of a Movement), Taipei: Shibao, 1986, p. 241.

2. Ibid., p. 240. See also the section titled "Taiwan jingyan" (Taiwan experience) in Chiao Hsiung-Ping, ed., *New Taiwan Cinema*, Taipei: Shibao, 1990, pp. 281–313. This section includes reviews of earlier films made by important directors such as Hou Hsiao-Hsien, Edward Yang, and Wang Tong. Both Chiao's introduction and an essay by Luo Wei-Ming on films in 1983 emphasize the theme of "coming-of-age."

3. Chiao Hsiung-Ping, "The Distinct Taiwanese and Hong Kong Cinemas," in *Perspectives on Chinese Cinema*, edited by Chris Berry, London: BFI Publishing, 1991, p. 158.

4. William Tay, "The Ideology of Initiation," in *New Chinese Cinemas: Forms, Identities, Politics*, edited by Nick Browne, Paul G. Pickowicz, Vivian Sobchack, and Esther Yau, Cambridge, England: Cambridge University Press, 1994, p. 158.

5. June Yip, "Constructing a Nation: Taiwanese History and the Films of Hou Hsiao-hsien" in *Transnational Chinese Cinemas: Identity, Nationhood, Gender*, edited by Sheldon Hsiao-peng Lu, Honolulu: University of Hawaii Press, 1997, p. 143.

6. Ibid., p. 140.

7. Ibid., p. 160.

8. Wu Chi-Yan, "Taiwan jingyan de yingxiang shuzao" (The Visualization of the Taiwan Experience), *Film Appreciation*, vol. 8, no. 2, March 1990, pp. 51–52.

9. Chen Kuan-Hsing, "Why Is 'Great Reconciliation' Im/Possible?: De-Cold War/Decolonization, or Modernity and Its Tears," *Taiwan: A Radical Quarterly in Social Studies*, no. 43, September 2001, p. 55. There is an earlier version of this essay in English. See Chen, "Why is 'great reconciliation' im/possible? De-Cold War/decolonization, or modernity and its tears," in two parts in *Inter-Asia Cultural Studies*, vol. 3, no. 1, 2002, pp. 77–99, and no. 2, 2003, pp. 235–251.

10. Ibid., Cui Kuei-fen, "Response to 'the Great Reconciliation?'" no. 3, p. 128.

11. Ibid., Chu Tien-Hsin, "Response to 'the Great Reconciliation?'" no. 2, pp. 118–199.

12. Ibid., Zheng Hong-Shen, "Response to "the Great Reconciliation?' " no. 4, p. 140.

13. See reviews on Wang's earlier films between 1983 and 1985, collected in Chiao's *New Taiwan Cinema*, pp. 221–231, especially Huang, p. 230, and Chiao, p. 225.

14. Chen Feibao, *The Art of Taiwan Film Directors*, Taipei: The Association of Taiwan Film Directors, 1999, p. 174.

15. Critics are keen to do just that. In a special issue on "Ethnicity, Memory, Subjectivity: A Special Issue on [Wang Tong's] *Red Persimmons*" in *Chung Wai Literary Monthly*, vol. 31, no. 11, April 2003, six out of the seven essays make extensive comments on this image. All three essays I quote here are from that volume.

16. Chu Hsiang-Chun, "*Red Persimmons*, Benjamin and Memory," pp. 45–46.

17. Tsai Chia-Chin, "Redemption through Memory: On Wang Tong's *Red Persimmons*," pp. 75–76.

18. Liao Chao-Yang, "Reflexivity and Separation: Wang Tong's *Red Persimmons*," pp. 25–26.

19. David Bordwell, for one, has commented on how the opening credit sequence is often the most self-conscious of a fiction film. It works to address its audience directly to set the course for its ensuing narrational act that will in turn be performed in a more transparent and seamless realist style. See Bordwell, *Narration in the Fiction Film*, Madison, Wisconsin: University of Wisconsin Press, 1985, especially pp. 59–61 and pp. 160–161.

20. Tsai, "Redemption through Memory," p. 89.

21. Liao Chaoyang, "*Hill of No Return*: The Experience of Land and National Space," *Chung Wai Literary Monthly*, vol. 22, no. 8, January 1994, pp. 52–53. One of Liao's major arguments in this essay is also to establish that the so-called "Taiwanese people" are in fact also another group of immigrants from China whose presence in Taiwan is always already that of the colonizer. I will focus only on the colonial politics between Taiwanese and Japanese here, as I have elaborated on this additional level of complexity in the previous section on the "native Taiwanese" and " emigrant Mainlanders" debate.

22. I elaborate the condition of the will-have-been as a salient feature of colonial modernity in a different context in "Framing Time: *New Women* and the Cinematic Representation of Colonial Modernity in 1930s Shanghai," *positions: east asia culture critique*, vol. 15, no. 3, pp. 553–579.

23. Lu, *Taiwan Cinema: Politics, Economy, Aesthetics, 1949–1994*, Taipei: Yuanliu, 1998, pp. 390–391.

24. Ibid.

6   Anywhere but Here: The Postcolonial City in Tsai Ming-Liang's Taipei Trilogy

1. It is important to note that Tsai already had at that time a very impressive resume with many theater, television and documentary productions as well as film screenwriting to his credit. For a complete list of Tsai works

before 2002, see Wen Tian-Xiang, *Guangying dingge: Tsai Ming-liang de xinling changyu* (Freeze-Frame in Light and Shadow: The Spiritual Site of Tsai Ming-Liang). Taipei: Hengxing, 2002, pp. 238–251.

2. Chiao Hsiung-Ping, from the transcript of the jury deliberation for the Fifth Annual Film Awards presented by *China Evening News* on November 8, 1992. See *Dangdai gongtai dianying, 1988–1992* (Contemporary Hong Kong and Taiwan Cinemas, 1988–1992), vol. 2, edited by Huang Wu-Lan, Taipei: Shibao, 1992, p. 178.

3. Interestingly, *Rebels* won this recognition before its theatrical release. Also interestingly, even though Tsai won the best director award in 1993's Golden Horse Award, *Rebels* was not even nominated in the Best Film category. This other jury, apparently, had voted against change.

4. Xiao Ye and Lu Feii quoted in *Contemporary Hong Kong and Taiwan Cinema, 1988–1992*, pp. 176–177.

5. In discussing Tsai's next film, *Vive L'Amour*, Hsiao-Hung Chang and Wang Chih-Hung also highlight the film's "refusal [of] nostalgia." I will discuss this essay in greater detail in the next section on *Vive L'Amour*. See Chang and Wang, "Mapping Taipei's Landscape of Desire: Deterritorialization and Reterritorialization of the Family/Park" in *Focus on Taipei through Cinema, 1950–1990*, edited by Ru-Shou Robert Chen and Gene-Fon Liao, Taipei: Wangxiang, 1995, pp. 124–125.

6. Wen Tian-Xiang, *Freeze-Frame*, p. 9.

7. Yomi Braester, "If We Could Remember Everything, We Would Be Able to Fly: Taipei's Cinematic Poetics of Demolition," in *Modern Chinese Literature and Culture*, vol. 15, no. 1, Spring 2003, p. 32.

8. Carlos Rojas, "'Nezha Was Here': Structures of Dis/placement in Tsai Ming-Liang's *Rebels of the Neon God*," in *Modern Chinese Literature and Culture*, vol. 15, no. 1, Spring 2003, p. 71.

9. Ackbar Abbas, *Hong Kong: Culture and the Politics of Disappearance*, Minneapolis and London: University of Minnesota Press, 1997, pp. 8–12. In these particular pages, Abbas engages very closely with issues of representation, including self-representation, in Hong Kong. In some ways similar to the local/global dilemma, the problematic of self-representation—that is, how to represent a Hong Kong subject when "Hong Kong" itself is on the verge of becoming a non-location—demands a way of thinking that focuses less on what is than what is *not*. In other words, a productive way to imagine what the cultural space of Hong Kong is may well be to see it as "transient" (8), as "cultural translation" (12).

10. The Benjaminian notion of "homogenous, empty time," I must add, serves to critique a simplistic historicist notion of time as linear progression, as progress. And this linear thinking of time has in fact forced our consciousness of history out of the *experiential* realm of the Now—the clear and distinctive presence of the historical subject, of subjectivity in history.

11. As an installment of a series on AIDS in Asia, this documentary focuses on male patients in Taiwan while other subjects and regions are also represented, such as Hong Kong, Japan, and women and AIDS. Another interesting point to note is that, because of the double social stigma still associated

with AIDS and homosexuality, Tsai Ming-Liang works out specific forms of representation in order to protect his subjects' privacy. For example, the patients' faces are never shown in full frontal and their voices are mechanically manipulated to become non-recognizable. Tsai himself, however, does not hide behind the camera; instead, he often is the photographic object even when his role as the director is conducting the interview. In an interview with Wen Tian-Xiang, Tsai speaks briefly about this project. See Wen, *Freeze-Frame*, pp. 126–29, 222–223.

12. Even though Rojas' point fares well with a slightly too hygienic interpretation of this seemingly odd act, I would prefer not to shy away from both the denotative and connotative use of this "figure" of AIDS: an ill wish, a deadly curse that is loaded with sickness, filth, and, most importantly and concretely (as opposed to "abstractly"), shame.

13. Rojas, " 'Nezha Was Here'," pp. 64–65.

14. Critics of this film often note this shot as a visual protest of Taiwan's stifling educational system. See, for example, Xiao Ye, "Dang zhanglang yudao zhanglang" (When a Cockroach Meets Another Cockroach), *China Times*, Nov. 13, 1992, and Wen Tian-Xiang, *Freeze-Frame*, p. 77.

15. Rojas, pp. 70–71.

16. Jean Ma, *Melancholy Drift: Marking Time in Chinese Cinema*, Hong Kong: Hong Kong University Press, 2010, p. 87.

17. Wen, *Freeze-Frame*, p. 78.

18. Edmund K. Y. Wong, "Aiqing yisi, gudu wansui" (Love is Dead, Viva la Solitude), in *Vive L'Amour*, Tsai Ming-Liang et al., Taipei: Wanxiang, 1994, pp. 187–90.

19. For an excellent analysis of Taipei's architecture and urbanism in relation to the legacy of Taiwan's multiple colonial histories, see Hsia Chu-Joe's "Building Colonial Modernity: Rewriting Histories of Architecture and Urbanism in the Colonial Taiwan," *Taiwan: A Radical Quarterly in Social Studies*, no. 40, September 2000, pp. 47–82. Because of the untidy and enmeshed colonial histories of Taiwan—the Dutch, the Spanish, the Japanese, and, with even greater complexity, Mainland China—one key characteristic of postcolonial Taiwan is as "a space of fragmented, discontinuous and heterogeneous places" (52). Each regime has tried to exert its power by redesigning and reinterpreting Taipei's urban structure and architectural meanings. This period since the late 1970s that Braester focuses on must be placed within this larger historical context.

20. Yomi Braester, "Taipei's Cinematic Poetics of Demolition," pp. 30–31.

21. Ibid. p. 32.

22. Ibid. p. 33.

23. See Braester's essay for a summary of the change of policy and its resulting controversy, pp. 49–52.

24. Indeed, the park has since become an important venue for the municipal government to stage various social, cultural, and political events, ranging from outdoor film festivals, to arts and crafts fairs, to the location of the Emergency Control Headquarters after a major earthquake disaster in 1999.

25. Meanwhile, it is worth noting, Xiao Kang climbs out from under the bed and begins to leave when he decides to lie down on the bed with the still fast-asleep Ah Rong. After much hesitation and struggle, shown in a bird's-eye medium close-up, Xiao Kang finally moves in and kisses Ah Rong ever so briefly on the lips before he exits from the frame, leaving only the half-turned face of Ah Rong, in total incognizance of this boldest and yet saddest act of desire. The theme of non-reciprocated desire will take yet another and further perverted twist in the next film I will discuss.

26. Chris Berry, "Where is the Love?: The Paradox of Performing Loneliness in Tsai Ming-Liang's *Vive L'Amour*," in *Falling for You: Essays on Cinema and Performance*, edited by Lesley Stern and George Kouvarous, Sydney: Power Publications, 1999, pp. 147–175.

27. Chang and Wang, "Mapping Taipei's Landscape of Desire," in *Focus on Taipei through Cinema*, pp. 124–125. Essays in this volume—itself a rather elaborate program note for a special film series for the Golden Horse International Film Festival in 1995—are published in both Chinese and English. The texts quoted here are the original English translation in the book.

28. This point is further justified when Tsai's 2002 film *What Time Is It There?* regroups once more the three characters.

29. Taichung is the third largest city in Taiwan, about a hundred miles south of Taipei. It is interesting to note that the climactic event (which I will discuss later) takes place, as a matter of fact, *outside* Taipei. I will invoke in the Afterword some possible readings of this interesting shift of locations in Tsai's films in particular and in later Taiwan cinema in general.

30. Daniele Riviere, "Scouting," an interview with Tsai Ming-Liang, in *Tsai Ming-Liang*, p. 98.

31. Hsiao-Hung Chang quoted in Zhang Aizhu, "Piabo de zaiti: Cai Mingliang dianying de shenti juchang yu yuwang changyu" (Imagining Queer Bodies: The Erotic Site/Sight of Tsai Ming-Liang's Films), *Chung Wai Literary Monthly*, vol. 30, no. 10, March 2002, pp. 88–89.

32. Zhang Aizhu, p. 89–93.

33. Li Qing-Zhi, "Pintu dushi: xunzhao dianyingzhong de taibei" (Puzzle City: Looking for Taipei through Film) in *Jainzhu dianyingxue* (Architecture and Film), Taipei: Chuangxing, 1996, pp. 136–138.

34. Much more could be said about Tsai's use of those musical sequences. In a private conversation, Andrew F. Jones, for example, suggested that these sequences provide an odd, cinematically and pop musically mediated sense of a lost or disjointed history by playing on nostalgia for the old Shanghai and Hong Kong's Mandarin cinema and its music.

Afterword to the Paperback Edition

1. Wei De-Sheng interviewed on *Nangfang Dialy* on May 8, 2012, after the premiere of *Seedig Bale* in China. See http://www.chinataiwan.org/xwzx/dlzl/201205/t20120508_2526141.htm

Works Cited

Abbas, Ackbar, *Hong Kong: Culture and the Politics of Disappearance*, Minneapolis and London: University of Minnesota Press, 1997.

Adorno, Theodor W., *The Culture Industry: Selected Essays on Mass Culture*, edited and with an introduction by J. M. Bernstein, London and New York: Routledge, 1991.

Anderson, John, *Edward Yang*, Urbana and Chicago: University of Illinois Press, 2005.

Andrew, Dudley, "Islands in the Sea of Cinema," in *National Cinemas and World Cinema*, edited by Kevin Rockett and John Hill, Dublin, Ireland: Four Courts Press, 2006.

Armes, Roy, *Third World Film Making and the West*, Berkeley and Los Angeles: University of California Press, 1987.

Bazin, André, "An Aesthetic of Reality: Neorealism," *What Is Cinema?* vol. II, Berkeley, Los Angeles and London: University of California Press, 1971.

Berry, Chris, "Where Is the Love?: The Paradox of Performing Loneliness in Tsai Ming-Liang's *Vive L'Amour*," in *Falling for You: Essays on Cinema and Performance*, edited by Lesley Stern and George Kouvarous, Sydney: Power Publications, 1999.

———, "If China Can Say No, Can China Make Movies? Or, Do Movies Make China? Rethinking National Cinema and National Agency," in *Modern Chinese Literary and Cultural Studies in the Age of Theory: Reimagining a Field*, edited by Rey Chow, Durham and London: Duke University Press, 2000.

Berry, Chris, and Mary Farquhar, *China on Screen: Cinema and Nation*, New York: Columbia University Press, 2006.

Bhabha, Homi, "DissemiNation: Time, Narrative, and the Margins of the Modern Nation," in *Nation and Narrative*, edited by Homi Bhabha, London and New York: Routledge, 1990.

Bordwell, David, *Narration in the Fiction Film*. Madison, Wisconsin: University of Wisconsin Press, 1985.

Braester, Yomi, "If We Could Remember Everything, We Would Be Able to Fly: Taipei's Cinematic Poetics of Demolition," in *Modern Chinese Literature and Culture*, vol. 15, no. 1, Spring 2003.

Butler, Judith, *Precarious Life: The Powers of Mourning and Violence*, London and New York: Verso, 2004.

Chang Xiao-Hung, and Wang Chih-Hung, "Mapping Taipei's Landscape of Desire: Deterritorialization and Reterritorialization of the Family/Park," in *Focus on Taipei through Cinema, 1950–1990*, edited by Ru-shou Robert Chen and Gene-Fon Liao, Taipei: Wangxiang, 1995.

Chen Feibao, *Taiwan dianying shihua* (A History of Taiwan Cinema), Beijing: Zhongguo dianying chubanshe, 1988.

———, *Taiwan dianying daoyan yishu* (The Art of Taiwan's Film Directors), Taipei: The Association of Taiwan Film Directors, 1999.

Chen Kuan-Hsing, "Why Is 'Great Reconciliation' Im/Possible?: De-Cold War/ Decolonization, or Modernity and Its Tears," *Taiwan: A Radical Quarterly in Social Studies*, no. 43, September 2001.

———, "Why Is 'Great Reconciliation' Im/Possible? De-Cold War/Decolonization, or Modernity and Its Tears," in two parts in *Inter-Asia Cultural Studies*, vol. 3, no. 1, 2002, and no. 2, 2003.

———, "Taiwan New Cinema, or a Global Nativism?" in *Theorizing National Cinema*, edited by Valentina Vitali and Paul Willemen, London: BFI Publishing, 2006.

Chen Long-Ting, "Image and Identification of Taiwan in Taiwanese Dialect Cinema," in *Essays on Taiwanese Dialect Cinema*, Taipei: National Cheng-Chi University, 2007.

Chen, Robert Ru-Shuo, *Taiwan xingdianying de lishi wenhua jingyan* (The Historical and Cultural Experience of New Taiwan Cinema), Taipei: Wanxiang, 1993.

Cheng Ming-Lee, ed., *Politics and Contemporary Taiwanese Literature*, Taipei: Shibao, 1994.

Cheshire, Godfrey, "Time Span: The Cinema of Hou Hsiao-Hsien," *Film Comment*, vol. 29, no. 6, November–December 1993.

Chiang Kai-Shek, in *San Min Chu I: The Three Principles of the People* by Sun Yat-Sen, "Two Supplementary Chapters" by Chiang, Taipei: Government Information Office, 1990.

Chiao Hsiung-Ping, "The Year of Breaking Through," *Dianying Biweekly*, no. 179, January, 1986.

———, "The Year of Turning Point," *Dianying Biweekly*, no. 179, January, 1986.

———, "Achievements against the Odds," *Lien-Ho Literature Monthly*, February, 1987.

———, ed., *Taiwan xin dianying* (New Taiwan Cinema), Taipei: Shibao, 1990.

———, "The Distinct Taiwanese and Hong Kong Cinemas," in *Perspectives on Chinese Cinema*, edited by Chris Berry, London: BFI Publishing, 1991.

———, *Shidai xianying: zhongxi dianying lunxu* (Images of Time: Discourses on Chinese and Western Films), Taipei: Yuanliu, 1998.

Ching, Leo T. S., *Becoming "Japanese": Colonial Taiwan and the Politics of Identity Formation*, Berkeley and Los Angeles: University of California Press, 2001.

Chu Hsiang-Chun, "*Red Persimmons*, Benjamin and Memory," in *Chung Wai Literary Monthly*, vol. 31, no. 11, April 2003.

Clifford, James, *The Predicament of Culture: Twentieth-Century Ethnography, Literature, and Art*, Cambridge, Massachusetts: Harvard University Press, 1988.

Crofts, Stephen, "Reconceptualizing National Cinema/s," in *Film and Nationalism*, edited and with an introduction by Alan Williams, New Brunswick, New Jersey, and London: Rutgers University Press, 2002.

Deslandes, Jeanne, "Dancing Shadows of Film Exhibition: Taiwan and the Japanese Influence," in *Screening the Past*, November 2000. http://www.latrobe.edu.au/screeningthepast/.

Du Yun-Zhi, *Zhongguo dianying shi* (The Film History of China), Taipei: Taiwan Commercial Press, 1972.

———, *Zhonghua minguo dianying shi* (The Film History of the Republic of China), Taipei: The Council for Cultural Affairs, Administrative Yuan, 1988.

Farquhar, Mary, and Chris Berry, "Shadow Opera: Towards a New Archaeology of the Chinese Cinema," in *Post Script*, vol. 20, nos. 2 and 3.

Guo Dai-Xuan, "Taiyu dianying ui huxing gecu xushi yanjiu" (Studies of Song Narration in Taiwanese Dialect Cinema and Popular Music), in *Essays on Taiwanese Dialect Cinema*, Taipei: National Cheng-Chi University, 2007, pp. 128–139.

Hasumi, Shiguehiko, "Dangxia de xiangchou" (Homesickness Now), in *Hou Hsiao-Hsien*, Taipei: National Film Archive, 2000.

Heyse, Paul, "Letter to Georg Brandes March 3, 1882," quoted in Sigrid von Moisy, *Paul Heyse: Münchner Dichterfürst im bürgerlichen Zeitalter. Ausstellung in der Bayerischen Staatsbibliothek 23. Januar bis 11. April 1981*, München: C. H. Beck, 1981.

Higson, Andrew, "The Concept of National Cinema," in *Screen*, vol. 30, no. 4, 1989, pp. 36–46.

———, "The Limiting Imagination of National Cinema," in *Cinema and Nation*, edited by Mette Hjort and Scott Kenzie, London and New York: Routledge, 2000.

Hong Guo-Juin, "Strategies of Defiance: Towards a Thesis on Anti-Realist Documentary," in *Film Appreciation Journal*, no. 111, April–June 2002.

———, "Framing Time: *New Women* and the Cinematic Representation of Colonial Modernity in 1930s Shanghai," in *positions: east asia cultures critique*, vol. 15, no. 3, Winter 2007.

Hsia Chu-Joe, "Building Colonial Modernity: Rewriting Histories of Architecture and Urbanism in the Colonial Taiwan," in *Taiwan: A Radical Quarterly in Social Studies*, no. 40, September 2000.

Hu, Brian, "7 Reflections on *Cape No. 7*," *Asia Pacific Arts*, October 31, 2008. http://www.asiaarts.ucla.edu/article.asp?parentid=99915.

Huang, Ren, ed., *Xinzhe yingji: Lixing, dianying, wushi nian* (Tracing a Journeyman's Shadow: Fifty Years of Lee Hsing's Films), Taipei: Shibao, 1999.

Huang, Ren and Wang Wei, eds., *One Hundred Years of Taiwan Cinema*, Taipei: Chinese Film Critic Association, 2004.

Huang Wu-Lan, ed., *Dangdai gongtai dianying, 1988–1992* (Contemporary Hong Kong and Taiwan Cinemas, 1988–1992), vol. 2, Taipei: Shibao, 1992.

Huang, Vivian, "Taiwan's Social Realism," in *The Independent*, vol. 13, no.1, January–February 1990.

Jameson, Fredric, *The Political Unconscious: Narrative as a Socially Symbolic Act*, Ithaca, New York: Cornell University Press, 1981.

——, "Remapping Taipei," *New Chinese Cinemas*, New York: Cambridge University Press, 1994.

Jay, Martin, *Adorno*, Cambridge, Massachusetts: Harvard University Press, 1984.

Jen, Hong-Zhi, "Taiwan xindianying de lailu yu chulu" (The Past and Future of New Taiwan Cinema), in *New Taiwanese Cinema*, edited by Chiao Hsiung-Ping, Taipei: Shibao, 1990.

Jones, Andrew F., *Yellow Music: Media Culture and Colonial Modernity in the Chinese Jazz Age*, Durham: Duke University Press, 2001.

Karl, Rebecca, *Staging the World: Chinese Nationalism at the Turn of the Twentieth Century*, Durham: Duke University Press, 2002.

Lamley, Harry J., "Taiwan under Japanese Rule, 1895–1945: The Vicissitudes of Colonialism," in *Taiwan: A New History*, edited by Murray A. Rubinstein, Armonk, New York, and London: M. E. Sharpe, 1999.

Lee Daw-Ming, "Dianying shi ruhe laidao Taiwan de?" (How Did Film Arrive in Taiwan?), in *Film Appreciation*, no. 16, pp. 3–6.

—— , "The First Chapter of Taiwan's Film History: 1900–1915," in *Film Appreciation*, no. 73, pp. 28–44.

——, "Riben tongzhi shiqi dianying yu zhengzhi de guanxi" (The Relationship between Film and Politics during the Japanese Colonization), in *History Monthly*, no. 94, November 1995, pp. 123–128.

Lent, John, *The Asian Film Industry*, London: Christopher Helm, 1990.

Li Qing-Zhi, "Pintu dushi: xunzhao dianyingzhong de taibei" (Puzzle City: Looking for Taipei through Film), in *Jainzhu dianyingxue* (Architecture and Film), Taipei: Chuangxing, 1996.

Li Tian-Duo, *Taiwanese Cinema, Society, and History*, Taipei: The Society for Chinese Cinema Studies, 1997.

Li You-Hsin, ed., *Gangtai liuda daoyan* (Six Major Directors of Hong Kong and Taiwan), Taipei: Zili wanbaoshe, 1986.

Liao Chaoyang, "*Hill of No Return*: The Experience of Land and National Space," in *Chung Wai Literary Monthly*, vol. 22, no. 8, January 1994.

——, "Reflexivity and Separation: Wang Tung's *Red Persimmons*," in *Chung Wai Literary Monthly*, vol. 31, no. 11, April 2003.

Liao Gene-Fon, "Towards a Definition of Healthy Realist Films: Memorandum on Taiwan's Film History," in *Film Appreciation Bi-Monthly*, no. 72, 1994.

——, *Xiaoshi de yingxiang: taiyupian de dianying zaixian yu wenhua rentong* (Fading Sight and Sound: Cinematic Representation and Cultural Identity in Taiwanese Dialect Cinema), Taipei: Yuanliu, 2001.

Lin Bo-Wei, *Taiwan wehua xiehui cangsang* (The History of Taiwan Cultural Association), Taichung, Taiwan: Taiyuan, 1993.

Lin Wenchi, "Hou xiaoxian zaoqi dianying zhong de xieshi fengge yu xushi" (The Realist Style and Narrative in Hou Hsiao-Hsien's Early Films), in *Ximeng rensheng: Hou xiaoxien dianying yanjiu* (The Puppet Master: Studies of Hou Hsiao-Hsien's Cinema), edited by Lin Wenchi, Sheng Shiao-Yin, and Li Zhen-Ya, Taipei: Maitian, 2000, pp. 93–111.

Liu Xian-Cheng, "Liuling niandai Taiwan jiankang xieshi yingpian zhi shehui lishi fenxi" (A Socio-Historical Analysis of Taiwan's Healthy Realist Films in the 1960s), in *Film Appreciation*, no. 72, pp. 48–58.

Lu Feii, *Taiwan Cinema: Politics, Economy, Aesthetics, 1949–1994*, Taipei: Yuanliu, 1998.

Lu Su-Shang, *Taiwan dianying xiju shi* (The History of Taiwan's Film and Drama), Taipei: Yin-Hua Publishing, 1961.

Lu, Tonglin, *Confronting Modernity in the Cinemas of Taiwan and Mainland China*, New York and Cambridge, UK: Cambridge University Press, 2002.

Ma, Jean, *Melancholy Drift: Marking Time in Chinese Cinema*, Hong Kong: Hong Kong University Press, 2010.

McGrath, Jason, *Postsocialist Modernity: Chinese Cinema, Literature, and Criticism in the Market Age*," Stanford, California: Stanford University Press, 2008.

Mi Zhou, and Liang Xin-Hua, eds., *Xindianying zhi si* (The Death of New Cinema), Taipei: Tangshan, 1991.

Misawa, Mamie, *Silver Screen in the Colony: Research on Taiwan Governor Office's Film Policies, 1895–1942*, Taipei: Avanguard, 2002.

Nornes, Abe Mark, "For an Abusive Subtitling," in *The Translation Studies Reader*, edited by Lawrence Venuti, New York and London: Routledge, 2000.

Phillips, Steven, "Between Assimilation and Independence: Taiwanese Political Aspirations Under National Chinese Rule, 1945–1948," in *Taiwan: A New History*, edited by Murray A. Rubinstein, Armonk, New York, and London: M. E. Sharpe, 1999.

Ritchie, Donald, *A Hundred Years of Japanese Cinema: A Concise History*, Tokyo, New York and London: Kodansha International, 2001.

Rojas, Carlos, " 'Nezha Was Here': Structures of Dis/placement in Tsai Ming-Liang's *Rebels of the Neon God*," in *Modern Chinese Literature and Culture*, vol. 15, no. 1, Spring 2003.

Roy, Denny, *Taiwan: A Political History*, Ithaca, New York, and London: Cornell University Press, 2003.

Shih, Shu-Mei, "Globalisation and the (In)Significance of Taiwan," in *Postcolonial Studies*, vol. 6, no. 2, 2003.

Sklar, Robert, *A World History of Film*, New York: Harry N. Abrams, Inc., 2001.

Standish, Isolde, "Mediators of Modernity: 'Photo-interpreters' in Japanese Silent Cinema," in *Oral Tradition*, vol. 20, no. 1, March 2005, pp. 93–110.

Tay, William, "The Ideology of Initiation," in *New Chinese Cinemas: Forms, Identities, Politics*, edited by Nick Browne, Paul G. Pickowicz, Vivian Sobchack, and Esther Yau, Cambridge, England: Cambridge University Press, 1994.

Thompson, Kristin, and David Bordwell, *Film History: An Introduction*, New York: McGraw-Hill, Inc., 1993, 2003, 2009.

Tsai Chia-Chin, "Redemption through Memory: On Wang Tung's *Red Persimmons*," in *Chung Wai Literary Monthly*, vol. 31, no. 11, April 2003.

Tsai Pei-Huo, *et al.*, *Taiwan mingzu yundongshi* (History of Taiwan's National Movement), Taipei: Zili wanbaoshe, 1971.

Udden, James, "Taiwanese Popular Cinema and the Strange Apprenticeship of Hou Hsiao-Hsien," in *Modern Chinese Literature and Culture*, vol. 15, no. 1, Spring 2003.

Wang, Yiman, "Screening Asia: Passing, Performative Translation, and Reconfiguration," in *positions: east asia cultures critique*, vol. 15, no. 2, Fall 2007.

Wen Tian-Xiang, *Guangying dingge: Tsai Ming-liang de xinling changyu* (Freeze-frame in Light and Shadow: The Spiritual Site of Tsai Ming-Liang), Taipei: Hengxing, 2002.

Wong, Edmund K. Y., "The Last Beam of Morning Light," in *Dianying Biweekly*, nos. 129–130, February, 1984.

———, "Edward Yang's *Taipei Story*," in *United News*, February 5, 1985.

———, "Aiqing yisi, gudu wansui" (Love Is Dead, Viva la solitude), in *Vive L'Amour*, Tsai Ming-Liang *et al.*, Taipei: Wanxiang, 1994.

———, ed., *The Chronicle of Taiwan Cinema 1898–2000*, Taipei: The Council for Cultural Affairs, Administrative Yuan, 2005.

Wu Chi-Yan, "Taiwan jingyan de yingxiang shuzao" (The Visualization of the Taiwan Experience), *Film Appreciation*, vol. 8, no. 2, March 1990.

———, *Didu kaifa de jiyi* (Memories of Underdevelopment), Taipei: Tangshan, 1993.

Wu Wen-Xing, ed., *Renshi Taiwan: huiwei 1895–2000* (Know Taiwan: Reminiscences between 1895–2000), Taipei: Yuanliu, 2005.

Xiao Ye, "Xindianying zhong de Taiwan jingyan" (Taiwanese Experience in the New Cinema), in *Yige yundong de kaishi* (The Beginning of a Movement), Taipei: Shibao, 1986.

———, "Dang zhanglang yudao zhanglang" (When a Cockroach Meets Another Cockroach), *China Times*, November 13, 1992.

Ye Long-Yan, *Guangfu chuqi Taiwan dianying shi* (Taiwan Film History in the Early Years after Restoration), Taipei: National Film Archive, 1994.

———, *Hsinchushi dianyingshi* (The Film History of Hsinchu City), Hsinchu, Taiwan: Hsinchu Municipal Cultural Center, 1996.

———, *Riju shiqi Taiwan dianyingshi* (The History of Taiwanese Movies During the Japanese Colonization), Taipei: Yushanshe, 1998.

———, *Zhengzong taiyu dianying xingshuailu* (The Orthodox Chronicles of the Vicissitudes of Taiwanese-Dialect Films), Taipei: Boyang, 1999.

Ye, Emilie Yue-yu, *Gesheng meiying: gechu xushi yu zhongwen dianying* (Phantom of the Music: Song Narration and Chinese-Language Cinema), Taipei: Yuanliu, 2000.

Yip, June, "Constructing a Nation: Taiwanese History and the Films of Hou Hsiao-hsien," in *Transnational Chinese Cinemas: Identity, Nationhood,*

Gender, edited by Sheldon Hsiao-peng Lu, Honolulu: University of Hawaii Press, 1997.

————, *Envisioning Taiwan: Fiction, Cinema, and the Nation in the Cultural Imaginary*, Durham, North Carolina, and London: Duke University Press, 2004.

Zhang Aizhu, "Piabo de zaiti: Cai Mingliang dianying de shenti juchang yu yuwang changyu" (Imagining Queer Bodies: The Erotic Site/Sight of Tsai Ming-Liang's Films), in *Chung Wai Literary Monthly*, vol. 30, no. 10, March 2002.

Zhang Jing-Pei, "Miandui dangdai daoyan Lixing" (Face to Face with Director Lee Hsing), in *Xinzhe yingji: Lixing, dianying, wushi nian* (Tracing a Journeyman's Shadow: Fifty Years of Lee Hsing's Films), edited by Huang Ren, Taipei: Shibao, 1999.

Zhang Sheng, *"Descendants of the Yellow Emperor," United News*, Arts and Literature Section, March 1, 1957.

Zhang Xian-Yan, "Taiwan wenhua xiehui de chengli yu fenlie" (The Establishment and Disbandment of the Taiwan Cultural Association), in *Taiwanshi lunwen xunji* (Selected Essays on Taiwan History), Taipei: Yushangshe, 1996.

Zhang, Yingjin, *Chinese National Cinema*, New York and London: Routledge, 2004.

Index

Printed in the United States of America